Neil Kaminsky, LCSW

When It's Time to Leave Your Lover
A Guide for Gay Men

*Pre-publication
REVIEWS,
COMMENTARIES,
EVALUATIONS . . .*

"**K**aminsky has provided a much-needed and very practical combination of psychological insight and advice to all gay men facing this difficult transition. A unique and useful book."

Robert H. Hopcke, LMFT
Director,
Center for Symbolic Studies;
Co-Editor of *Same-Sex Love:
A Path to Wholeness*

"**I**n a perfect world, relationships would always work out and we would all live happily ever after. In reality, not all relationships do work out. It's sad, but true. Can my relationship be saved? Should I leave him? What will I do without him? For anyone who has asked questions like these, *When It's Time to Leave Your Lover: A Guide for Gay Men* should provide some answers.

A guide needs to be insightful and practical. Kaminsky's book is both of these things without reading like a textbook. From deciding to leave and separating to being newly single and starting to date again, this guide acknowledges that ending a relationship can be devastating. It also provides the hope needed to survive a gay divorce. In a community that often has a 'get over it' attitude, it is nice to find a book for gay men that is sympathetic and supportive."

Rick Roberts, MA
Department of Communication Studies,
University of San Francisco

When It's Time to Leave Your Lover

A Guide for Gay Men

HAWORTH Gay & Lesbian Studies
John P. De Cecco, PhD
Editor in Chief

When It's Time to Leave Your Lover
A Guide for Gay Men

Neil Kaminsky, LCSW

Harrington Park Press
An Imprint of The Haworth Press, Inc.
New York • London • Oxford

Published by

Harrington Park Press, an imprint of The Haworth Press, Inc., 10 Alice Street, Binghamton, NY 13904-1580

Cover design by Marylouise E. Doyle.

Cover photo © 1999 by Mark V. Lynch and Latent Images Photography. This photograph may not be copied, reproduced, or used in any manner whatsoever without prior written permission from: Mark V. Lynch • 6402 Evangeline Trail, Austin, TX 78727 • USA Phone (512) 250-2106 • email mark@latentimages.com. Federal law provides penalties for copyright infringement. 1-800-944-4946 http://latentimages.com.

The Library of Congress has cataloged the hardcover edition of this book as:

Kaminsky, Neil, 1951-
    When it's time to leave your lover : a guide for gay men / Neil Kaminsky.
        p.   cm.
    Includes bibliographical references and index.
    ISBN 0-7890-0497-6 (alk. paper)
    1. Gay male couples. 2. Separation (Psychology) 3. Gay men—Psychology. I. Title.
HQ76.K32 1999
306.76′6—DC21   99-14373
                                                                                                                    CIP

ISBN: 1-56023-938-7 (pbk.)

In memory of my ex-partner,
Calvin Martin Lowery, 1959-1995;

in memory of my aunt, Tillie Young,
1904-1995 (my "other mother");

and to my mom, Gussie Kaminsky,
the very best mother in the whole world.

ABOUT THE AUTHOR

Neil Kaminsky, LCSW, is a licensed clinical social worker in California and holds a social work license in New York State. Practicing in social work for over twenty years, Mr. Kaminsky has worked in diverse areas of the field throughout his career, including school social work, foster care, inpatient psychiatry, adolescent residential treatment, forensic psychiatry, and medical social work. He has also been in private practice in both New York City and San Francisco, working primarily with gay men. He has had significant experience with clients struggling with relationship, self-esteem, and HIV/AIDS issues. Mr. Kaminsky has written several articles that address various topics impacting the gay male community, including HIV/AIDS, spousal relationships, coming out, homophobia, antigay violence, and racism. Mr. Kaminsky currently resides in San Francisco, California, where he is pursuing other writing projects.

CONTENTS

Acknowledgments

Writing a book has numerous rewards. One of the greatest pleasures I experienced with this project was the eagerness of so many people to share their time, expertise, and emotional support.

My gratitude is expressed to Robert H. Hopcke, MFCC, who guided me through the fascinating and for me uncharted world of writing and publishing. His vast knowledge and experience has been invaluable. I am grateful to Rik Isensee, LCSW, who graciously invited me to speak about the topic of this book to his class on gay male relationships at City College in San Francisco. His encouragement and the positive energy I felt from his students augmented my excitement about the book. I am grateful to Greg Merrill, MSW, for taking the time to share his insight on gay domestic violence. I learned a great deal from him. Thanks to Thomas J. Caldarola, MFCC, for sharing his knowledge on gay male relationships from his work with gay couples in private practice. My appreciation is expressed to Matthew McKay, PhD, for critiquing the early manuscript, and probably for a million other reasons! His unwavering support and enthusiasm for this project helped motivate me during the difficult times. Thanks to Al Ferrer, MD, for providing psychiatric feedback and other good suggestions. He has never hesitated to offer help when I needed it, and for that I am truly grateful.

A number of gay men were gracious enough to invite me into their lives and recount their uncoupling stories. Some of what they told me appears as quotes in this book. To protect privacy I will not mention their names. I am especially appreciative of this group. As busy as we all are, these men did not hesitate to share their valuable time. They had the courage to disclose very intimate facets of their lives. They revisited sadness and broken dreams and deeply painful memories so that others could benefit from their experiences. That takes a very special spirit, and it deeply impressed me.

Thanks to Bill Palmer, managing editor at The Haworth Press, for giving me the opportunity to make the idea of this book become a reality. My appreciation is expressed to John P. De Cecco, senior editor, for his warm support during the writing of the manuscript. I am very appreciative of Melissa J. Devendorf, administrative assistant, for being consistently pleasant and patient with my innumerable questions about the publishing process. Thanks to Andrew R. Roy, production editor, for his excellent feedback and clear direction. At the time of this writing there are still others at The Haworth Press with whom I have not yet had the pleasure of working. I look forward to my association with them.

I am very blessed with many wonderful friends. In my view it is the quality of one's relationships that governs the quality of one's life. My friends have enriched my life in profoundly meaningful ways.

Thank you, Harry Williams, for being the best buddy (and "psychoanalyst") anyone could ever ask for. What would Sunday mornings be without a three-hour long-distance conversation with you? Thank you, Kelvin Fincher, for your emotional support, and for editing some of the manuscript, but especially for hugging me almost to the point of asphyxiation when I told you I had the book contract! I will also never forget our drive along Highway 1. Thank you, Randy Wade, for being in my life. How did we ever spend a year and a half apart? You are very dear to me, Randy, and will forever hold a very special place in my soul. My fervent gratitude to the rest of my wonderful friends—Eddie Kunofsky, Rick Roberts, Chucky Hughes, Gordon Gilbert, Tracy Millard, Jerry McLaughlin, Richard Ramaseur, and Milford Chang. You are simply the greatest.

Introduction

You may have been searching for a lover with an insatiable hunger. Perhaps you had finally had given up trying, only to unexpectedly, and literally perhaps, crash into him. Conceivably you had no plans for love, putting all of your energies elsewhere, only to have Cupid sting you with the certitude that other plans were afoot in the universe. Whatever the situation, the occurrence of your coming together was as unique as it was jubilant. In time, or perhaps at first sight, you fell in love, a feeling universally acknowledged and ubiquitously mystical. Mental health professionals such as myself, for all our so-called expertise on human behavior, are hard pressed to define the "chemistry" of love. Why is it that we can meet people who have all the "right stuff," only to discover that there are no sparks? Therapists, like everyone else, are unable to definitively answer that question. The chemistry of love is one of the mysteries of humanity that remains awe-inspiring in its unwillingness to be empirically scrutinized.

Being in love, like a priceless gem, is extraordinary in no small part because it's so rare. We meet thousands of people throughout life. We fall in love with very few. Certainly, we can increase our chances of meeting a mate. We can position ourselves in the right places at hopefully the right times. But some luck has to be on our side for him to walk into our lives.

"You Can't Hurry Love."[1] It's certainly true. You can hurry affairs, sex, and delusions of romance. But you can't hurry *love*.

Being in love in a committed relationship becomes a principle part of a person's life. It becomes a vital source of emotional nourishment. Much of what you do, feel, plan, and dream involves your lover. He becomes, in a sense, an extension of you and family to you. You create a history and a life together that brings fulfillment and joy in a way nothing else can or ever will.

Given that, few of us, rationally, would want to let go of it without a considerable fight.

And we shouldn't. All relationships create stress. Whenever two people are together there will be differences and conflicts and hurt feelings. To talk about endings at the first sign of problems is foolhardy indeed. There are innumerable ways to negotiate problems and keep a relationship healthy and gratifying.

Breaking up when there is hope is as destructive as remaining together when there is none. While the reasons for precipitous uncouplings among gay men cannot be exhaustively addressed here, suffice to say there are societal forces working against gay relationship longevity. Among them are homophobia, which preaches that gay relationships are inherently defective, ambivalence in our own community's support of relationships, a dearth of positive role models, and the lack of societal institutions (such as legal marriage) that support long-term relationships. Gay men have been criticized for precipitously uncoupling, and there is merit to that argument. Betty Berzon, in her book *Permanent Partners: Building Gay and Lesbian Relationships That Last,*[2] talks about this (and breakups within the lesbian community) when she takes issue with "the gay national anthem"—our readiness to threaten a breakup as a way to deal with problems.

That being said, there is an equally important issue to examine, one which we have focused very little attention on in the gay community. Some gay men do not leave relationships when they actually should.

Without a doubt, gay relationships, like all relationships, reach plateaus and serious dilemmas. Sometimes the partners in those relationships can resolve the problems on their own, or employ a therapist to help them do it. The relationship survives, and it grows stronger. *But not always. Relationships don't always come back to life. Some relationships cease working and are never able to work again. Some relationships never worked in the first place.* What determines "nonviability" is an important question that I will be addressing in this book.

When a relationship is no longer viable, the people in it should no longer be there. Men who remain together when they ought not live in a shell of what once was. They may call themselves lovers, but the word is a mockery of their reality. These men experience abysmal disappointment and emotional numbness as they go through the motions of what no longer has any meaning for them. Sometimes there is betrayal and other high drama, other times just a quiet eating away of the soul. Often there is silence where there was communication, sorrow and resentment where there was once wonderment and love. This is a sad and tragic picture indeed.

WHO COULD BENEFIT FROM THIS BOOK

If you are a gay man considering a breakup or in the process of one, this book is for you. The book examines, specifically for gay men, the full gamut of the breaking-up process. It addresses the decision to leave, outer societal and gay community pressures against uncoupling, grieving loss, emotional and social ramifications of a breakup, "rebounding," coping and healing, and the components of a healthy, viable relationship. Although the book's perspective is that of the person doing the leaving, a good deal of material is applicable to the man who has been left.

Perhaps you are a single gay man, but have unfinished business from a previous relationship. This book could help you revisit the past, and give you clarity about what took place. This can aid in your closure and thus ability to move on in your life.

You may be in a relationship currently, and something is beginning to make you uncomfortable. Since I describe many of the circumstances that indicate serious dysfunction in a gay male relationship, the book may help you figure out what is going wrong. Your problems may still be resolvable, and your relationship still viable. If problems are left unattended, they are likely to grow past the point of resolvability, much like a terminal disease.

You may be the friend of a gay man who is in a problematic relationship, or who is going through a breakup. This book may assist you in understanding what your friend is experiencing, and enable you to support to him in a more meaningful way.

You may be a therapist working with gay men, or in professional training to become a counselor. This book addresses in considerable detail the emotional and social aspects of gay male uncoupling, and the tools to cope and grow. I describe a variety of techniques that clients can use, such as journal writing, visualization, and challenging negative, unrealistic thoughts (cognitive behavior therapy model). This could assist you both in your understanding of this experience, and your day-to-day work with this population. If you are currently working with a gay man in the process of uncoupling or who is considering a breakup, it may also be helpful for your client to read the book as you work with him.

VALUE-FREE DESCRIPTIONS OF HUMAN BEHAVIOR DO NOT EXIST

Writing about human behavior under the guise of a value-free perspective is not possible. When one explores others, one cannot avoid seeing "what is" without looking through a lens of personal values, prejudices, life experiences, and so on. I am certainly no different.

While it may be obvious that I value the dissolution of an unviable relationship, it's also true that I strongly support the institution of gay and lesbian long-term relationships. My point is that the relationship should be or have the potential to become healthy, and that we should not remain together for the sake of remaining together. I present the view that one of the benefits of ending a nonviable relationship is that it frees you to be with someone with whom you can truly experience happiness.

WHAT I DO NOT ADDRESS IN THIS BOOK

Tackling an area as vast as gay uncoupling means there are many issues that will not be addressed. I have little personal and professional experience with lesbians, and therefore do not examine uncoupling within the lesbian community. My experience with the bisexual community is about the same. I have no professional experience with the transgender community and am not able to address problems specific to that community. Age, class, and racial differences, gay men with children, and differences in the length of relationships, are all topics that may be worthy of books in themselves. I therefore make no attempt to investigate these areas because of the vastness and complexity of the material. I would not be doing justice to them. I do recognize, however, that these are very significant variables that will affect the uncoupling process. I do discuss gay domestic violence because that is a major indication of relationship dysfunction. However, this is also a very complex topic, and it merits more depth than the space of this book will allow. I am also *not* an expert in domestic violence. Please see the bibliography for further reading on this subject.

I grew up in New York City, and at the time of the writing of this book, I have lived for the past eleven years in San Francisco, California. I recognize that the experience of living in these two very large, openly gay environments is different from living in other cities and small towns. My perspective is thus unavoidably affected by my experience. I recognize that there may be issues specific to the kind of community you live in that may not be addressed in this book.

THE TERM "GAY COMMUNITY"

There are of course class, economic, cultural, psychological, racial, and many other differences among us. Thus, the term "gay community" is somewhat inaccurate (I am using "gay community" to be synonymous with "gay men." I refer to lesbians as the "lesbian community"). However, as gay men we do share some similarities in how we relate romantically to one another, and what we struggle with during the uncoupling process. Thus, while not a "pure" term, I do believe its use is appropriate in describing the people about whom this book is written.

HOW TO USE, AND HOW NOT TO USE, THIS BOOK

This is a "how to" book. You will learn how to make an assessment of your relationship, how to constructively leave if that's what you choose, and how to cope and grow from your uncoupling experience. You will learn what to expect and how to manage the social and psychological ramifications of a breakup. I will discuss some of the major characteristics of healthy relationships. I will give advice and make suggestions throughout, and I will strongly argue my points. I will provide vignettes, a detailed story of two gay men in a destructive relationship (Chapter 1), and quotes from gay men. I will quote some professionals. At times I will provide examples of how to do something (e.g., communicating with your ex when you want to reestablish contact). But you are the one who decides what you should do. The $64,000 question I cannot, of course, answer—*should you or should you not break up with him?* I will discuss a wide range of "red flags" or indications of serious relationship problems. I will supply you with a lot of information and explanations, and hopefully that decision will become relatively clear. But in the final analysis, you are responsible for yourself, and you will be making that decision.

You may not agree with some of what I say, and it makes no sense to do that which does not feel right for you. I do ask you, however, to keep an open mind, and consider what at first may seem foreign and not applicable to your experience. Even if you continue to disagree, there is merit in viewing a different perspective and forcing yourself to think about it.

This book covers a wide range of time in the uncoupling experience, from first assessing the decision to leave to working through the loss and being ready for a new relationship. You may not have begun to seriously consider a breakup, or you may have left him long ago. Wherever you are in this process, there is something you can learn, even if it means revisiting what happened long ago. The book unfolds in chronological sequence, and I believe you can get the most out of it if you read it cover to cover, in that order. You may want to go back to the topics that affect you the most after that. By looking at the whole picture your understanding will be deepened because the various areas are interrelated.

A book can certainly help improve one's life, but it's never the last word nor the only word. I will be covering some very serious topics. Among them are depression, codependency, severe control in relationships, and violence. *This book is not meant to be a tool to help you self-diagnose anything. If you feel depressed, for example, you need to get to a competent mental health professional forthwith. If you are violent or the victim of violence, you must get competent help immediately. In no way is this book meant to be a substitute for any form of psychotherapy or any other kind of professional help. At times I refer to medical and legal issues. Please be advised that I have no medical training nor any legal training and no form of medical nor legal advice is being given nor implied. This book may be used as an adjunct to professional help, such as psychotherapy. You need to discuss that with the person you are working with.*

Use of Vignettes and Quotes

Quotes come from interviews by the author of gay men over twenty-one years of age. Identifying information about these people has been altered to protect privacy. The detailed story in Chapter 1 is based on real people, although identifying information and other information in the story is fictitious. The professionals are quoted and identified by their actual names and affiliations. The other vignettes are purely fictitious. However, they are based on the author's personal and professional experience.

CHAPTER OUTLINE

The book consists of eleven chapters presented in the order of the breaking-up process. For example, it begins with making a decision whether or not to uncouple (after Chapter 1, which describes the rise and fall of a relationship) and later discusses reconnecting with an ex after the grieving period. A brief description of the chapters is as follows:

Chapter 1, "Lovesick," traces a twelve-year relationship from its inception to its very destructive ending.

Chapter 2, "Reinventing Your Life: Making the Decision to Leave Him," examines some of the forces, both general and specific to our community, that pressures one not to uncouple. It then addresses nineteen red flags, or indications of significant problems. For example, lack of trust, lack of separateness, incompatibility, fantasy confusion about who your lover is, and lack of emotional support are among the issues covered.

Chapter 3, "How to Break Up Like a Grown-Up: Healthy Ways of Saying Good-Bye," gives very specific advice on how to actually go about breaking up in the most constructive and least emotionally damaging manner. It also addresses the issue of moving out.

Chapter 4, "A Time of Pain: Dealing with the Emotional Aftermath of a Gay Divorce," examines the numerous psychological effects of uncoupling, such as sadness, guilt, anger, confusion, and so on. It gives practical advice on how to cope with these painful feelings.

Chapter 5, "You No Longer Live Here: Social and Other Life Changes of Breaking Up," addresses the social changes you will experience post-breakup, such as running into your ex in the community, dealing with friends, and relationship secrets being shared with others.

Chapter 6, "Creating the Ex-Relationship: Developing the Kind of Contact You Want," addresses under what conditions it is appropriate to try to reconnect (not as lovers), and how to go about doing it. It also describes the kind of situations (severe control, violence) that mandate avoidance of future contact.

Chapter 7, "Remembering the Misery: Why You Shouldn't Go Back," demonstrates how some gay men return to their former relationship (as lovers) because, among other issues, they have difficulty tolerating the discomfort of the breakup. This can be highly destructive because the reasons for the breakup often still remain. This chapter examines this issue, and gives advice on how to avoid the trap. It also explores the circumstances where it would be appropriate to return to a former relationship.

Chapter 8, "Alone Again: Facing the Difficulties, Appreciating the Benefits," addresses some of the pain of "being alone," and how to cope. It also points out the benefits and encourages the reader to take advantage of them.

Chapter 9, "How to Say No to the Rebound Trap: Taking a Relationship Vacation," describes what rebounding is, and why it is destructive. It gives the reader advice on how to avoid engaging in it.

Chapter 10, "Learning the Lessons of Your Ex-Relationship," helps the reader revisit the mistakes of his ex-relationship, with the goal of providing a rich learning experience.

Chapter 11, "Starting Over: Loving a Man," explores some of the principle characteristics of healthy romantic relationships between gay men.

AMBIVALENCE AND UNCOUPLING

It's likely that many who read this book are thinking about leaving their lovers. Whenever one is faced with such a monumental decision, there is apt to be significant ambivalence.

Some relationships that come apart have been extremely dysfunctional, laden with violence and substance abuse, and many other extreme problems. Although the participants may breathe a collective sigh of relief when they uncouple, it doesn't mean that they won't walk away with some ambivalent feelings. A "horrific," even life-threatening relationship doesn't preclude the possibility, indeed the likelihood, that it had/has some good aspects. The bottom line of *love* is that it feels very good, even if the relationship conceived of that passion is destroying the lovers. If your problems don't fall in the extreme category, which may be the case for many of you who are reading this, your ambivalence is apt to be more intense. Acknowledging and embracing that ambivalence is the most important first step in making a rational assessment of the future of your relationship. Ambivalence causes considerable anxiety. When you are in such a state, you may use faulty judgment to eliminate your emotional pain rapidly. To refuse to make peace with your ambivalence thus can result in either backing away from the scary thoughts of breaking up, or cause you to exit in a quick, blazing explosion. Either of those methods will come back to haunt you. Backing away may simply be a postponement of the inevitable, with years of unnecessary, mutual disenchantment. Moving out the furniture while he is at work will certainly deny closure, with attendant emotional suffering that could last for years. You need to slow down and accept that deciding whether you should leave him, just like the act itself, is a process.

COUPLES THERAPY AND STAYING TOGETHER

If you have never met with a professional counselor, you may want to consider that option if you are considering a breakup. Couples therapy can sometimes "save" a relationship in the sense that the therapist can facilitate communication. Although this is a book about breaking up, some relationships can end for the wrong reasons and need not. One such scenario is when two men are very locked into distorted views of one another based on "childhood baggage." A therapist can provide a safe environment to separate the childhood distortions from reality, and enable the men to successfully negotiate the present. This is just one of many ways couples therapy can help improve a relationship, and avoid a precipitous uncoupling.

Of course, an equally legitimate function of couples therapy is to help a couple recognize that their relationship must end. A therapist can assist partners in coming to terms with this fact, and enable them to separate in a constructive manner.

HOMOPHOBIA AND (I'M NOT PARANOID) OUR ENEMIES

Given the immense lack of support for relationships that gay men endure in this very homophobic society, it is a wonder that there are any gay relationships at all. As a therapist who has worked with gay men for over twenty years, and as a man who has been gay for a lot longer than that, I am continually heartened by the strengths I have witnessed in the gay men I have known. I am equally impressed by the immense power we demonstrate as a community in our ability to love and bond in healthy, enduring relationships, despite the appalling pressures of homophobia and HIV.

But one can always view a description of problematic gay relationships as evidence of a vintage homophobic concept, namely that gay relationships are *inherently "sick" and unable to endure.* Given the nature of homophobia, this is unavoidable. Facts, of course, never matter when it comes to dogmatism; reality can be perverted into pseudo "evidence" to support intolerance.

Relationships between gay men, as between any people, do not work at times. To remain with someone in a union that is emotionally and spiritually dead is an exercise in futility and self-destructiveness. Homophobic precepts about our relationships have perhaps forced us into a position to avoid objectively addressing this issue. Who among us would want to provide any ammunition to those who would like nothing better than to hurt us? However, to grow as individuals and as a community, we must look at the good, the bad, and the uncomfortable. This is what builds strength. This is how we stay healthy and empowered. Few, if any, would with argue the position that it serves our community to deny the difficulty *some gay men* have with practicing safer sex, or who have problems with substance abuse. I believe the same prevails with dysfunctional, nonviable relationships. Homophobic monsters will always be out there, reveling in an orgy of information perversion, bigotry, and hatred. They will always do their best to misconstrue the real story of our lives. Developing our individual strength makes us a more viable and healthy community, and ultimately, a much more potent force to be reckoned with.

Chapter 1

Lovesick

Since the Stonewall riots in New York City in June 1969, the lesbian and gay communities in the United States have made significant strides in debunking prejudicial myths and stereotypes. The struggle is far from over, and antigay sentiment and oppression remain part of the American landscape. But our world is very different from that of previous generations. Like the massive technological changes of the past 100 years, there is no going back to invisibility and second-class citizenship.

As the millennium approaches, we are unafraid to put our energies, our dollars, and our lives on the line. We demand equality before the law. We demand the freedom to work and live where we choose. We will not settle for partial equality, for indeed the concept is an oxymoron.

I believe we will continue to survive and grow in the twenty-first century. We will raise children if we so desire. We will continue to develop loving, long-term relationships. Legalized gay and lesbian marriage will one day become a reality.

Being in love will profoundly enhance your life. It will render depth and color and joyousness to your existence that no other experience may ever provide. Finding a life partner with whom to experience such feelings is a dream spawned early in life. It becomes a procurable goal during adulthood. We, as gay men, share in this vision, despite pervasive homophobic beliefs that depict us as inherently flawed and incapable of mature love.

Leaving your partner is one of the most difficult and painful decisions you will ever have to make. It's probably one of the most agonizing experiences you will ever have to endure.

Gay spousal relationships are gaining and will continue to gain legitimacy in the twenty-first century. Our well-merited delight, however, should not blind us to the fact that such relationships, like all relationships, remain complicated social systems. Sometimes these relationships cease to work, or never were able to in the first place. We bond at times for the worst of reasons—we want the parent we never had, we fear the world, we want to deny existential loneliness and death. Other times life simply gets in the way. He is not who he used to be and neither are you. What once made sense, sadly, no longer does. Often it's a combination of many factors. But whatever the reasons, some gay relationships should not, and more to the point, *cannot* be "saved."

Our legacy of living in a homophobic culture that says all such relationships cannot survive should not blind us to the fact that *some* really can't. Resistance to breaking up for fear of "living out" the stereotype cannot make an unworkable relationship work. When we try to hold on to what is no longer there, we risk destroying ourselves.

The following story does not involve homophobia per se, but demonstrates a host of other reasons that impeded a much-needed parting of the ways for two gay men. The story of Anthony and Steven poignantly illustrates just how wrong something that once seemed "so right" can become.

Anthony is forty-five years old. He is a medical doctor and lives in Chicago. If you ask him what he remembers most about Steven, he begins to talk about the middle of the night.

The middle of the night during the good times. Magical times for Anthony. "Didn't we take each other to a place where no one's ever been?"[1] conveys Anthony's feelings about that experience most distinctly. Anthony generally did not sleep well. When he'd awaken to find Steven next to him, a sublime sense of joy and well-being would overtake him. He would entangle himself around Steven, putting his face into the center of Steven's back. He would feel warmth emanating from a special spot below Steven's shoulder blades. He would also place his ear against Steven, and listen to the flow of oxygen surging through his lungs. He would even smell and lick Steven, laughing softly as his lover remained deeply asleep. During these times, in the dead of the night, Anthony felt as if no one else on earth existed, nor needed to.

He met Steven on a snowy December evening in the early 1980s, in a Chicago nightclub. Anthony felt depressed that evening. He had recently ended a brief affair and was feeling especially lonely and vulnerable. The holidays were coming, and his best friend Bryan was vacationing in Amsterdam. Holidays had always been difficult for Anthony, and the prospect of a lonely Christmas troubled him. His plan on this night was the same he had executed many times before when he was in this mood. First he would have a few drinks, just to get him a little high. Then he would talk to Michael, the coat check person. Michael made him laugh, especially when he critiqued the way some of the patrons looked. He did not know Michael outside of the bar, but he felt very comfortable with him nonetheless. After that, he would leave the club and call his favorite hustler, Chico. One hour of a massage/jerk-off session with Chico was all that he needed. Then it was home to sleep, and awake at seven, in plenty of time for his first patient.

After his second beer, he walked near the dance floor and immediately noticed Steven. Steven was watching the people dance. He appeared somewhat uncomfortable and innocent, almost as if he had never been to a club before. This, for some reason, turned Anthony on, and he had a fleeting urge to walk over to him. But he aborted the thought immediately. He didn't feel he had the energy or the motivation to engage in small talk. "Probably a shithead anyway," he told himself.

For the next hour, Anthony walked around the club, drinking more beers, passing the same people, feeling increasingly depressed and disgusted. He finally succeeded in giving himself an upset stomach. He then decided to leave. "No time to even talk to Michael," he thought. As he approached the coat check booth to simply get his coat, he observed that Steven was talking to Michael. He watched the interaction for a while and found himself feeling attracted again to Steven. He mentally debated whether to break into the conversation. His debate did not last long. Rather abruptly, Steven stopped talking, turned in Anthony's direction, and proceeded to walk toward him. Anthony felt mildly anxious, wondering if this stranger had been aware he was watching him. Steven positioned himself directly in front of Anthony. Instead of saying anything about staring, he asked Anthony why he liked to wear red bow ties. Anthony was confused, wondering what on earth this was about. Why would a stranger ask him a question like this? And besides, he never wore bow ties, red or otherwise. When he told Steven this, Steven responded that he had to make something up; he just wanted to talk with him! In fact, he had been telling Michael about how much he wanted to meet him. He had been following Anthony around the club for the past hour trying to get up the nerve to say something!

Anthony was impressed. His despondent emotions vaporized as he asked Steven to join him for a drink (7Up for Anthony) in a quiet, candlelit booth away from the crowd. Anthony soon learned that Steven was a criminal defense attorney, that he had moved to Chicago only a year previously, and that he was unattached. They sat in this booth sharing their life stories until the "ugly lights" came on, signaling that the club was closing. But they weren't finished. They drove to an all-night diner and ate and talked for the next four hours. Anthony woke up his assistant and told him to cancel all of his appointments. It usually took illness to keep Anthony from his patients, and he was quite surprised at how easy it was for him to do this. When they finally parted with the morning sun illuminating the Chicago skyline, they had made a date to visit a museum on the weekend.

Anthony returned home and climbed into bed. But sleep was flat-out impossible. He was intensely excited. At first he thought he was experiencing an infatuation that would pass. But he knew, upon further reflection, that this was different. He realized that he had somehow crossed a threshold, that the feeling he had was materially different from any feeling he had ever experienced. Somehow he knew that life for him would never be the same.

It never was. He fell in love with Steven. They would be lovers for the next twelve years.

Within six months of that evening, Steven moved into Anthony's apartment. A year later they purchased a home in a fashionable district of Chicago.

Friends joked with them about being the "model gay American couple." They were young (Anthony was thirty, Steven twenty-eight), successful, in love, and apparently happy.

On one level, Anthony was very happy. Being with Steven, doing "nothing," brought him immeasurable pleasure. He especially loved frigid Sunday afternoons, curled in front of their fireplace, reading *The Chicago Times* together.

Birthdays, during their early years together, were also very joyful. They would take each other out for dinner, and "surprise" each other by secretly telling the waiters to sing "Happy Birthday" when the dessert came. (The waiters would come out singing with a lit candle in a piece of cake.) Anthony started the tradition, and before long it became a running joke. Steven would make it difficult for Anthony by saying he didn't want a dessert, even though he loved sweets and was known to put sugar in soft drinks. So one year Anthony got very creative. He arranged for a cabaret performer to sing "Happy Birthday" to Steven. No dinner, no dessert, and even more important, it was a month before Steven's birthday! Steven conceded that he owed him one, as he planted a kiss on Anthony's mouth. The crowd broke out in applause.

Steven and Anthony also traveled the world, having extraordinary, but sometimes frightening, experiences.

Greece, in the summer of 1984, topped their list.

Their visit to the island of Naxos (which they later renamed "Obnoxious") began as fun. On their second day, they rented scooters early in the morning to tour the island. They were enjoying their view of the Aegean Sea when Anthony's scooter unexpectedly ran out of gas. The gauge was broken, indicating half a tank when the machine came to a stop. "No problem," thought Anthony. He pulled the lever labeled "emergency supply" but was then surprised to discover a very big problem. The emergency supply was empty! Anthony borrowed Steven's scooter, located a gas station about a mile away, and filled a plastic container with gasoline. On the ride back to Steven, he nearly had a very serious accident. For reasons unknown to this day, his scooter literally split into two pieces as he was traveling about twenty miles per hour! Anthony was thrown head first onto the road. The container of gasoline flew out of his hand and rolled along the ground ahead of him. Miraculously, Anthony sustained only minor bruises. The container of gasoline came to a stop at the base of a tree.

Anthony was dazed and sat on the ground until Steven found him. Steven had become worried when Anthony did not return, and walked the disabled scooter along the road until he reached Antho-

ny. A passerby in a pickup truck brought them and what was left of
the scooters back to town.

When they told the merchant what happened, instead of an apology, he screamed at them. Although he was screaming in Greek, it
didn't take long for them to figure out what he was saying. They
destroyed his property and he wanted 500 American dollars for the
scooter. He was in possession of Steven's passport, and was not
returning it until he received the money. Steven, the tough young
criminal defense attorney everyone in Chicago feared, meekly
asked Anthony if he could "do something." Seeing Steven in such
fear energized Anthony. Without hesitation he told the merchant
that if he wanted to avoid an international incident, and the wrath of
his father, a high official in the U.S. State Department (actually a
bus driver for the City of Los Angeles), he had better hand over the
passport. The merchant didn't have a clue as to what he was talking
about and kept screaming in Greek. And Anthony continued the
international incident angle, eventually implying that he was going
to call President Reagan. This caused Steven to burst out laughing.
Which made the merchant even louder and more angry. But then,
unexpectedly, the merchant stopped yelling. He pulled the passport
out of a drawer and flung it at Anthony. In perfect English he added,
"filthy American swine."

Anthony and Steven tried to leave the store without laughing, but
did not succeed. In fact, they began laughing hysterically, which
caused the merchant to pick up a large stick and come at them.
Which caused them to run out of the store at light speed! They
didn't stop until they reached their hotel three blocks away. The
merchant actually stopped a few yards from his store. They were
still laughing when they reached their hotel room.

This kind of joy and treasured memories that Anthony experienced with Steven contributed, ironically, to denial of what came
later on. Insidiously, over many years, their relationship deteriorated.
Eventually, Steven would emotionally abuse Anthony. What was
once very beautiful transformed into a living nightmare. Throughout,
Anthony held on to images of Greece and other happy times like
frozen visions that could somehow obliterate his day-to-day torment.
He did not want to accept that things had changed, and that life with
Steven had become impossible. Part of his resistance was appropri-

ate. He did not want to let go of someone he loved. Anthony remained in love with Steven up to and even after the bitter end. The other part was quite disturbing. He believed on a very deep level that he had to be with Steven to survive. The image of the relationship ending created a feeling of ghastly, intolerable, overwhelming pain for him.

Before I illustrate what happened, I want to describe Anthony's background. We will also explore Steven's past in a more limited way. Their backgrounds hold clues to why they created the kind of relationship they did. It also explains to large degree why Anthony remained long after he should have left.

Steven and Anthony are both white men, who were raised in the Midwest. Steven grew up in South Bend, Indiana, and Anthony in Kansas City, Missouri. Anthony was raised in a middle-class family. Steven's parents were wealthy.

Anthony was the youngest of four boys. His mother was chronically depressed and withdrawn. Essentially, she was emotionally unavailable. His father took on the "mothering" role and was especially protective of his youngest. Too protective. He was infantilizing and would "take over" in a manner that prevented Anthony from experiencing his own strengths and skills.

He approached children who did not want to be Anthony's friends and tried to change their minds. If Anthony had a minor problem with a teacher, he was visiting the school. If Anthony forgot to return a library book his father would bring it back. His father even made his doctor appointments until Anthony was twenty, and visited the doctor with him. The doctor finally told his father in no uncertain terms that he didn't want him to accompany Anthony any longer.

His intentions were truly good. The effect on Anthony's self-esteem was very bad. Anthony often rebelled against this control and psychological engulfment. That was the healthy part of him "talking." Although he was unable to articulate this, he very much wanted to confront his own challenges and see himself through on his own steam. But with his anger came guilt and distortion of his own judgment. He was unable to see that his rebellion was a healthy attempt to develop his individuality. He was, in his own eyes, a bad boy for being so angry with his father. After all, look at how much his father was doing for him. How could he bite the hand that literally fed him? What was even more psychologically destructive was that he developed the belief that he could not rely on himself. Fundamentally, he considered as given that he had little internal strength. If his father had to do so many things for him, obviously he could not do them himself. Compounding this was his father's view of the world as a dangerous, unpredictable environment that no one could easily negotiate. Anthony internalized, or in the psychological vernacular "introjected," that view. These conditions were ideal for the development of a host of very significant and dangerous psychological problems that would plague him as an adult. They were: (1) inappropriate dependency; (2) an aberrant fear of abandonment; (3) inappropriate guilt, especially related to anger; (4) severely impoverished self-esteem; and (5) distrust of self-judgment.

The above were also the fundamental dynamics of the relationship between Anthony and his father. As Anthony matured, the relationship also became "internalized." It served as a blueprint of sorts for the way he would form an intimate relationship with another adult. Anthony's father was never intentionally malevolent, as Steven would later become. However, Anthony's dependency, fear of abandonment, invalidation and guilt related to anger, and questioning his own judgment in relation to Steven were similar to what he experienced with his father.

Despite his self-esteem difficulties, Anthony was extremely intelligent and excelled academically. He was ahead as early as elementary school, and became valedictorian in high school. He was accepted by a good college on a full scholarship, and later had no trouble getting into an excellent medical school. He became a family practitioner and was a very good doctor. He cared about his patients and they knew it. He was also a plainly superior physician; he was very bright and knew what he was doing. His private practice skyrocketed early in his career, and he was highly regarded by colleagues and patients alike. None of this, unfortunately, made a dent in his poor self-esteem. Inside he still viewed himself as a tiny, powerless, terrified, bad boy. His only gift, as he saw it, was an ability to fool everyone.

Steven grew up in a very different environment. Both of his parents neglected him. As they were wealthy, they often traveled and hired others to care for Steven and his mentally retarded brother. They truly regretted that they had ever had children. Steven essentially raised himself and his brother. He learned to trust no one and depend on himself for everything. Because he felt so dependent upon himself for his survival, he had supreme difficulty admitting, even to himself, that he was ever needy. This did not change when he became an adult. He could still never be wrong or "unable"; that would be too threatening to his sense of safety.

He also felt unloved by his parents, and as a result he was unable to feel love from others (even though Anthony did love him). He had a profound distrust of others (he did not trust his parents' proclamations of concern for him, which was accurate), and he grew up learning to behave dishonestly toward others.

When Anthony and Steven first coupled, their childhood roles fit together perfectly. Dysfunctional complementary roles often feel comfortable in the beginning because they are so familiar and therefore feel safe. For example, Anthony was "weak and incompetent" and Steven was "Mr. Know-It-All." What better combination? Unfortunately, it was a perfect fit only in fantasy. When you don't live in reality very bad things are likely to happen. It did for them. These roles severely interfered with their ability to negotiate as adults and grow together. It destroyed their chances of developing intimacy and contributed ultimately to deep resentments and chaos.

The beginning of their problems could be traced to the way Steven kept Anthony waiting when they had an agreement to meet at a certain time. Steven was chronically late, and Anthony would often wait for over an hour. Often, it was on a street corner. When Steven would finally arrive, the following scenario would usually ensue: Anthony would yell at Steven for being late, and Steven would yell at Anthony for overreacting. Obviously, any reasonable person would conclude that Anthony's anger was justified, especially since Steven was chronically late. But something else was going on. Whenever Steven did not appear when he was supposed to, Anthony would become overwhelmed with catastrophic thoughts that something terrible had happened to Steven (such as being killed by a car). As unlikely as this was, and as predictable as Steven's tardiness was, he could not shake these catastrophic thoughts whenever Steven was late.

This was his pathological fear of abandonment operating, and it overrode his rational judgment. On a cognitive level, he knew that his fear was far-fetched, but that wasn't enough to reign in his emotions. Furthermore, this knowledge worked against him once Steven finally arrived and the emotional storm was over. For a moment, he would operate in reality and express justifiable anger at Steven for being late once again. But then he would go on the attack *against himself* for having needlessly worried and "overreacted in his anger." Inside he would call himself "weak," "acting ridiculous," "hysterical," and "bad."

It may seem hard to believe that someone as intelligent and otherwise sane as Anthony could operate this way. This is the malignant power of psychological difficulties.

This dynamic then was "used" by Steven. When he finally did arrive, Steven took no responsibility for being late (remember, he could never be wrong or "deficient"). Instead, he shifted the focus to Anthony, blaming him for ruining the day by starting an argument. This resonated perfectly with what Anthony was thinking. Within moments Anthony was on the defensive, apologizing for what he had done. His thoughts went something like this: "I am always hysterical—I was being hysterical just now. Of course, nothing terrible happened to him. How can I believe the same crazy shit over and over again? And so what if he is late? So what if it happens often? So he's not perfect. What's the big deal anyway? I am screaming at him not because he's late but because I have this ridiculous fear. I am a bad schmuck for reacting this way. Steven is *real* angry; he wouldn't be this mad for nothing. I don't know what I am doing. All this crazy shit is going to make him leave me. God I better stop this . . . maybe I will get him so angry that he will leave me. . . . Then what would I do? I screwed up again. Better make it up to him . . . fast."

The fact of Steven's chronic lateness, which was a serious form of disrespect for Anthony, became totally ignored. Anthony remained weak, incompetent, and out of control. Steven remained flawless as usual.

The lateness problem took on more malignant forms as the years passed. Steven would come home at three or four o'clock in the morning without calling, after having told Anthony he would be home much earlier. Ironically, Anthony did not suspect that Steven was with other men, which in fact he was. Anthony was in very deep denial; he could not believe that Steven was cheating. To do that would be to acknowledge that they had serious problems. Instead, he would became obsessed again that "something terrible may have happened" to Steven. He would not be able to sleep and would pace across his living room. He would work himself into a panic, looking out of the window for Steven, eventually convincing himself that Steven would be found dead in the street.

When Steven finally did walk through the door, Anthony would experience the same combination of emotions he had when Steven was late meeting him on the street—first righteous anger, then self-reproach and terror that he would lose Steven. After Anthony would confront Steven for being late, Steven would turn around and walk out the door in disgust. Anthony's terror would return. He would think: "I just let Steven slip through my fingers. If only I could have kept my big mouth shut. Now Steven will be killed on the street in the middle of the night and it will be *my fault*." So he would run after Steven in the street, begging him to come back to their safe house, apologizing for what he had done. He had over-reacted again.

This dynamic between Anthony and Steven became even more toxic in their later years.

Steven would have "friends" come to town, men Anthony never met or spoke to. He never had any idea who they were or how Steven met them. Anthony was never "permitted" to ask those questions—he was "prying" if he did. Steven would often stay out all night with these people. If Anthony objected, Steven would call him a controlling, selfish bitch. If Anthony raised the possibility that Steven was having affairs (Anthony still did not actually be-lieve this, but he would say it in a state of anger), Steven went ballistic. He would accuse Anthony of cheating, call him paranoid, and imply he was thinking of leaving him. Terrified, once again Anthony convinced himself that he had committed a mortal sin and begged for redemption. If he could only be more liberal, he told himself. Why was he basing his relationship on heterosexual val-ues? (As though only heterosexuals would get upset when their partners were out all night with unknown people!) Couldn't he just let Steven be Steven?

At a party nine years into their relationship, Steven's infidelity was displayed before Anthony's eyes. Still the power of his denial prevailed.

Another guest at the party, who did not know them, commented to Anthony about how good-looking Steven appeared. He then went on to say that a friend of his had been *dating* Steven and that he was very jealous of his friend. Anthony did not even consider the possibility that this was true. Instead, he announced that he was Steven's lover, and told the man that his friend was a "fuckin' asshole liar." He added that he "would kick the living shit out of him" for spreading false stories. The man excused himself, saying he had to go to the bathroom. He agreed that his friend was probably lying, and apologized for saying anything. But even under his veil of denial, Anthony was able to discern the expression on the man's face, which said something like, "Boy, is this poor queen missing the boat."

A system of denial can prevail only so long. When denial has lasted a very long time reality can feel brutal and overwhelming.

Denial ended for Anthony in the winter of 1994. He had been feeling sick throughout the month of January. Although he was a doctor, he was a very bad patient. He thought he was just run-down from working too hard and did not bother to see another physician. But when he woke up one morning to find his tongue covered with thrush, he knew he had to do something. A colleague who examined him told him to get an HIV test. He had tested negative a few years previously, and never bothered to get another test. He had been safe with Steven most of the time, and besides, he thought, how could he contract HIV from Steven? Steven had tested negative a few years previously, and he was assuming Steven was not sleeping with anyone but him. Anthony also wasn't sleeping with anyone else. Nevertheless, Anthony got tested. He was HIV positive. It had to be a false positive, he told himself. He was retested. The results were positive again.

At first, Steven was very supportive. He told Anthony they would face the challenge together. He was allegedly tested again and told Anthony that he tested negative. But he refused to permit

Anthony to speak with his doctor. Anthony was accused of being paranoid and prying again.

It didn't take very long for Steven's so-called support to vaporize. He became increasingly distant, and refused to listen when Anthony told him how frightened he was. He continued to deny that anything was amiss—that is, until a cold Sunday morning three weeks after Anthony's test results came in.

Steven told Anthony to turn the phone off because he had something very important to say. Then it came out of him with lightning speed. He was involved with another guy; he had been involved with him for the past three years. They had a two-year-old son from this man's previous marriage. He loved the man; he loved their son. They were his family and he was leaving Anthony to be with them. He was leaving. That afternoon!

It seemed like a bad dream to Anthony. Steven could not have said this. At first, Anthony just repeated his sentences, trying to get it straight, almost like trying to comprehend the instructions in a VCR manual. But soon he was out of control, telling Steven he couldn't mean this, begging him not to leave, pleading that he had HIV and did not want to die alone. He unraveled quite rapidly, crying like a five-year-old, telling Steven he was sorry for everything and that he would be "better from now on." Steven had little to say. He had made up his mind and he was leaving. Steven took about an hour to pack two suitcases. He told Anthony he would be in touch and then proceeded to leave. Anthony tried to stop him by placing himself in front of the door. Steven shoved him out of the way and went out. Anthony ran after him into the street. Steven jumped into a cab and Anthony ran in front of the car. The driver told him he was going to call the police if he didn't get out of the way. Finally he relented, and the cab drove away. Anthony stood there howling, tears streaming down his face, only dimly aware that a small crowd of people had gathered and were staring at him. The cold finally startled him, however. It was thirty degrees, there was snow on the ground, and he was wearing only gym shorts, a T-shirt, and socks. He was three blocks from his house and had not closed the door. He ran back home.

Anthony did not know where Steven had gone, but tried to reach him at his job. He would take no calls. The next day, Anthony went to the law firm and waited three hours until Steven arrived. Steven refused to speak with him. He told him to leave or he would call the police.

For the next two weeks, Anthony tried in vain to speak with Steven.

Steven never communicated with him again. Although he owned a considerable amount of property with Anthony, he simply walked away from all of it.

Steven's story of another man and a child was true. Anthony learned that the man's name was Gregory and that he was also an attorney. Six months after the breakup, Anthony learned from a mutual friend that Steven had moved to Seattle with him and the child. His relationship with Anthony appeared to be erased from his life.

The kind of turn this relationship took would be extremely difficult for anyone to handle. Anthony's poor sense of self and years of refusing to see flashing red flags made this experience all the more horrendous. Added to all of this, of course, was the fact that he had recently learned he was HIV positive.

It took little time for him to psychologically decompensate.

The evening after Steven left, Anthony called his best friend Bryan. Bryan came over immediately and stayed with Anthony until the next morning. They talked for many hours, and Bryan tried to reassure him that everything would work out for the best. But Anthony was inconsolable. He believed that his life was over. Ironically, he focused very little on his HIV status. His feelings about his medical condition actually paled against the emotional distress he was experiencing over the loss of Steven.

The next few days deteriorated into a living nightmare. Anthony stopped going to work and gave little information to his office assistant or the hospital as to what was going on. He also had tortured dreams that he was calling the "Lymphoma Society." An elderly woman answered the phone. He did not have HIV—he had a brand new disease and they had not even begun to do research on it.

Another week passed and he stopped sleeping altogether. Eating became virtually impossible. Hospital staff and his office assistant, Kevin, continued to call. He told them to leave him alone. Kevin finally came to his house. He wouldn't let him in and told him to go away or he would call the police.

Anthony grew very agitated; he would pace across his living room floor hundreds of times. He would also do the opposite; he would sit in a chair for hours and stare out into space. Bryan begged him to get psychiatric help but he was not interested.

Anthony deteriorated even further. His thinking slowed and he began to have a masklike expression. His movements were dilatory and robotic. As he sank deeper into the abyss, he believed he had gained insight. He was the lowest creature on earth. He was an inherent fuckup; otherwise none of this would have occurred. He realized that he had never done anything in his life without an evil motive. He was a diabolical, miserable, rotten-to-the-core shit who passed for a human being.

Anthony was suffering from serious clinical depression. Typical of serious depression is an unrealistic negative appraisal of the self, including a sense of responsibility and level of self-blame that does not match reality. Eating and sleeping disturbances are common. Emotional filtering out of positive experiences is usually present; one feels that life has always been terrible and will always remain that way. A person's ability to perceive constructive options is also severely limited, which can result in believing that suicide is the only option.

This was Anthony's conclusion. He had a variety of medications in his home, including barbiturates, and he knew how much he would need to kill himself. Four weeks after Steven left, Anthony overdosed. He had no last-minute ambivalence. He made no calls, he wrote no letters. He just wanted the pain to go away.

Luckily his friend Bryan had run out of patience.

As Anthony was ingesting barbiturates, Bryan was driving in Friday morning Chicago traffic rather dangerously. His mission was to get Anthony to a psychiatrist now. Not tomorrow, not in the afternoon, but *now*. He was not taking no for an answer, and if he had to physically drag Anthony into his van he would do it. He had already made the appointment with a well-known psychiatrist re-ferred by a mutual physician friend. Bryan had keys and let himself in when Anthony did not answer. He found him unconscious in his bed. He called 911, and Anthony was rushed to the hospital. He was very lucky. He survived, but it had been a very close call.

After he was medically stable, Anthony entered a psychiatric hospital. He was still at high risk for suicide. He remained hospitalized for another five days and the acute suicide risk passed. He was medicated with Elavil, an antidepressant. Although no longer acutely suicidal when he was discharged, it was weeks before the antidepressant began to have an effect (which is typical). Anthony also agreed to begin outpatient psychotherapy. Bryan moved in with him after he was discharged and stayed with him for two weeks. Anthony did not return to his medical practice for a year.

The antidepressant, along with psychotherapy, pulled Anthony out of the depths of his depression. As his functioning returned, he began to see through his denial for the first time in his life. Deeply shaken and still missing Steven on one level, he was astonished to see how he had abdicated his needs for so many years. He was particularly flabbergasted at what he called his "ass-backward reality." What he had considered safe was dangerous. Steven's presence felt like security to him, which he now believed should have felt like life-threatening danger. Anthony was extremely angry at Steven, and amazed that it had all happened. How, he asked himself over and over, could he have tolerated such long-term abuse? How could he have believed that he could not live without Steven? Why did he not see how indescribably miserable he was? How did he stand for the disrespect, the lack of intimacy, the distrust, the incompatibility, the absence of joy? Why did he live in the past and discount the present? And what the hell was he afraid of anyway?

Unsteady and facing an uncertain future with HIV disease, Anthony nevertheless felt hopeful and confident. He knew he had his work cut out for him but he was motivated to do what it would take. He would never return to denial and self-destructiveness. He would never return to the kind of relationship he had with Steven. He was at peace, perhaps for the first time in his life.

Chapter 2

Reinventing Your Life:
Making the Decision to Leave Him

I never felt like we were actually partners in the relationship. We were kind of individuals who were doing things and we kind of had some type of companionship but it wasn't . . . you know . . . it didn't seem like we were building things together.

Antonio, 29, management consultant
Boston, Massachusetts

The problem with Kurt was that it became more and more obvious that he and I were two very different people. . . . The differences between us, personality-wise, came through more and more as time progressed.

Chet, 37, high school teacher
Chicago, Illinois

Ending your relationship—leaving your lover—how do you make such a monumental decision? Are you very angry and want to punish him? Is it a way to shock him, to be able to finally communicate how unhappy you have been? Do you really know what you are doing? You can't go back once you go forward. Are you about to do something that you will regret for the rest of your life?

And what about the scene out there? Do you really want to have to go through all that dating stuff again? Do you fancy meeting the long line of fools, losers, and liars? Will you really be better off? Is now the time to be single, in the age of HIV? Maybe the problem is all inside your head. Perhaps you are throwing out the best thing you ever had.

These are not simple questions, and it is imperative that they be addressed before you make a decision that will alter your life forever.

Breaking up can be a mistake and it can profoundly harm you. It's a decision that should never be taken lightly, nor impulsively. Furthermore, even if your decision is appropriate, it will be difficult—saying good-bye to a lover, changing your life, facing the unknown—none of that is effortless or uncomplicated. However, it may be *necessary*; necessary to save your happiness, your peace of mind, your sanity, and your future. It may even be requisite for your survival.

In this chapter, we will explore some of the major relationship "red flags." While there is no formula that can tell you whether or not to break up, there are many indications that signify serious problems. Making a decision to leave rests on being able to see these problems, concluding that they are beyond help, and most important, caring enough about yourself to demand a better life. Before we address those red flags, however, it's important to take a look at some of the difficulties we all face when contemplating a breakup.

RESISTANCE TO LETTING GO

We pursue relationships to enhance our lives. We chase love to be nurtured and feel special. No one wishes to meet the man of his dreams so he can be unhappy. Nevertheless, many of us stay in relationships that no longer provide what we need. What's going on here? Aren't we the people who change boyfriends faster than underwear?

Some of us do. But this widely held notion can actually play a role in making us remain when we ought to be leaving. Indeed, a number of significant pressures can create obstacles to uncoupling.

Homophobia

Oppressed people, at times, will do anything to discredit a pejorative stereotype describing their group. They will do the opposite, come hell or high water, even if it is destructive. Thus, people from a group described as "passive" may behave very aggressively. Those considered "shiftless and lazy" may be workaholic. And gay men may hold onto a relationship that has long ago died. We may not even be aware of what we are doing because consciously we reject homophobic stereotypes. "That's antigay garbage" we cry as we hear Pat Robertson speak. But we also don't want to tell Mom and Uncle Burt and the world at large that we split up. We don't want to live out the precept that says "homosexual relationships never last."

Internalized homophobia is operating in such a scenario. While we may, thankfully, reject most homophobia as bigoted and untrue, exposure to this kind of thinking, especially during our formative years, does have its effect.

The process of internalizing homophobia[1] comes from a variety of sources. Our society condemns homosexuality in the most virulent way. We are depicted as sick, criminal, immoral, child molesters, perverted, sinners, immature, weak, dirty, diseased, woman-hating, antifamily, and a threat to society as we know it. *I'm just starting!* The list of horrors is endless. The salient point is that to be gay is to be very, very bad. Less than, inferior, shameful, *disgusting*. Learning this from the time you could first comprehend these concepts will have a damaging effect when you realize you are "one of them."

But society conspires in even more ways to make the internalization of homophobia certain.

• Misinformation about who we are and how we live our lives permeates our culture. As we grow up, just like everyone else, we internalize this misinformation. Misinformation not only comes in the form of a "horror list" as indicated above, but in the form of missing information. We learn little about the reality of gay men's lives, let alone the positive aspects of our lifestyle. Thus, it's difficult to embrace "living gay" as a satisfactory option.

• Although we have had a considerable presence in the news and other forms of mass media, particularly during the past two decades (due in large part to the HIV pandemic), there has been a tradition of silence, blindness, and denial in America about homosexuality. Furthermore, due to prejudicial concepts of what we look like, where we can be found, and how we behave, we are largely invisible and treated as such. When was the last time you were assumed to be heterosexual? Have you had the experience of being told "you're just kidding" when you told them you weren't? This contributes to self-invalidation. If the world denies your existence, how good can you feel about yourself?

• Although much is changing, generations of us have lived, and *had to live,* in secrecy. We have therefore been deprived of positive role models, and have been denied the opportunity for normative courtship experimentation during adolescence. Indeed, the case can be made that we have been denied our adolescence. Because our families live in the same homophobic society that we live in, they have been unavailable to us for support against such a barrage of oppression. The isolation and fear and hiding has kept us from growing up with peers who could also provide support for positive self-regard.

• Societal institutions further support our oppression. From the criminalization of our sexual behavior, to the denial of our basic civil rights, to our condemnation by religion as sinners, to the psychiatric profession, which until 1973 considered homosexuality a psychiatric illness[2] (and homophobia stills exists within the psychotherapeutic community, which I will discuss in more detail later in this book), we are up against potent powers that make living gay, and a positive gay identity, exceedingly difficult.

Yet despite all of the above, we have been able to create a strong community and succeed in loving ourselves and each other. We have developed mutual support for one another within our community, and many of us have been able to release many of the false beliefs about us. Nevertheless, given this kind of assault, it is foolhardy to believe that all of this could be expunged from our collective psyche.

Thus, it's no surprise that we may fear what we have been warned about. We may question, at times, if indeed the admonitions are true. You may therefore ask whether gay relationships are inherently defective and doomed to failure. That's a classic homophobic precept. By developing a long track record of remaining together (no matter how miserable you are!) you in effect neutralize that concern and bad feeling about "a gay man being unable to sustain a relationship."

Another form of internalized homophobia is the "lonely homosexual" myth. Leaving him may feel like it will bring you one step closer to "ending up old and alone."

This feeling comes not only from having been told this probably a million times by the time we reach adulthood (which in itself can have a palpable effect). Our homophobic culture creates a *real* loneliness for most of us because homosexuality is considered anathema throughout our society. Many of us walk together open and proud in my community of San Francisco, California, but this is far from the norm in most of America, and absent throughout most of the twentieth century. Invisibility, isolation from one another, and closet living (if you want to call that living) can cause profound feelings of loneliness. During our childhood and adolescence, when we have the fewest options, our loneliness can be most severe. How many of us grew up thinking we were "the only one"? How much abuse did we (do we) experience at the hands of our adolescent peers? Have you taken a look at the suicide rate among lesbian and gay youth? According to Advocates for Youth, an organization located in Washington, DC, gay, lesbian, bisexual, and transgender youth are two to three times more likely to attempt suicide than their heterosexual peers. Lesbian, gay, bisexual, and transgender youth may make up to 30 percent of completed adolescent suicides annually, making suicide the leading cause of death in this age group.[3]

These appalling experiences can create deep psychological wounds related to being alone. To contemplate leaving one's lover may activate a feeling of profound and paralyzing loneliness. This may, thus, impede leaving when you have to.

> I grew up feeling very alone, very isolated . . . the idea of giving that up [leaving his lover] is absolutely just the most horrible thing . . . I know there are other gay men . . . but that doesn't change how you feel. The feelings are still there of isolation and loneliness. There's no question that's the most painful thing about not being with him.
>
> Michael, 47, lawyer
> Washington, DC

> . . . the idea that you'll always be alone. And here I am sort of a self-prophecy type thing. I initiated this breakup for what? To be alone? To prove everyone right, that a gay man will always

be alone? . . . So much so that I was even questioning . . . well maybe I should just go back to the other life because at least I don't have to deal with all these roller coaster emotions.

Juan, 44, research psychologist
New York City

HIV

HIV powerfully affects life as a gay man and makes ending relationships significantly more complicated. How do you leave someone who is ill? What if you are sick? How do you begin thinking about radically changing your life if your future is very uncertain? There are no easy answers to these questions, and each individual has to answer them for himself. Some men could never leave a sick lover, no matter how unhappy they are. This may be appropriate for them not just because of some societal moral standard, but because they couldn't live with themselves if they did. On the other hand, pressures from illness sometimes lead to violence, and in such a scenario uncoupling may be necessary to save both men. In still another scenario, one who is ill may appreciate time in a profoundly more significant way, and would loathe sharing that time with a man he no longer was in love with.

These are but a fraction of the issues HIV raises. It is beyond the scope of this book to address the myriad roles HIV may play in the uncoupling process. As I will mention at different places throughout this book, certain problems require the intervention of a mental health professional. If HIV is playing a significant role in your difficulties with your lover and/or your questions about breaking up, I strongly suggest you consult with a mental health professional who is familiar with these issues.

Our Coupled Culture

The norm in our culture, whether you are gay or heterosexual, is to be with a partner. If you are "alone," the question you will probably hear is "Why is someone like you (with all your strengths) not snatched up already?" The question you are less likely to hear is "Exactly what is wrong with you?"

Being without a partner is thought of as unfulfilling, sad, pathetic, and lonely, not to mention that *something is wrong*. We don't just have our mothers nagging us with "So are you seeing anyone yet, Mikey?" Most messages in our culture nag us in the same way! Try an experiment. Take yourself out to dinner *by yourself* on a Saturday night. Note how you feel as you sit there among the couples and groups of people. Or, if you see somebody alone on a Saturday night in a restaurant or the theater, make note of what you are thinking about him or her.

Leaving your lover means choosing, at least for a while (unless you "rebound," which I will discuss in detail in Chapter 9), to be without a partner. Pejorative societal messages about being single, together with a culture designed for couples, can make that choice difficult to make.

Pain Avoidance

Our societal propensity to bypass pain at any cost is another roadblock to ending a relationship. From food and sex to cocaine and heroin, we have a very destructive love affair with emotional pain avoidance. Uncoupling, by its very nature, is an experience laden with pain. Unless you are in a coma, you are going to hurt very badly when your union unravels. This is a major life change with no rain check. There will be sadness, confusion, anger, and ambivalence. You will experience major loss and have to grieve that loss. There will be uncertainty, fear, stumbling, newness, and loneliness. Your day-to-day life will change. Where you live and how much money you have in your pocket may also shift. And no matter how much support you get from those who love you, it is a solo act. No one but you will be living this experience. In a society that encourages pain avoidance, this will be a difficult option to embrace.

The Gay Single Scene

Being single is a double-edged sword. It can be exciting and free, but it's also scary and lonely.

Meeting new people, at least initially, often depends a great deal on physical appearance and youth. If you feel you do not measure up very well in those areas, it can be terribly threatening to be "out there." Furthermore, developing new relationships requires work. You can no longer depend on your "routine" for emotional companionship, and will have to actively seek it. Getting to know a new person and letting him get to know you requires a high level of social skill. The dating scene is also rife with disappointment. You may like him more than he likes you. When he doesn't call back, when he doesn't show up, when you see him with another guy, all of that is going to be very difficult to tolerate. If you have been out of the loop for a long time, you may feel very "rusty," and indeed it may be significantly more difficult for you to reenter the arena.

These thoughts are likely to cross your mind as you consider leaving him, and can scare you away from objectively assessing the need to do so.

But Staying Together May Be Much More Painful

That all being said, the cost of staying when you should be leaving will be much higher. I underscore some of the difficulties you will face so that you will not let those pressures deter you from what you need to do, if breaking up is what you need to do. And now those red flags. . . .

CONFUSION FROM THE START

I just wanted to conform to what was considered the heterosexual norm of a relationship. . . . I just did it because that's what was expected . . . that all little good girls are supposed to grow up and get married and have a family. And that I was supposed to be one of those little good girls [chuckle]. It didn't matter who I chose to be in a relationship with or who I married that as long as I was with somebody—that's how it was, that's how it's supposed to be.

Lamont, 27, waiter
Dallas, Texas

Most of us recognize the immense importance of clearly thinking through a major decision before we proceed. If you buy a car, for example, you have probably done some research on a number of different types of autos, and know what is good quality within your price range. You are very likely to be clear as to what you want in a car—for example, automatic transmission versus stick, two-door versus four, and so on. You would also know why you want to purchase a new car at the time you are doing it—the old one has died, your new job requires extensive road travel, Grandma Helen left you money.

Although a relationship will affect your life in far more important ways than a car ever will, you are likely to do a lot less homework when it comes to "the man of your dreams."

Part of this has to do with our emotional brain operating. Love and romance are quite alluring, and when we get stung it's difficult to put on the brakes. Who wants to plan and "think through" when riding on such intensity?

We also have a lot of half-baked ideas in this society about what really goes on in a romantic union, especially in a long-term relationship.

We observe a lot of the splendor of romance on the screen, but we learn little in this culture about the nuts and bolts of day-to-day partnership. What, for example, is real intimacy? How scary does it become, and how do you *not* sabotage your relationship when you get frightened? What is compromise all about? What is trust when you have to trust your emotional well-being with another? What is domestic violence, especially psychological domestic violence? When is the line crossed from an argument in which "the wrong things were said" to frank emotional abuse?

Heterosexuals are, by and large, at a loss with this also, so you could probably double that problem when it comes to us. We have problems specific to our community, and specific pressures and difficulties because of the daily oppression we face. How sad it is that Relationships 101, both heterosexual and gay, is not a part of required school curricula.

If you walk into a relationship blind and unprepared, you may find yourself tripping over red flags. After the music stops, you may discover that you are living something you never expected, planned for, desired, nor are prepared to handle. It's like waking up in a foreign country and wondering how on earth you ever got there.

A CHANGE IN NEEDS

All of us, hopefully, change throughout our lives. Traditionally, psychology has focused on the different developmental stages we pass through during childhood. But life is a continuous process, and the desires and needs you have at one point in your adult development may be very different years later.

A relationship sometimes accommodates those changing needs. For example, one man may earn considerably more money than his partner in the beginning of their relationship. Years later, this changes; the man making less is promoted, the other one starts a new career. This significantly alters the dynamics of the relationship they started with. There may be shifts in power, self-concept, and a change in the daily routine of the household. For example, the man who earned less may have had more responsibility for household chores in order to "pull his weight." Now he may no longer feel comfortable remaining in that role. The other man may have had more of a dominating role in the relationship. Money and power in this society are often equated. Now this may have to change.

If both men are self-aware, flexible, and are able to talk about what's going on, the relationship may fare well. The dynamics must still change, but no one has to be left out in the cold. The man who now earns less may accept that his partner does fewer household chores. Maybe he has to do more in the house now. Perhaps he has to do some soul-searching about his former "dominance," and make peace with the fact that things have changed. Or maybe he can maintain a certain dominance in his new role with doing more for the house, and his partner will be OK with that. Power shifts are usually complex, and the men will therefore need to continually negotiate as their changing relationship unfolds. But as I said, if they are flexible and open and communicating, this is not impossible to achieve. Furthermore, these possible arrangements are but a fraction of options they have. The bottom line is that both men need to feel their respective needs are still being adequately met for the relationship to remain viable.

Obviously, this is not always the case when needs change. People sometimes begin a relationship with powerful needs that are not easily abdicated. If one man undergoes major growth and a shift in needs, and the other does not, there can be irreconcilable differences.

Sometimes this occurs when there's a vast difference in age. Although this was true for Kyle and Lester, as I am about to describe, this problem can manifest without a significant age variance.

Kyle and Lester live in Indianapolis, Indiana. Kyle is now twenty-nine, Lester is fifty-four. They met seven years ago when Kyle was in his last year in college.

Kyle never had a significant relationship with a man before he met Lester. In fact, he had had no significant romantic experiences with anyone. He went out with a few women in his late teens, but all of the experiences turned into disasters. He was strictly gay, and although he tried to fight it by dating women, it became increasingly clear to him that he wasn't interested in women. He found men to be just the opposite. At age twenty, he began to have his first sexual experiences with men. Most were "tricks" whom he met on the street or in bars. He had a few short affairs with men he met through newspaper ads. None of these encounters were particularly satisfying. Although they met his sexual needs somewhat, emotionally he was miserable.

Kyle was a very passive young man, and had always been that way. He could not easily assert his needs; often he wasn't even aware of what his needs were. As a boy he was shy and had few friends. He had a brother two years older who was athletic (he was on the high school football team) and very popular with both boys and girls. His father clearly favored his older brother Tony, and it appeared to Kyle that his father was embarrassed to be his dad. His mother was quite nurturing, but she was also timid and shy and had her own problems. She struggled with bouts of clinical depression, and her own mother was very ill. Many times she was simply unable to be emotionally available to Kyle.

Kyle got along well with teachers and did fairly well academically. But he was often ridiculed by peers. He was called "Tony's little faggy brother." Tony, like his dad, seemed uncomfortable to be associated with Kyle. Although he did love Kyle and would associate with him at home, he distanced himself in public, especially during adolescence. He was of no help to him with the children at school who taunted him.

When Kyle first began to pursue men, he found the "gay world" frightening. It wasn't easy for him to visit a stranger's house, and he often felt physically threatened. Although muscular and six feet tall, he did not perceive himself as strong. He also found one-night stands uncomfortable and empty but believed that was all he could expect as a gay man. He was also terrified of contracting AIDS. Often, when he had sex, he felt quite anxious and behaved awkwardly. On more than one occasion he was derided by a sexual partner for being "so uptight."

When he met Lester, it seemed as if all his dreams were answered. Lester was extremely nurturing and supportive, and he helped Kyle feel safe. He had been out for many years and presented a radically different view of the gay community. Lester brought him to parties and gay-affirmative social events (Lester was very involved in raising money for HIV research and treatment), and for the first time Kyle socialized in non-sexually pressured environments. He met friends of Lester, many of whom were professionals and who appeared to be stable and "normal." They, like Lester, were considerably older than Kyle. This appealed to him.

Lester had quite a dominating personality. Whereas Kyle was shy, he was extremely outgoing and self-assured. This suited Kyle fine. He didn't need to meet people—Lester did it for him. Lester could probably strike up a conversation with a corpse, he would joke to himself.

Because Kyle had never enjoyed his sexual experiences very much, he had no problem when Lester proposed that they have a monogamous relationship. In fact, he agreed to it without giving it a moment's thought.

Lester was an upper-level manager of a large corporation. He made a very good salary and was accustomed to the finer things in life. He owned an exquisite home, and he was very happy to share what he had with Kyle. Kyle moved in with Lester after six months. Kyle felt somewhat guilty for living in such luxury, but Lester told him not to worry about it.

Lester was used to being in a dominating role—whether in his job (there were a hundred people under him), his volunteer activities, or in his social life. For the first two years this worked out well for him and Kyle. He made most of the decisions for both of them. This fit in with Kyle's passivity. Lester was essentially his life, and he felt very beholden to him. Thus, what Lester wanted, Lester got.

Kyle worked in a large law firm (as a receptionist initially, even though he was a college graduate) and contributed a fraction of the money to pay the bills. He did little outside of his life with Lester. On occasion, he would go for a drink with a co-worker after work. At those few times Lester asked a lot of questions about who he was with. Kyle found it odd and somewhat irritating, but he did not express his feelings. He simply answered Lester's questions.

Kyle received a number of promotions in his job, and by the third year he was promoted to supervisor. He had significant new responsibilities and had to interface with a large number of people. He found it challenging but enjoyable. He was pleased to discover that he could relate well to most people, even when he had to direct them and evaluate their work. He became less shy and slowly developed more confidence in his social abilities. He also began to make some friends at work. These people were interested in socializing with him outside of the job. As he began to spend time with others, he found that he had to go through the "third degree" whenever he came home. Lester would ask him numerous questions about who these people were, what he was doing with them, and so on. He began to feel more and more uncomfortable with this. When he tried to explain that he needed to have his own friends, Lester would respond with, "We're a couple, I should know who your friends are. Why can't we all hang out together?" Kyle had no answer to give him, but he knew in his gut that he did not want them to "all hang out together." He wanted to "hang out" with them without Lester.

Throughout the years, Kyle grew more and more uncomfortable with their relationship. At the same time, he became increasingly at ease with being gay. He developed a consciousness about homophobia, and felt a deep resentment for having to hide and feel so bad for so long. He became open with co-workers and finally came out to his parents. He no longer saw the gay community as the scary place he once believed it to be. He therefore viewed Lester's "protection" of him as less and less attractive. In fact, he began to resent it. No longer did it feel good to hide from fellow gay men in the comfort of Lester's presence—on the contrary, he wanted to be around them more and more on his own terms.

When he decided to join a gay hiking club, Lester wanted to join it with him. He then decided to forgo his plan. When they socialized together in public, Lester was constantly warning him about all the men who wanted to "get into his pants." He would say he was telling him this only for his protection, but Kyle no longer felt he needed protection. He often didn't agree with Lester's assessment in the first place, and felt suffocated. Kyle repeatedly told Lester that he could take care of himself, and to back off. Lester ignored his wishes.

Kyle also found Lester's daunting influence over people increasingly unpalatable. When they attended a party, he'd be offended by Lester's domination of every conversation. They would be talking with someone, for example, and Kyle wouldn't be able to get a word in edgewise. He'd then walk away from Lester and start up a conversation with someone else. Lester would join him within minutes, and before long, Kyle was no longer in the conversation!

Kyle also began to become aware of a strong sexual desire for other men. No longer did he associate sex with the lurid and empty experiences of years past. He longed to experiment sexually, but he would not cheat on Lester. He finally broached the topic of opening up their relationship, but Lester would not hear of it. Indeed, he became extremely angry with Kyle for even thinking about it. "What do you think you're going to find out there—nothing but AIDS!" he thundered. Kyle remained faithful, but his frustration and resentment grew wider and deeper. Eventually he could not bring himself to have sex with Lester. Eventually he could no longer bring himself to tolerate the relationship. He left him.

Seven years after Kyle met Lester, he had radically different needs. This is not to say his needs in the beginning were "dysfunctional" or less than authentic. He was frightened of the gay world at twenty-two. He knew little about the community and needed someone to show him the way. Lester was the perfect tour guide. He was shy and reticent and Lester's gregarious personality worked as a perfect balance. He needed a stable romantic relationship and Lester was able to provide it. He wanted to get away from multiple sex partners, and Lester supported that. He needed none of this seven years later. Lester needed to be a caretaker and to dominate. He needed to be in super control. His needs did not change in seven years, and when Kyle's did, nuclear fission was created. The relationship became unworkable and had to end. Although Kyle left Lester, one can easily make the argument that uncoupling was in both of their best interests.

You can discover if a red flag exists for you in this area by evaluating your own needs. Get a piece of paper and a pen. Write out the primary needs that you had when you first met, and that he was able to meet. This may take a little time. Try to describe those needs in a word or a short sentence. Thus, you may write "security," "share experiences with someone," and so on. Next to each need write a "yes" or "no" in relation to what is going on today. If he doesn't meet the need or if you no longer have it, your answer is "no." Please note that I don't mean that he has to meet the need 100 percent—no one can do that, and much of your needs may actually have to be met internally. For example, a lover can meet the need for security on some level, but a sense of security in life is primarily an internal job.

On another sheet of paper, write out the major needs in your life right now. Again, this will take some time. Note how similar or different they are from the needs you had when you first met him. Now, next to each one of those needs on this second piece of paper answer (with "yes" or "no"), whether he meets the need or does not, and if not, whether he interferes with it. Stay completely way from moral judgments and try to answer the question as a scientist would. For example, if you would like to get a job that would enable you to travel a great deal, and your lover would strongly protest this, he is interfering with that need. Forget that his feeling is understandable and legitimate, which it may be. The simple fact is that you have that need and he is an impediment to meeting it. People sometimes have trouble self-validating when they are able to justify their lover's viewpoint. They recognize his legitimate concern but in that process *forget that they have a legitimate need nonetheless.* Remember, we are talking about your life, and if he is getting in the way of what you desire, you are missing out no matter how nice he is, and no matter how legitimate his reasons are.

By doing this exercise, you can get a good look at the landscape of your needs, past and present, and where your lover fits into this. Obviously, if you have a lot of primary needs that he does not meet and may even impede, you have a red flag.

SEPARATION/INDIVIDUATION VERSUS MERGING

An issue all of us face in a relationship is the desire to be very close with our lover while at the same time maintaining boundaries. His pain is your pain; he knows you and you know him like no other. But you would never want him physically attached to you or able to see inside your brain. Your love for him is indisputable, but you cherish possession of your individuality even more. In the final analysis, there has to be a "you" before there can be a "you and him."

In the beginning of a romantic relationship we tend to be very merged and like it that way. A Sunday without your new love is tantamount to disaster. A weekend away will feel like years in San Quentin. And your friends . . . what friends? They wistfully hope that one day you will be seen again in public.

When you are psychologically healthy that day eventually arrives. It doesn't mean that you and your partner are having problems. On the contrary, a normal change is occurring, and in fact the feelings between the two of you are likely to be deeper.

Some people, however, do not tolerate the individuation of their partner or for that matter themselves. A host of reasons can create this, and usually poor self-esteem is at the core. When this happens there may be terrible conflict. One partner wants to assert his individuation and the other one wants to crush it. An awful cycle may develop in which one man tries harder and harder to control his lover while the other pushes adamantly to get way from the control. Sometimes both guys desire enmeshment, but that does not make the relationship work any better. Loss of self has high costs. Among them are loss of freedom, stunted personal growth, depression, and resentment.

The following is a list of some problems you may be having that have enmeshment issues at their core. When I use the term "he" I am referring to either one or both of you.

- He tells you how to dress, how to speak, and whom you can and cannot be friends with.
- He needs an accounting of all the time that you are not with him. He expresses a nagging sense that you are doing something wrong when you are out of his sight.
- He gets upset when you spend time talking with friends on the phone. He cross-examines you about who you were speaking to, what you were talking about, why you were on so long, etc.
- He dislikes all of your friends.
- He accuses people you know of trying to turn you against him.
- He has a "we" identity. Goals, plans, experiences, etc. are thought of from a couple perspective almost all of the time.
- He wants to spend most of his time with you to the exclusion of others. He wants the same from you. He's missing a life.
- At times he will finish your sentences.
- He will respond to a question asked to you.
- He will accuse you of something bad (you don't care about him, you are not being a good enough lover, you are cheating, etc.) if you want to spend time alone or with anyone else.
- He will belittle opinions, preferences, desires, and needs of yours that he does not share.
- He experiences time away from you as terribly painful. He will try to manipulate events to prevent this from happening.
- He is upset about something and becomes angry with you because you are not also upset.
- He is angry with a particular person and wants you to stop talking to that person.

LOVING A FANTASY

I wanted him to be really stable and he wasn't.

Jack, pet store owner
Miami Beach, Florida

Falling in love involves, to some degree, creating a person who is not really there. This is particularly common in the beginning of a relationship. Your lover is Mr. Right and he is flawless. This is the essence of romance, and it is a wonderful experience. In time you get to know your partner better, and the picture becomes more balanced. Mr. Right may become Mr. Pretty Damn Good. Or you may discover that he is not really the man you want and the relationship comes to an end. Sometimes.

A person may have such a strong need for a particular kind of person in his life that the partner "becomes" that person, real or not. This is a prescription for a relationship that is laden with incessant blaming, disappointments, and marathon arguing. Vast reserves of energy become invested in anger and attempts to make a person into what he is simply not. Seth and Leon illustrate a poignant example of this problem.

These men are an interracial couple. They have been together for two years. Seth is white and Leon is African American. They live in separate apartments in San Francisco, California, each with a roommate. Seth keeps talking about getting a house together, about "years down the road," about maybe adopting a child one day. Leon laughs about this, saying, "You are a dreamer, but such a cute dreamer." Recently Leon's parents came to visit him from Winston-Salem, North Carolina. Seth had never spoken to Leon's parents, nor did Leon speak much about them to Seth. Seth was certain they knew all about him and was very excited to meet them. He was in for the shock of his life. They did not know that he existed! Seth became very angry when he learned this and told Leon that he felt that this disrespected their relationship. After all, wasn't he Leon's partner? Leon answered, "No." "Then what the hell are we?" Seth demanded. "We are involved, we are having a good time now . . . that's it." "What about all of our dreams, our plans?" Seth pleaded to know. Leon answered coldly, "They are your dreams, not mine."

TRUST

As far as him sleeping with someone else, it didn't really matter. It was the betrayal of the agreement that really pissed me off.

Jack, pet store owner
Miami Beach, Florida

... deliberately misrepresenting something to your partner is a form of emotional abuse.

Greg Merrill, MSW
Director of Client and Advocacy Services
Community United Against Violence
San Francisco, California

John is an area manager for a California bank. His job involves frequent overnight travel. He has been with his lover Perry for six years and they have a monogamous agreement. They share a home in San Francisco, California. When John is away, he worries that Perry is cheating. Perry vehemently denies this and resents the interrogation each time John returns from a trip.

During a trip to San Diego recently, John could not sleep and became obsessed with the thought that Perry was having sex with someone at that very moment (it was three in the morning). He had no evidence to back this, simply a feeling. Finally, he could control his anxiety no longer, and called Perry. Somehow if he heard Perry's voice, he believed, he would feel better. Unfortunately, the phone simply kept ringing. He tried three times with the same result. John panicked. It made no sense for Perry not to answer in the middle of the night, he thought. He concluded that he was definitely sleeping with someone—probably at that person's home. He made an arrangement for an 8 a.m. return flight, even though his job in San Diego had not been completed. When he arrived home he called Perry at work and accused him of cheating. Perry told him he didn't know what he was talking about and hung up on him. Perry was so upset, however, that he left work. He came home and a three-hour "discussion" ensued that almost became violent. Perry said he forgot to reset the answering machine, and the ringer on the phone had been turned off. He was alone at home, asleep, end of story. Not for John. He called Perry a liar and accused him of having sex with a guy they had both met at a party the previous weekend. Perry told John that he was paranoid and "totally crazy" and belonged in a mental institution. John called Perry a "gutter-level slut homo spic" who deserved to get HIV.

John has not apologized for what he said; indeed he feels justified and continues to mistrust Perry. Perry has not tried to revisit this incident with John (as with others when he was unfairly accused of betrayal). Perry feels increasingly angry and unhappy with their relationship.

Nigel loves Philip very much. Their sex life has been bad for years, however. Philip does not want to deal with this and changes the subject whenever Nigel brings it up. Nigel has even pleaded with him to go for couples counseling, but Philip refuses. Philip also refuses to consider a nonmonogamous relationship.

For the past six months, Nigel has been having sexual liaisons with other men, unbeknownst to Philip. The first time it happened he felt he had lost control. He made a promise to himself that it would never occur again. But a week later he was having sex with the same man. He then reframed his self-assessment and justified his behavior because of Philip's stubbornness. He continued the pattern with other men, and "made peace" with his decision. He found further comfort in the thought that "what Philip doesn't know won't hurt him."

Trust is a prerequisite for intimacy. Being in love means being able to connect with your partner on a level that is deeper than with anyone else. You may wear a thousand masks and play numerous roles with the outside world. But with him it is a different story. He knows the real you. He knows what you really think of your boss and your job. He knows about your dreams and fears, how you pulled your penis out in class in fourth grade to frighten one of the girls, how your hemorrhoids hurt throughout your trip to Pakistan.

If you don't feel trust for your lover (based on real or imagined betrayal), or if you are in reality dishonest with him, the structure of your intimacy is fractured. How can you feel secure and let down the masks if you are not certain he is sincere with you? Or, taken from the other viewpoint, how can you feel close to someone you know you are lying to?

I am not talking about morality. I am talking about what dishonesty and lack of trust does to the quality of your relationship.

Justification in the arena of cheating is always rationalization. Nothing merits lying, and no excuse for dishonesty will prevent the loss of intimacy both of you will suffer. In the above example,

Philip is obviously difficult to negotiate with. But Nigel still has a choice. He can tell Philip flat out that he needs and will pursue other sexual relationships if nothing changes between them. It may be the ultimatum Philip needs to get him to change, or it may mean the relationship ends at that point. In either of those scenarios, honesty will prevail, and both Philip and Nigel will know what is happening. One can make the case that even if they uncouple because of this, their intimacy is preserved. By lying, on the other hand, and omission is a form of lying, Nigel has created a false understanding between them. Philip continues to believe they are remaining monogamous, which in fact is not the case. This can only serve to push them further apart. Since intimacy is the cornerstone of a relationship, anything that erodes intimacy erodes the relationship, indeed compromises the foundation of the relationship. There is just no getting around this. The concept of "getting away with cheating" is a common but irrational belief. Just who is "getting away" with what if the relationship is being poisoned? The one who is cheating and the one who is being lied to both pay a high price.

The case of unjustifiable mistrust is equally problematic. Perry indeed is *not* cheating, and John's mistrust is an internal problem. Nevertheless, if he is not able to resolve it, a red flag exists for both, just as if real deceit existed. Trust, like honesty, is inseparable from relationship viability.

WHAT LOVE CAN'T DO

Our culture is pervaded with mythology surrounding what love does for the individual. The song "Touch Me in the Morning" illustrates this: as she is saying good-bye to her beloved, she tells him to "leave me as you found me, *empty* [my emphasis] like before."[4]

This says the following: Before she met him she was "empty," his love for her made her "full," and now as he leaves she is empty all over again.

Her access to a worthwhile existence depends on this guy being there! This does not say much about the guy either. He falls in love with an "empty" woman, holds enormous power over her, and assumes enormous responsibility for her life! I would call that pretty dysfunctional, not to mention devoid of logic. This is not the worst-case scenario. How about the songs that say "I can't live without you?"

You may say that they are just songs. They are. But they do express deeply held convictions in our culture. We believe that a relationship can take care of what is missing in the individual. If you are depressed, a lover will pull you out of your depression. If you are anxious, he will make you calm.

It really doesn't work this way, despite the hundreds of thousands of messages to the contrary. When you have low self-esteem, when you are not feeling good inside your own skin, very few "externals" can change that. The task is for you to go "inside," certainly with help, but ultimately it is your job to change your perception of yourself. The problem is that we often don't recognize low self-esteem as the core issue. We desperately scour the environment for relief from our pain. But you can never achieve internal contentment this way. He cannot get inside you and make it all better, no matter how tight he holds you!

If you try this, you will not only fail, but you can self-destruct in the process. Your self-esteem will be eroded even further as your own life takes a back seat to the relationship. Life will become very precarious; if he ever leaves you your fragile self-esteem will go with him. He therefore cannot die, you have no option to leave him, and you had better never make him angry or disinterested in you. The result will be two very unhappy individuals in an unbalanced power relationship who resent each other. This is what happened to Anthony and Steven.

Some examples of trying to use a relationship to cure internal problems are:

- Not wanting, fearing, or dreading to be alone. Needing a lover to "take away" feelings of loneliness.
- Wanting security, an underlying belief that you are unable to care for, protect, and/or adequately direct your life.
- Feeling you are not good enough; a basic feeling of inadequacy as a human being.
- General disenchantment with your life. You have pervasive difficulty enjoying experiences and believe it is because there is no man in your life.

- Difficulty negotiating the complexities of the world; believing a lover can make that easier.
- Wanting to replace an ex-lover or other significant losses in your life.
- Fearing illness or being ill and wanting to be taken care of.
- Wanting to be taken care of without any issues of illness.
- Wanting to "be with someone." You are the "relationship type" and it is not OK to be single.
- Vintage internal homophobia; dreading to "end up old and alone."
- Your friends are in relationships. You feel inferior because you don't have a lover also.
- Your ex has a lover. You want to even the score.
- Preoccupation with aging.
- Obsessive reliving "the good old times" in a former relationship. You are obsessed with wanting to bring those feelings back.
- Wanting to impress your family and/or others. You are not the lonely stereotypical homosexual.
- Needing sexual release and having difficulty satisfying that need outside of a relationship.
- Desire to "rescue" someone so that you will feel worthwhile.

FRIENDS BEFORE LOVERS

Jethro is a Los Angeles fireman. He has been together with Sam for six years. Sam works in an upscale clothing boutique in West Hollywood. Both men feel they have been arguing with each other for as long as they can remember. Sam likes to stay up late and go to clubs. Jethro likes to be in bed by ten. Sam is a low-fat fanatic. Jethro seems to be on a mission to clog his arteries before he turns forty. Sam thinks flirting is harmless. Jethro thinks it's immoral and disgusting.

A major fight took place at a party recently. Sam danced closely with another guy and Jethro told Sam "to go fuck himself." It turned into a nasty scene and Jethro left the party without Sam.

The worst "World War III," according to Sam, broke out a month before Christmas when he announced to Jethro that he was going to spend the holiday with his mother in Indiana. Jethro told Sam that he should spend the holiday with him, that holidays should be spent with one's lover. Sam said he never knew about that rule and he simply wanted to be with his mother this time. What was the big deal? he asked. Jethro told him it was proof that Sam didn't love him, in fact, proof that he *never* loved him. How could he even consider not spending Christmas with him? When the day finally came for Sam to leave, they once again went at it. Jethro's final words to Sam as he was leaving the house for the airport were, "I hope your fuckin' plane crashes."

Opposites do not, often, attract. We become and remain involved with people who are compatible with us. This is relatively easy to observe in a friendship. One does not voluntarily spend time with people whose values and beliefs are alien to one's own.

When it comes to love, compatibility is even more important because of the depth of the relationship. But it is precisely the intensity of emotions in amour that can obscure a compatibility problem. Deep feelings of romance can mask the fact that you really *do not like your lover or have much in common with him.*

The excitement of a new love can hide the compatibility issue. Happy are those who can quickly recognize incompatibility and gracefully bow out. Some, however, do not, and refuse to recognize compatibility problems for years.

Some questions you can ask yourself to assess your compatibility are:

- Do we enjoy spending time together? Do we enjoy similar activities? Do we spend more time laughing than arguing?
- Without thinking for more than a second or so, does time together feel more like fun or more like work?
- What are my expectations of a relationship? What are his?
- What is really important to me? What are my basic values? What does he believe in?
- What are my goals for the next five years? Do I see him as a support or an impediment to those goals?
- Is it easy to get across to him what I want to communicate or does he often misinterpret what I am saying?

- Do we misinterpret our motivations? Do we often accuse each other of having hidden agendas?
- How do we perceive the amount of time together? Do I feel we spend too much time together, while he feels we don't see each other enough (or vice versa)?
- Do I have difficulty understanding why he behaves the way he does?
- Do I have difficulty accepting his needs and desires as legitimate?
- What do I feel about his friends? On a scale from "love to be friends with them also" to "can't stand them," where do I fall?
- Does he find boring what I find exciting? Or vice versa?
- Do I find him boring?
- Do I like him?
- Do I dislike him?
- Do I consider him a friend, in addition to being my lover?

DENIAL

Denial refers to a defense mechanism in which a significant portion of mental awareness is blocked out or "denied." It is often described as a "primitive" defense mechanism because it is seen early in the human developmental cycle. For example, a young child may put his hands over his eyes if he is frightened. You would not see this in a normal ten-year-old under normal conditions. Under abnormal conditions, such as a traumatic event, older children and adults can regress and employ this defense mechanism. Example: a mother learns that her son has been murdered. She becomes concerned about the dirt in the carpet and begins to vacuum.

Defense mechanisms are very useful; their purpose is to defend. The child needs to reduce his overwhelming fear. The mother needs a "break" from the horrific news in order to process it. In psychological terms, defense mechanisms preserve ego homeostasis. They prevent us from freaking out.

Denial becomes very problematic when it operates as a style of coping with a painful reality. Often this problem has its roots in the so-called dysfunctional family. Denial in this sense is one of the hallmarks of that system. Example: A father is sexually abusing his nine-year-old daughter, the mother is intoxicated each day before 4 p.m., and the twelve-year-old son is failing in school. The family becomes focused on the youngster's failings. The spotlight is on his poor study habits, his laziness, how he needs to be grounded. The real pathology is not addressed. It is denied.

Denial in a relationship is very harmful. What you do not know *can* hurt you. Reality has a nasty way of eventually raising its ugly head.

Denial does not mean you have a complete block on reality. People in recovery will often report that on some level they really did know what was going on. Think about it. Do you have a sense that something is amiss in your relationship but it seems a little too frightening to explore it further? Do you tell yourself that you need to deal with a particular problem with your lover but then "forget" to do it? Do you have a general sense of unease with your partner but don't seem to be clear about why? It may be a good idea to check in with a trusted friend. It also may help to consult with a mental health professional. Some of examples of denial operating in a relationship are:

- Believing you are in a monogamous relationship when in fact your lover is having multiple affairs.
- You are cheating on your lover but you do not think that you are doing anything destructive.
- You are physically and/or verbally abused. You believe this is the normal downside of being in a relationship.
- You feel your lover is your protector whom you cannot live without. But you are actually taking care of him emotionally and/or in other very significant ways (financially, acting as his "parent," etc.).
- You do not feel free. You believe that this is an acceptable compromise.
- You often think of good times you had with your lover in the past but spend little or no time thinking about what has been going on recently (which is not "good").
- You know you are unhappy and don't love him but can't leave him because _____ (fill in the blank).

- Your lover is a drug addict and/or an alcoholic. He tells you he will be better from now on. He says he needs no outside help. You believe him.
- You take responsibility for your lover's behavior. He drops a glass dish. You made him nervous. It's really your fault, he tells you. You accept that.
- You have same the same kind of argument over and over. You believe the overt issue you are arguing about is the real issue.
- You are not happy but you think it will get better "eventually." You don't know how or when "eventually" will come. But that word seems to make you feel better.

CHEMICALS AND PHYSICAL VIOLENCE

Abuse of alcohol and drugs and violence do not necessarily manifest together, although they often do. I mention them in the same line because they are two relationship red flags that either alone or in combination can kill. I repeat—*can kill.* If you are experiencing these kinds of problems with your partner, you have, in a sense, a simple decision to make. Either the problem, the relationship, or you end. If you are violent and/or chemically dependent, you need professional help whether or not you break up with your partner. These kinds of difficulties are very serious and do not go away without professional intervention.

> It was too intense, too much alcohol and violence. . . . We were drinking a lot together. He had a real problem with flipping out after about three drinks or so. . . . We were in a bar together, we were drinking, and the bartender started giving me free drinks. He got really upset. He was yelling at the bartender and the security guard came over and hit him with a club on top of the head. And his blood started squirting all over. I jumped the security guard and then the police came and we got arrested for assault and battery and being drunk. When I got out of jail, I just said, "You have to move; I'm over it." So he moved the next day.
>
> It was very sad . . . I remember helping him move out with the stuff and feeling really sad and thinking maybe I'm making

a mistake and then deciding that I just could not get involved and go to jail again. I'd never been in jail. It was crazy. We had neighbors complaining about the fights. I just realized that it was going to kill us. I felt like it was the best thing that I could do for both of us.

Jack, 56, pet store owner
Miami Beach, Florida

Violence

Disagreements, arguing, and being angry are all part of a relationship. When you are very close to someone, tension and conflict are inevitable. Indeed, if a couple does not exhibit discord at times, that in itself is a problem. It's very likely the feelings are present, and probable that the men are fearful of expressing them. Underground is not a good place for those kinds of feelings to live.

Anger and disagreements are thus normal. Physical violence of any sort and threats of physical violence *are not*. *Never.* It may be difficult for some of us to truly believe this because of our experiences while growing up. If you were raised in a family where people hit each other, violence may appear to be a natural way to problem solve.

Domestic violence does not exist in a societal vacuum. American culture plays a major role in it. Despite all of our expressions of concern and moral indignation, violence in America is as traditional as Thanksgiving. Our culture teaches us to "manage" frustration and to problem "solve" by hitting and killing. Is it any wonder we bring this attitude to our relationships?

While exposure to violence as a child in the home may contribute to one's involvement with a violent spouse, this is not always the case. Men who have never been abused also become victims of domestic violence.

Two major dynamics often operate when people remain in violent relationships: The battered person loves his partner, and believes the situation will get better. The belief, often, is a fantasy. Without intervention, it's next to an impossibility.

Men who are victims of violence often live in social isolation from others. Thus, as the behavior gets more out of control and more crazy, there are no others around to serve as reality checks. Victims also become desensitized to the violence after a while.

If you are a victim, you are likely to be in denial. For example, you may see his behavior in the following way: He has broken the television set but he has not broken you. He has smacked you but you have not bled. You have bled but at least he did not break a bone.

All of the above are serious assaults, and the fact that something worse has not occurred is meaningless. To not perceive the extreme gravity of any of those acts means you are in denial.

Violence is potentially lethal for two primary reasons. It can be uncontrollable. (There is controversy about this. Some believe battering is premeditated.) For example, he meant to smash the television set and you happened to get in the way. It's also progressive. A shove today is likely to turn into a slap tomorrow. The next time it's a punch. The next time it's the emergency room.

I include verbal threats of violence as "violence" because being threatened is terrorizing and is therefore violent. Verbal threats can also escalate into behavior.

If you are being battered, it's likely that other areas of your life have also unraveled. This is often the pattern, and it serves to limit your options. Perhaps you have lost your job and will now find it financially difficult to leave. You may have lost your friends, and thus another avenue of escape no longer exists.

Violence does not get better without outside intervention. There is no way around this. Denial can be very strong and you may actually believe it will stop, especially when he has been so remorseful and apologetic. That remorseful and "calming" phase is part of the cycle, and you shouldn't be fooled by it. The violence will come back. If you feel all will be OK now, I strongly suggest that you totally disregard those feelings and go for professional help immediately.

Help for gay men is, unfortunately, limited. One reason is societal resistance of recognizing that men can be battered. Battering is traditionally thought of as a male-upon-female act. There are also few professional agencies in this country serving victims of gay domestic violence. Please consult the list of gay community resources in this book for some of what does exist. In any event, you still must find a way to get help. Your life could literally depend on it.

If you consult a psychotherapist, make certain that he or she has had adequate training to work with victims of gay domestic violence. Sometimes well-intentioned therapists (who unfortunately don't know what they're doing) do couples therapy when the violence is still very much out of control. That may actually serve to increase the violence.

Chemical Dependency

As with violence, denial rules the day with people who are out of control with alcohol and/or chemicals. Frequently those close to such people collude in the denial. They are referred to as "enablers"—they enable or at least support continuation of the destructive behavior. Denial has thousands of faces. It is the abuser proclaiming that he isn't drinking "too much," or explaining to you that it has been a particularly stressful week, and that is why he is so stoned. It's you pouring alcohol down the sink, or flushing cocaine down the toilet, or again threatening to leave him unless he stops. When denial is operative there is no chance for recovery because the real issues are not being addressed. Stress is not responsible for intoxication. Addicts underestimate and/or lie about how much they use. Throwing out booze is like trying to drain the ocean. Issuing meaningless threats is a form of verbal diarrhea. Only intervention that confronts the out-of-control behavior is consequential. In her book *Beyond Codependency and Getting Better All the Time,* Melody Beattie states: "We may have spent years trying to negotiate with people who didn't play fair. Diseases such as alcoholism don't negotiate. They win—until recovery begins."[5]

NEVER FORGIVEN

Gregory, the marketing director of a clothing store in Dallas, was honored as employee of the year. The company went all out, arranging a black-tie dinner at a very fancy restaurant. The company is gay positive. Mark had been with Gregory for three years at the time, and had been to numerous company functions with him prior to this. He was known and well liked by many of Gregory's co-workers. Gregory had been with the company for ten years.

A seat was reserved for Mark next to Gregory at the table in front of the podium. After dinner Gregory was to give his acceptance speech from the podium. The people sitting at the table with Gregory could be seen by everyone else at the dinner. If someone was missing, it would be very obvious. Seventy-five people would attend.

It was held on a Friday night. Gregory went to the dinner without going home (he showered and changed clothes at a co-worker's home). The plan for Mark was to come home from work first, and then go to the restaurant.

Mark is a special education teacher, and had experienced a particularly difficult time during the week prior to this event. One of his students attempted suicide right in front of him (he stabbed himself in the neck). Mark had had a close relationship with this boy for a number of years, and felt devastated. He spent a considerable amount of time during that week (in addition to his normal teaching duties) visiting the boy in the hospital and attending meetings with various administrators. They were panicking over the bad publicity and a possible lawsuit by the boy's mother. When Mark returned home on Friday afternoon he was extremely tired but still looked forward to the dinner. He decided to relax in his favorite chair "for just five minutes" before taking a shower. The next thing he knew the phone was ringing and Gregory was on the other end of it screaming at him. It was ten p.m. and Gregory had just completed his acceptance speech! "Where the fuck have you been?" he bellowed over and over again in Mark's ear. "Why didn't you answer the phone?" Mark had been deeply asleep in the chair. Despite the fact that the lights were on, that the TV was blasting, and that the phone was ringing, he still slept soundly. Gregory had actually called five times!

Mark and Gregory are still together two years later, but this incident remains unresolved. Whenever Gregory gets angry at Mark he brings up the incident as if it happened yesterday. He tells Mark what a lowlife he is, how irresponsible he is, and how Gregory will never forgive him. When the incident first occurred, Mark felt terribly guilty and replayed the scenario in his mind hundreds of times. He "beat himself up" for being so "stupid," and wished over and over again that he could have done something different. But he finally made peace with himself. He had made a mistake and embarrassed Gregory but it was unintentional and there was nothing he could do to change it. He had been terribly fatigued that week and his body simply gave out. He was also angry with Gregory, who hadn't been able to appreciate what he had gone through. His anger has grown appreciably over the years as Gregory has refused to let go of the incident.

Responsibility is imperative in a relationship. So is accepting human fallibility and forgiving. Inability to forgive is a serious symptom of relationship dysfunction and unhealthy on a variety of levels.

Refusal to forgive may be symbolic of other more emotionally threatening problems. In the above example, Gregory questioned people's care and concern for him long before he met Mark. Although his anger with Mark for not showing up is justifiable and reality based to a degree, his not letting go of it is coming from another place.

Gregory's mother is an alcoholic, and he had been in and out of foster care throughout his childhood. He never knew his father. His mother is still alive and contacts him only when she needs money. She has absolutely no interest in Gregory's life. She never did. His chronic blaming of Mark for this incident is related to his feelings of abandonment and not being loved and cared for. It's a dysfunctional mode of expressing the appalling anguish he has lived with all of his life. In a sense it is also a form of avoidant behavior, because it enables him to "deal" with his pain without, in effect, dealing with his *real* pain. Aside from leaving a chronic wound in his emotional life, it creates, unfortunately, an additional destructive effect by eroding his relationship with Mark.

Whatever the cause, never forgiving has nothing to do with problem solving and everything to with individual and relationship destruction. Problem solving mandates a solution. You may be very angry, you may get over it, or you may break up, but there is ultimately a resolution. Chronic blaming has no resolution. It is designed *to attack the person, not his behavior, and to punish.* It doesn't give the accused an opportunity to change behavior or for the relationship dynamics to achieve a healthier equilibrium. It's a way to keep everything in the same miserable, stagnant state. There are further complications. The partner who is being blamed is likely to (a) be angry and act out either directly or passive aggressively; (b) accept the label of "bad lover" and create, in effect, a self-fulfilling prophecy; and (c) feel negative about the future of the relationship and be less motivated to do the work required to make the relationship thrive.

POWER AND CONTROL

Devon and Gary have been together for two years. They have been living in a house owned by Gary in Berkeley, California.

Devon is twenty-seven years old and is a graduate student at the University of California at Berkeley. Gary is forty-nine and works as a manager in an electronics store in the area. For the past year they have experienced increasing conflicts. Devon feels he is being suffocated by Gary. Gary complains that Devon is distant and "does not behave like a lover." A few of their recent battles:

- Gary repeatedly tells Devon that he loves him. When Devon doesn't say "I love you" in return, Gary becomes sullen and tells him to say it.
- Devon and Gary were invited to a party given by Gary's friend. Devon met Gary at his job so they could go to the party together. Devon was wearing faded jeans and Gary told him that they were going home first so Devon could change; he would not "permit" him to come to his friend's house dressed like that. They got into a screaming argument in the car and Devon jumped out while they were waiting for a red light. Neither one went to the party and Devon did not return home until the following day.
- Devon's friend from college invited him to visit her in San Diego for the weekend. When Devon told Gary about the trip and did not invite him he became enraged. He told Devon he was a selfish SOB and had no ability to love another human being. Devon complained that he had not seen his friend in a year and simply wanted some time alone with her. Gary said that was ridiculous and demanded to go. Devon did not visit his friend in San Diego

that weekend but instead left Gary. He moved in with a friend across the bay in San Francisco. Gary was in hysterics. Crying on the phone to Devon, he pleaded, "How can you do this to me?" And then, in a flash, his sadness transformed into righteous anger. "You are my lover . . . you can't leave me." Devon promptly hung up on him.

Power and control issues permeate many kinds of relationships. At times they can play functional roles. In a family where parents are able to define suitable boundaries for their children, their power and control works for the best interests of their children. In fact the absence of their power and control would be very dangerous. Young children would be more than happy to eat candy all day. Some teenagers would have no trouble staying out all night and not going to school.

This does not fare very well in an intimate relationship between two adults. There is no legitimate purpose for one adult to control another mentally competent adult. While certain expectations are developed between partners (we call once a day, we are monogamous, etc.), there is enormous difference between this kind of expectation and the belief that you have power to control your lover's behavior. An expectation in this sense is a mutually agreed-upon accord for a mutually agreed-upon goal. Example: You both want to be monogamous because you both believe it will best for the relationship. When there is an expectation, one still has the *option* to violate it. Of course there can be negative consequences. For example, if you agreed to be monogamous and you cheat, your lover may leave you. But he does not have the choice to beat you up and tell you that you can never do that again.

Believing you have power to control will wreak havoc. As in the case with Gary and Devon, ending a relationship can be a unilateral decision (actually, in a sense, it always is—I will address that in a later section) and the controller may be devastated with the sobering reality that he never really had any power to control what his lover did.

Absent a breakup, life for both men will be very unpleasant. Aside from making the controlled person miserable, controlling behavior is energy depleting for the controller, who has to work harder and harder at an impossible endeavor. There are simply no winners in such a situation. Furthermore, believing you legitimately have power and control over your partner can result (due to other factors also) in physical violence. This a very serious relationship red flag. Even in nonviolent relationships, loss of freedom and control over one's life is extremely unhealthy.

There is a sad irony in physically violent relationships. Batterers tend to be extremely jealous of any attention given to their partners. At the core of their violent behavior is an attempt to control due to terror of abandonment. This is likely to create, however, just that— the partner actually leaving.

> Battering in some ways is the ultimate dysfunctional behavior because the batterer is doing it so the person won't leave. And often that is exactly why the person does leave.
>
> Greg Merrill, MSW
> Director of Client and Advocacy Services
> Community United Against Violence
> San Francisco, California

JEALOUSY

Jealousy, particularly in the sexual arena, is common with many couples. We all struggle with possessive feelings and narcissistic issues. When it's appropriate, and when it's within limits, jealousy need not be a concern. Thus, you may be in a club with your lover, and if you flirt with a stranger, it's understandable that your lover may feel uncomfortable. If you don't have an agreement that this is OK, then you have something to work out.

Expression of his discomfort to you is one thing. Telling you what you can and cannot do, threatening to hurt you, and/or physically attacking you is quite another matter. As I mentioned in the previous section, there is a world of difference between an accord, a violation of an accord, and an order to behave in a certain manner.

Jealousy can cross the line from appropriate to inappropriate up to frankly psychotic. A man may feel jealous of any attention or even supposed attention that his lover is giving and receiving from others. For example, you may go out to buy groceries, and be accused by your lover of having sex with the store clerk (or some-one else). You may have to stay late at work, and be accused of having an affair. If there is no real basis for his feelings, that kind of jealousy is highly inappropriate and frankly scary.

Sometimes there is a blurry line between what is appropriate and inappropriate (or it may seem blurry to you), and it will be a judg-ment call. If you feel you have problems figuring out something like this, consult a good friend who you feel can be reasonably objective. You can also ask yourself a few questions. For example:

- Do I have a very high threshold for inappropriate behavior in general?
- How reasonable is his jealousy? Do I see how he could inter-pret the situation this way, or does it seem completely out of left field?
- How upset is he getting? Does his anger seem proportionate to the situation?
- Is he telling me what I can and cannot do?
- Is his jealousy impinging on my freedom?
- How often is he expressing these kinds of feelings?
- What is my gut feeling about all of this?

Be aware that in the early stages of inappropriate jealousy (which may also be at the beginning of your relationship), this may actually feel good to you. You may believe that this is a sign of how much he cares about you. "Wow, he's really crazy about me," you may think when he expresses anger that you were not home when he called. Yes, *crazy* is the operative word! Inappropriate jealousy says little about the person who is the object of the jealousy, and a lot about the one who is having the feeling. There is nothing to rejoice about if your lover (or a person who may become your lover) is behaving in this manner. He is not expressing love for you. He is expressing, among other issues, a serious problem with his self-esteem.

Inappropriate jealousy is another serious red flag. While this doesn't mean, necessarily, that your lover will eventually commit violence against you, this kind of jealousy is a significant dynamic in gay domestic violence. Greg Merrill, MSW, Director of Client and Advocacy Services at Community United Against Violence (CUAV), San Francisco, California, states:

Most of our clients' partners [the client is the battered spouse] are extremely jealous about any attention they [battered clients] receive from anyone, even the most innocent kind of interaction. . . . It almost borders on delusion . . .

DYSFUNCTIONAL NEEDS

All relationships meet certain needs. People sometimes uncouple when they realize that their relationship is not meeting their needs. But an equally legitimate reason to uncouple, although much more difficult to recognize and achieve, is when a relationship is meeting dysfunctional needs.

Ralph met Karl at a party in Manhattan in the summer of 1990. Karl was twenty-six, Ralph was thirty. Karl had recently moved to New York from Atlanta. He had abruptly left Atlanta after being fired from his job as a waiter. He had visited New York in the past and felt it could be a good place to live. But he never really thought it through much. He did even less planning. He had no job and only five hundred dollars in his pocket when he arrived at the Port Authority bus terminal on Forty-Second Street. Karl also left a lot of unfinished business in Atlanta. He was married and had two young sons, ages two and four. He never told his wife he was leaving and she did not know where he was for a month. She also had no idea that he had sexual relationships with men. Karl had problems with the law. He had been arrested on a variety of minor charges (such as shoplifting) and was out on bail at the time he left Atlanta. In addition, was alcoholic.

Ralph worked as a supervisor in the loan department of a well-known New York bank. He lived in a small one bedroom co-op in the West Village. He often became involved with men whose lives were not going well. His friends often referred to these guys as the "mess of the week."

The pattern with these men was always the same. Ralph would take care of his "boyfriend" by showering him with expensive gifts and dinners. He would be his boyfriend's emotional Rock of Gibraltar, always there to listen to his tale of woe no matter what time of the day or night. When friends would tell Ralph that the man was bad news and he should beware, Ralph would ignore them. Indeed, he would defend the man to the world, telling everyone how unkind life had been for him, how he had to get another chance, how no one really understood him but Ralph. Then, of course, Ralph's credit cards would be stolen. And there would be five hundred dollars worth of long-distance calls on his phone bill. Sometimes his television and stereo system would disappear. Eventually he would toss the man into the street, feeling betrayed and confused, wondering why this kept happening to him.

The same pattern began with Karl. But something dramatically different unfolded. Karl began attending AA after living with Ralph for six months. For the first time in his life, he began to confront issues that he had never been willing to face. He was physically and sexually abused by his father, and he had actually witnessed his father murdering his sister in a fit of rage (his father was convicted and died in prison). Although he was making little money as a waiter, he was able to find a very low-fee psychotherapy clinic staffed by interns. As he addressed more issues in therapy he was willing to accept less financial help from Ralph. Finally he told Ralph that he would be moving in with a person he had met at his job. He told Ralph that he was deeply appreciative but his recovery mandated that he take more responsibility for his life and move out (he would be sharing expenses with his new roommate). He was also in contact with his wife and the public defender in Atlanta, and was planning to return to face his legal problems.

Ralph was thrown off balance. The usual betrayal did not happen. The usual externalization of blame for his problems could not fly, although he certainly tried. Ralph became distant, furious, and frankly bizarre. He accused the therapist of turning Karl against him and threatened her with violence (he threatened to shoot her, although he didn't have access to a gun). He took every opportunity to ridicule Karl's recovery, often saying "once a drunk, always a drunk." Finally, Ralph lost control while he had been drinking and stabbed Karl with a kitchen knife. Fortunately, the wound was superficial, but Ralph was arrested. Karl, understandably, refused any further contact with Ralph.

The turn of events with Karl illustrates in bold relief Ralph's very unhealthy needs that were being met in his relationships. Caretaking with very needy and often dangerous young men was his way of feeling that he had any worth as a human being. His deep sense of worthlessness was what precluded him from engaging in mutually caring adult relationships. When the other men abused him he always focused on them—they were bad and ungrateful and treated him poorly—he was just being a good guy. He was able to obscure the deeper, more painful issue of why he was getting involved with these kinds of guys in the first place. When Karl wouldn't permit Ralph to take care of him any longer, the terrible pain of feeling worthless was activated. Unfortunately, instead of being able to get in touch with it and use that information to begin to develop more satisfying relationships, he acted out in a dangerous manner to mitigate the pain.

SELF-IMAGE AND SECOND-CLASS RELATIONSHIP

Perhaps nothing more profoundly affects our lives than the manner in which we view ourselves. If we feel good about who we are, we are likely to make choices that are nurturing. We are equally likely to be intolerant of people and situations that are toxic or at least not serving our best interests. Such choices are congruent with the image that we are good, therefore we deserve good. Unfortunately, this is not the scenario for vast numbers. We in the gay community who start off being defined by society as an abomination certainly have our share of self-image problems.

Children who receive enough pejorative messages from people significant to them often internalize these messages into basic beliefs about themselves. What is particularly tragic about this is that they are then likely to behave in a manner consistent with the belief, which will often bring forth more messages from the environment that reinforce the belief. For example, the child who believes he is a "bad boy" will act out in the classroom, earning the wrath of the teacher and principal, who will then label him a "bad boy." This is the same process for other internalized beliefs such as lazy, stupid, undeserving, unable, and so on. Beliefs that become solidified become the basic lens through which the child and later the adult views the world. This mandates behavior in accordance with the belief and difficulty with perceiving evidence to the contrary. Thus, if you believe you are stupid, you may unconsciously set up a situation (e.g., attempt to perform a task that you do not have proper training for) in which you fail, which then confirms the belief that you are stupid. When you are able to perform a different task successfully, you may tell yourself that anyone could do it, or you really didn't do it that well, or that it doesn't matter (nonperception of contrary evidence).

Basic beliefs about ourselves and the world are termed "schemas" by cognitive behavior therapists. While cognitive therapy can help people dramatically change their schemas, without professional intervention these core beliefs are difficult if not impossible to crack.

When we fall in love, our schemas, especially about ourselves, play a major role in who we pick as a partner and what we will tolerate. If we feel "less than" and believe we cannot and should not expect much in a partner, that is pretty much what we will get. In more extreme cases people will tolerate physical and emotional abuse. In a certain sense, the benign cases are considerably more troubling because they are subtle and one may be less likely to act. For example, if your lover has sent you to the emergency room, you may leave him in order to survive. But if you feel a chronic sense of frustration and emptiness you may tell yourself that you are "just being a whiner again" and that you can't expect "pie in the sky." The fact that you are justifiably unhappy is not validated in your own mind. Your schema de-legitimizes your needs as "expecting too much."

If you suffer from low self-esteem, I strongly encourage you to consult a mental health professional. Your relationship may be an external manifestation of your bad feelings about yourself. You are seeing the world in shades of limitations and negativity and you are therefore creating such a world for yourself. It may be very difficult to get into a satisfying relationship because such a relationship would not fit in with your perception of yourself. You are missing out on a lot for no good reason!

Being with a lover should never be a "settle for" experience. The man you are with should be the man of your dreams. No, I didn't say a perfect man. That does not exist. Profound fulfillment with a lover, however, does. There is much in life we must settle for because it is the hand we are dealt. Such is never the case with a partner. We have control over whom we bond with, and what we have to accept from him. "First class" in love is the only class you should ever embrace.

OBLIGATION VERSUS DESIRE

Roger and Michael have been together for three years and live in New York City. Both are busy young professional men. Although they live together, they are like ships passing in the night. Michael is employed by an advertising agency on Third Avenue and works twelve-hour days. Roger is an editor in a publishing firm. They are both off on weekends but have developed an inflexible routine on those days. Saturday is for doing house chores. Saturday night is dinner out. Sunday is brunch with Michael's friends (most of whom Roger does not like) and then reading *The Sunday Times.* Sunday evening is an early dinner and then early to bed. Roger has longed to break out of this routine. When he told Michael he'd like to "fuck the chores" one Saturday and take a drive to Philadelphia, he was accused of being lazy and irresponsible. When he told Michael that he is not particularly fond of Michael's friends whom they go to brunch with, Michael called him an ingrate and a snob (he was reminded how some of those friends have done favors for them over the years). Recently Roger told Michael that he did not want to go to sleep early on Sunday and was going to take a walk. Michael complained that this was not normal; that Roger should not be "walking the streets alone" while he slept. This was just not what couples did, he declared. Roger then invited him to come along. Michael told him that was ridiculous because "at least someone in this house has to be responsible with his job." When Roger insisted that he was going to go anyway, Michael accused him of really planning to go to a bar so "he could get fucked like a cheap slut." Exasperated, Roger gave up and joined Michael in the bed. But he could not sleep at all. He felt guilty about his fantasies. He had a vision of hacking Michael to death with an ax.

Compromise is a salient aspect of any relationship. You do not have the same freedom that you did when there was no one else to consider. But compromise involves a desire to limit freedom because your stronger desire is for your relationship to work. The limitation is seen as reasonable and you are invested in it. Thus, you may have no trouble calling your lover to tell him that you are working late or going to have a drink with a friend. He may wonder where you are if you don't, and you don't want to worry him. This is dramatically different from obligatory behavior in which you have no investment in what you are doing but feel you simply must.

Roger has long ago lost his investment in their arrangements, but continues to participate because he feels he is supposed to. He has lost sight of the fact that a relationship is a voluntary creation that exists for the purpose of enhancing the lives of both partners. This is not enhancing his life. It's making him miserable.

Behavior that evolves from internal acceptance and a desire to empower both of you is part of the growing process of a relationship. Behavior based on obligation is part of the resentment growing/relationship dying process. If much of what you participate in with your lover is obligatory, you have discovered a red flag.

THE OPPOSITE OF EMOTIONAL SUPPORT

A relationship should serve as a buffer against a painful world. If your don't get the promotion you want, it's your lover who takes you out to dinner and tells you what a sorry mistake your company made. If you're being sued, your mother is sick, and your dog has just died, it's your lover who assures you that it will all pass.

That's the way it should be. But what if it isn't? What if, in fact, the reverse is even true? What if time with your lover is generally uncomfortable, and more support seems to come from the outside world?

> I wasn't receiving the support of . . . I guess the empathy that I guess I feel like I deserve from a partner. More along the lines of getting direction and reprimands and being told what I needed to do and not being able to make those choices on my own. . . . If I was having a problem at work . . . he would come back and say, "Well, I think you need to do this, in fact, why don't you go ahead and do this" and tell me what I needed to do, instead of letting me make those decisions on my own.
>
> Lamont, 27, waiter
> Dallas, Texas

I always felt like I could never do enough for him. . . . It basically became a negative spiral where, you know, I never got feedback about how wonderful I was. Now he says, "Oh you're a wonderful person" and all that, but . . . it's really too late, it's really, really too late.

Antonio, 29, management consultant
Boston, Massachusetts

Intimacy means your partner knows your vulnerabilities and is affected by them. Sometimes those vulnerabilities may annoy him to the point where he can't be understanding and could even go on the attack. Example: You are afraid of flying, and your lover experiences stress trying to calm you down each time you travel. One time he loses it and says, "Why the hell don't you get over this, you baby?"

Occasionally, under reasonable conditions (he's had a horrible week and he's on his last neuron) this kind of behavior is not a concern. When it begins to define your relationship, however, you then have a serious problem.

Dynamics are sometimes created in a couple in which one partner becomes increasingly dissatisfied and can see very little good in the other. The stage is then set for a relationship in which support is scarce and attack flourishes.

The attacker doesn't seek help nor leave the relationship. He'd rather sit there and revel in his "righteous" anger. The one attacked may have self-image problems and endure this kind of treatment for years.

There may be considerable reality behind the criticism. One partner may need an excessive amount of reassurance, for example, and the other is sick and tired of having to give it. So he attacks his lover for being such a drain and a wimp and can demonstrate example after example of how his lover demands inordinate attention. That never justifies, however, becoming someone's whipping boy.

Attacking someone does not serve a useful purpose. The insecure man will not require less reassurance because his lover told him how flawed he is for needing it! But more important, no one should tolerate excessive criticism and verbal attack no matter how "bad" one is. That kind of treatment is emotionally abusive, damages self-image, and is the antithesis of what one should expect from one's partner.

Do any of the following describe your relationship?

- You expect to receive no support from your partner when you are emotionally needy. You'd rather keep quiet about your feelings.
- There is an unspoken assumption on his part that you are a fuckup and constantly do the wrong thing.
- His mistakes are not as bad as your mistakes. He would never do *that*.
- Most problems in the relationship are your problems, according to him.
- Your behavior is not criticized. You are. There is something inherently wrong with *you*.
- You want to take a risk in order to better yourself (e.g., get a new job). He doesn't disagree with your decision. He puts you down for your decision.
- He really can't seem to hear or understand how you *feel*.
- He does not touch you (nonsexually) when you need it. You are crying. He continues to watch TV.
- He can't seem to perceive your strengths. He is indifferent or tells you there is nothing particularly special about them. You tell him about an accomplishment at work and he says, "Well, that's your job."
- If something really horrible happened you wouldn't think of calling him first. Maybe not at all.
- You feel you are being constantly attacked.
- He insults you in the presence of others.
- He breaks his promise to you about something that was very important to you. He was going to visit your mother with you. He backs out. He was tired. "What's the problem?" he asks.

SEX

Perhaps nothing could be finer than the man of your dreams being the perfect sexual partner. He would be forever adorable, and sex with him would be flawless. You'd always be equally excited, and both of you, without fail, would want to make love at the same time. Sex would invariably border on, if not surpass, a deeply religious experience. He would also play out any fantasy that your imagination could spawn. He would be the cable installation man, your Boy Scout buddy on an overnight in the mountains, your friend Lonnie in the shower in high school.

Since you and your lover do not live in porno video, you are willing to accept a lot less than what I just described. This is very good. Gay men, at times, needlessly destroy or hinder the development of a relationship because their sexual expectations are out of sync with reality. They buy into gay mythology about super sexuality which, when viewed in a sober light, has precious little association with life as we know it.

To be grounded in reality is a good sign. To experience sexual difficulties at times and to work on them as a couple is fine also. Indeed, it is imperative if there's any chance of the relationship lasting. Sexual problems between gay men occur all the time.

However, a very different problem may plague your relationship. Sometimes sexual interest between two men dies and *cannot be brought back to life*. When this occurs, or when the sexuality slows down significantly, the men may develop an agreement to be sexually satisfied outside of the relationship. There is nothing troubling about that, as long as both partners are *truly satisfied with that arrangement*. The problem comes when there is chronic dissatisfaction with sex and it is tolerated.

What may be very frightening to address is the possibility that the sexuality between you and your partner cannot be resurrected, and an outside agreement will not work for either one or both of you.

Another problem is chronic sexual incompatibility. What you want to do in bed he doesn't. It may be a matter of difference in what turns each of you on, or it may be due to anxiety. Fear of HIV is with us, and while we have a clear understanding of how the virus is transmitted, comfort level is still a very individual matter. Your partner may be uneasy with engaging in sexual behavior which, although posing low risk, is still too risky for him. Or you may feel that way. Is someone wrong or "bad" or inappropriate in such a scenario? I believe not. Many of us are quick to condemn someone who doesn't want what we want, but the fact is that individual sexual preferences and comfort levels are neither good nor bad. They just *are.* Occasionally people are able to change their preferences or expand their anxiety threshold, but it has to come from a desire on the part of the individual—you can't order your lover to "get over it." If he doesn't change, you are then faced with a sexual relationship that may be less than satisfactory for you.

Another problem is the question of whether or not your relationship should be open. Many couples face a serious dilemma with this question because there is little room for compromise. One partner strongly feels the need for outside experiences while the other is equally uncomfortable with such an arrangement. Again, it's very easy to cast blame ("you're promiscuous," "you're inhibited") but the fact of the matter is that neither man is wrong. Again, from time to time, people change and can embrace something they once rejected. *But not always.* Two men may continue to have different needs, and if they remain in the relationship, there may be no escaping the fact that one of them (or both) is going to be dissatisfied.

Our gay community overtly embraces and celebrates our sexuality. But we also come from, and remain part of, a society that feels very uncomfortable with human sexuality.

Most of us have deeply ambivalent feelings about enjoying sex, despite all the hoopla to the contrary. Although sexual innuendo seems to permeate every moment of our waking life, we are far from a sexually relaxed country. Indeed, we have a kind of schizophrenic relationship with sex. The laughter, the crude remarks, the red faces belie our discomfort, despite the fact that sex is everywhere. If you are a gay man, theoretically at least, your uneasiness should be tripled. Your sexual behavior is considered an abomination by millions of people. This has been drummed into your head since the day you were born. Let's not leave HIV out of the equation.

Deeply held beliefs about the inappropriateness of sexual enjoyment can manifest as an acceptance of a less than satisfying sexual life. This can cause you to miss the sexual red flag in your relationship. Your feelings may be unconscious, so on the surface you may be telling yourself it's not so bad, or it will get better, or somehow "this is what happens in a relationship." It's imperative, therefore, to sit yourself down and confront yourself with some hard questions. The first one, of course, is, are you happy with your sexual relationship? If not, how unhappy are you? How long has it been going on? What is causing the problem? Is the cause identifiable and resolvable? If so, what is causing it and how are you going to fix it? Are both of you talking about it? Have you gone for professional help?

Some other, more probing questions you can ask yourself are: Do I feel guilty about enjoying sex, and does this contribute to my acceptance of a less than satisfying sex life? Have I become so accustomed to dissatisfaction that I have forgotten what it is like to receive and give sexual pleasure? Have I adjusted to something that I truly don't like? That I abhor? Have I been fooling myself?

Sexual satisfaction is an important element not only of a healthy relationship, but of psychological well-being in general, and of being alive. Think about this for a moment: with all the shameful and confused feelings you may have about sexual pleasure, how would you feel if someone told you that your ability to have an erection and an orgasm would be taken away forever? Isn't that a ghastly thought? Missing enjoyable sex is missing a great deal, and should never be considered part of the normal give and take in a relationship. That's taking much too much.

THE ONE-PERSON RELATIONSHIP

You have been bickering with your lover for a very long time. It's reached the point where ten minutes with him dangerously raises your blood pressure. You do, however, know what's going on.

Both of you have been terribly hurt in former relationships and you are now expecting to be betrayed again. You are both really nice guys only trying to protect yourselves. In the process you are killing what you could have. You love this man dearly and it would be tragic to lose so much for such absurd reasons. It's time to give up this crazy game. You know that both of you are too angry at this point to make any sense with each other, so it's time for couples counseling. A therapist will help both of you calm down, learn how to communicate, and get back to where you once were.

All of this, of course, is *your* conclusion. And there is a problem with this. He doesn't buy it. But you know you can get him to see what's what.

So you talk and talk. Long hours of discussion that go late into the night and cause you to be sleepy the next day at work. You point out chapter and verse what you are doing to each other and that for the sake of what you have it's time to get help. But you have no customer.

No, it's not the both of you in his eyes. It's *you;* it's *your fault.* If you would just stop doing this and that everything would be fine. No, according to him, he has no problems with intimacy. No, he doesn't have that male problem. No, he won't go for couples counseling. Why should he?

One person in a couple may have good insight about what is wrong and may know what to do about it. But one person a relationship does not make! *Both* partners must acknowledge that they have a role in their difficulties and both must be motivated to resolve them. It's also not the job of one partner to convince the other of this fact. The best of all relationships take hard work, and at the core of a successful relationship is bilateral responsibility. If you are having serious difficulties and your lover doesn't think he has anything to do with it, you have nothing to work with.

PUTTING IT TOGETHER

We do not grow without significant risk and significant pain. Dreaming about reinventing your life is not enough. Without doing the hard work to make it happen, your dream will remain a mirage.

Perhaps you do not have many serious problems with your lover. Or maybe you have done little work to improve your relationship up to this point and you still can do more. If that is true, then by all means do try to make it work. But develop a plan, devise a way to assess if things are getting better, and set up some kind of time frame.

But perhaps you've come to a different conclusion. You realize that it is not going to work, but you do not feel you can *really* end it. Breaking up just seems too frightening, too uncomfortable, too unknown. Maybe someday, but not now. You're not ready for it now, you tell yourself.

If that is the case, consider this. If you are twenty years old, and you are very healthy, you are still unlikely to live more than another sixty years. After that, you will be dead for a very long time. Compared to the time that you will be dead, those sixty years are no bigger than a grain of sand that can vanish in a second.

Chances are you are much older than twenty, and have a lot less than sixty years left on this planet. Do you really have any years to throw away?

You may be falsely comforted by the "balance belief" our culture advances. It goes something like this: "If you are having a rough time now, there will be a better tomorrow. Just wait and see." Balance in life comes from a strong *commitment to create it,* not just an assumption that it will happen.

There will be a better tomorrow, thus, only if you exercise the enormous power you have over your life. Fate does not reward passivity, and you can be faced with a terrible rude awakening at the end of your life.

If you conclude on your deathbed that you missed out on finding happiness with a partner, trust me, my friend, there will be no redemption. At that time you may want to revel in your list of excuses that could stretch from San Francisco to a remote village in South America. You may try to explain to yourself and anyone who will listen the reasons why you didn't take risks and make changes. You may tell yourself that it was too difficult, that it was too scary, that you didn't have enough money, and so on. Your list of excuses could literally stretch around the world but it will still do you no good. No one comes down from the clouds and says, "Poor baby, you did miss out; here is another life." It just ends, and you did miss out, and end of story.

The power to direct your life for happiness or for unhappiness is all in your hands at this very moment in time. What are you going to do with that power?

Chapter 3

How to Break Up Like a Grown-Up: Healthy Ways of Saying Good-Bye

... I finally got the courage to say that it wasn't there anymore for me. And [sobbing] it felt like a foundation had broken. You could see the look in his face that he finally got that we were no longer what we were and that it was ending. ... I love him very much and never wanted to hurt him, and never wanted to admit to myself that I was not happy. And finally facing it, and seeing the hurt on his face was very difficult.

George, 32, automotive mechanic
West Hollywood, California

As important as it is to uncouple when your relationship is not viable, breaking up should never be taken lightly. At the very least you should have undergone the evaluation process outlined in the previous chapter. It is also usually helpful to share your feelings with a trusted friend, someone who can be reasonably objective. You may want to discuss this in a gay men's group. Or you may want to consult a professional psychotherapist. Be very aware of the amount of time it takes you to come to your decision. If you arrived at it in haste, step back, give it a little time, and reassess. Emotions may override logic, and time can function as a safeguard. Don't fool yourself with the belief that "if I don't do it now, I won't ever do it." If it really makes sense to leave him, and you are committed to doing what needs to be done, then you will leave. Nothing mandates that you uncouple this evening or tomorrow morning. Moreover, even if it is the correct decision, if you don't take the proper time to think it through, the way you try to bring this off may be disastrous.

There's a right and wrong way to leave a lover. What's more, should you change your mind, a decision like this will be very hard to retreat from. You are probably having many difficulties with your lover, and dropping a bomb like this and then doing an about-face will certainly add further problems (if not destroy what may have been saved).

But let's assume your decision was not created in haste. You have spent arduous days and sleepless nights analyzing your relationship. You have come to the painful but unequivocal conclusion that it is over.

But what do you mean by "it's over"? He's there just like he was there yesterday. Your world looks precisely the same. How on earth are you going to do this? And exactly . . . *what* are you going to do?

Coming to this decision has certainly been difficult, but the act of actually leaving him will be even be more complex. Your thoughts of breaking up have certainly played out in your fantasies, with you in the comfortable position of trying on scenarios with no real-life consequences. You and your partner may have actually discussed the possibility, considerably more risky, but it was still only a *discussion* of the *possibility*. This is no longer the case now. You are leaving the man. You will no longer identify as being in a relationship. Your daily life will be very different. Your social milieu, even your economic status, may be fundamentally transformed.

This is a time of high anxiety, a period when judgment can be impaired. Anxiety can also bring about a strong desire for action, a need to just *do something right now* to release that feeling of uneasiness. There is also a good chance that you are very angry with your soon-to-be ex, consciously and shamelessly desiring to punish him for all he has put you through. You may find your hand reaching for the phone, deciding to just let the bastard have the news on the phone. I strongly suggest that you move away from the telephone, take some slow, deep abdominal breaths, and do nothing . . . at least for the moment.

Here are a few examples of some men who let their impulses get the best of them, or simply could not face the uncoupling process directly:

• Rodney kissed his lover of three years, Keith, as he went off to work. When he came home that evening, all of Keith's belongings and most of the furniture had been moved out.

• Max was with his partner Adam, for eighteen months. Max was extremely angry with Adam, particularly because he had slept with a guy he met at the local Y. Max left a message on Adam's answering machine, telling him that he was finished with him. He told him not to even try calling back. Adam did, nevertheless, and discovered that Max had changed his number to an unlisted one. Adam went to Max's apartment. Max refused to speak with him, and told him to leave. When Adam persisted, Max threatened to call the police.

• Tommy was in Chicago at a software conference. He received a phone call from his lover of one year, Robert, at three in the morning. Both of the men live in New York. Awakened from sleep, Tommy was terrified. Robert ignored his fear and began to continue the argument that began before Tommy left for the trip. Robert felt that Tommy did not spend enough time with him, and that he let his job dominate his life. Robert went into a nonstop barrage of accusations. He ended the conversation by informing Tommy that they were no longer a couple.

• Jon was seeing Rex for a year and a half, but no longer wanted to be with him. He felt the chemistry had died. He was afraid to hurt Rex, so he could not imagine how he would actually tell him he did not want to be with him. He handled this by becoming more and more unavailable to Rex. He would let his answering machine pick up when Rex called, he would not call him back, and he even failed to show up at times when they had a date. He found different excuses for why he had less and less time to spend with Rex. Rex realized something was wrong and pleaded with Jon to tell him what it was. Jon kept denying that anything was wrong. Eventually Rex stopped calling. They have now uncoupled and never had a discussion about it.

THE BREAKUP FIGHT

This is a classic way to uncouple, and a very poor one at that. This is what ensued between Robert and Tommy.

For some couples, the ending comes in an impromptu argument in which one or both partners announce in the heat of battle that "this is not working anymore." In such a scenario, problems have been building over a long time, and the fight seems to be the final straw. It appears to be a moment of truth: "Yeah, I can't stand it anymore, I'm out of here."

This additional and final experience of misery with your partner may indeed create the moment of insight when you emotionally understand that there is no future. On the other hand, anger causes us to say things, from time to time, that we really don't mean. At the point of rage intense affect is in charge, which may lead you to ignore other feelings. Those other feelings, when examined in a state of calm reflection, may mean you really don't want to split up. However, once a statement like that is out of the bag, it may be very difficult to undo it. You may not want to admit that you were wrong. You lover may be flabbergasted and deeply hurt and his defenses are apt to be hardened. Even if you are able to say later on, "I really didn't meant that," he may say that he really does.

As important as it is to break up when it *needs* to happen, it's equally tragic to uncouple because pride and anger and hurt feelings foreclosed the ability to work things out. Men, as a group, have problems with "swallowing" pride and tolerating feelings of vulnerability. Announcements to break up are fighting words, and should never be expressed unless the one expressing them really means it. A safe rule of thumb is to never announce a decision to uncouple in the heat of rage.

This applies even if uncoupling is the right thing to do. The ending of a relationship is a very complicated process that, as we shall see shortly, involves a lot of planning and forethought. Much has to be accomplished both before and after the announcement. Responding to impulse (which is what you are doing when you are in a rage with him) means that you are not going about this in a planful manner (even though you may have been thinking about it a lot). Expression of anger in such an emotional state will also be an expression of attack and punishment. As we shall also see shortly, anger expressed in that manner during uncoupling is highly destructive for both of you.

And leaving your lover this way has still another serious complication. Breaking up may have been just too scary for you, and rage gave you courage to speak the unspeakable. This dynamic may be unconscious. When the smoke clears, it may once again feel too frightening (unconsciously) to deal with the complex and emotionally painful process of breaking up. So you forgo the process by convincing yourself that there's nothing more to talk about, that "it's over and time to move on." Nice end-of-the-twentieth-century buzzwords, but unfortunately, detrimental to your well-being. There is a great deal to talk about, and if you don't, it will be very difficult to successfully move on.

As with any major decision in life, the logical, rational part of your brain needs to rule the way you conduct business. I don't mean you should deny or suppress your strong feelings. But emotions alone should not determine behavior. Impulsive, drive-by divorce does not work psychologically. Developing your relationship was a process. Ending it will also be a process. Forgoing that process can be terribly destructive.

> It was shocking . . . I walked into the hallway and I saw his set of keys on the kitchen counter. . . . I immediately went through his side of the closet and everything was checked out, so to speak. And that's how he decided to end it. . . . I was pissed as hell and I called all of his telephone numbers that I had. . . . I left nasty messages for him. . . . He left without even having the courtesy of saying good-bye. . . . I felt very hurt. He was truly my first love, and I just felt very, very hurt by it.
>
> Juan, 44, research psychologist
> New York City

BREAKING UP IS YOUR DECISION

How you will inform your lover that you are breaking up should be carefully planned. But before we get into that, I want to take a moment to comment on what I mean by "how you inform your lover." It sounds like a unilateral decision. Wouldn't you want to talk this over with him?

Actually, *no.* You don't talk over the revealing of the decision to uncouple as you would talk over problems, with the goal of reaching a mutually agreed-upon resolution. Then you are mixing apples with grapes. In a sense, breaking up *is* a unilateral decision, needing only one person. It is reasonable to discuss serious problems with your partner *before* this day arrives. Sometimes such discussions (perhaps with the help of therapy) create significant change. A breakup may then become unnecessary. But neither one of you can take the cue from the other as to what each of you should do in the final analysis. Each of you individually makes a decision, and if one of you decides to break up, the relationship is over.

To say it in another way, it is necessary to be very clear about where you are with your decision when you meet with your lover to have the "good-bye talk." Certainly there are exceptions to all rules, and it never makes sense to be irrationally inflexible. But when you have reached the decision that uncoupling is necessary, *you have reached that decision.*

ACCEPTANCE

It's inescapable that this is going to be an uncomfortable experience. Accepting that is vital to making this talk successful, if not enabling it to take place at all. Accepting is an astounding method for decreasing emotional pain, because you are no longer fighting the reality of an immutable situation. I have had psychotherapy clients, relatively youthful people, lamenting over the fact that they didn't do this and that while they were younger. Unfortunately they were expending energy on capturing mirages, instead of investing that energy in what they could affect in the present. Analogously, when you accept the pain of a breakup discussion, you can expend your energy on your discussion of letting go, not on the dread of your facing this with your lover. This is not semantics. Lousy experiences are certainly lousy, but when you fight an unchangeable event, you feed and multiply your pain.

ANGER AND PUNISHMENT

Emotions will be very high at this time, and it's not unlikely that you will be very angry with your lover. Conceivably, you will want to use this "civilized, rational discussion" as a form of punishment—*I am leaving you because you are such a goddamn impossible bastard. This is what you have caused, this is what you get for all you did to me.* If you think about it, your punitive behavior never worked very well with him when you were together. It's not about to start working now.

Although it's very tempting to view a soon-to-be ex as evil incarnate, punitive behavior at the time of a breakup is an exercise in fruitlessness. Evil people often do not cause breakups; people who do not meet their partner's needs do. To attack is to miss the point and avoid a discussion of the real issue—that the relationship no longer works for you. By avoiding the real issue, you avoid the beginning of closure.

And what do I mean by closure? Closure in this sense is the successful result of working through issues so that you can have a feeling of completeness, a feeling of peace, and the ability to move on with your life. How we end a significant relationship will have profound effects on the way we integrate that experience in our personal history, and how we view a similar experience in the future. This is one of the reasons why the termination phase of psychotherapy is emphasized in professional training. It's crucial for the therapist to handle this in a planful manner, to maximize the benefits of the experience for the client. A successful termination enables the client to have a positive feeling about entering a therapeutic relationship in the future, should he need one.

Attacking and blaming is a proven method to harden defenses. If you attack it's likely you will be attacked in return. You'll spend time throwing bombs at each other, and accomplish nothing other than mutual emotional destruction.

When you uncouple, there are also likely to be a lot of sad feelings. You are losing an important part of your life, and with loss there is sadness and a need to grieve the loss. Anger is uncomfortable, but sadness and the sense of vulnerability that comes with that emotion is significantly more difficult to deal with. Added to the equation is the fact that you and your lover are two *men* who are socialized to avoid these more "feminine" kinds of feelings. Anger can work as perfect defense against those emotions, but at the high cost of debasing the closure process.

... I wish I didn't end it in such a mad way, such an angry way. I always told myself I would never want to be like my father [laughter]. After twenty-six years of living with my mom, their divorce was just so so so messy and dirty and nit-picking and every cent was counted. And to some degree, our breakup was like that.

Juan, 44, research psychologist
New York City

Of course, anger and sadness are not mutually exclusive feelings. The problem comes when one is used to cover up the other. It's OK, indeed essential, to express your anger and disappointment during this discussion. But it needs to be accomplished in a calm, direct, nonattacking way.

WHERE AND HOW TO DO IT: PRACTICAL CONSIDERATIONS

Uncoupling should involve a number of encounters with your lover. One discussion will not suffice; there is too much to talk about. Of course, you may not have cooperation from him, and if that is the case, you will have to work with what you have.

It essentially goes without saying (but I'll say it anyway to avoid any misunderstandings) that your rendezvous should be face to face without any interruptions. You don't need telephones ringing when you are in the midst of dealing with such emotionally loaded, life-changing issues. A public place such as a restaurant or park is not a good place to uncouple. There will be many distractions and a lack of privacy. Although problems can arise by meeting in either of your homes, or the home you both share if that is the case ("good old time" memory triggers, difficulty with ending the talk, etc.), a home is probably the best environment. I will address, shortly, the issue of what to do if the potential for violence exists.

You will need a considerable amount of time, so don't "pencil in" this conversation between other events. You will have a lot to think about after you finish talking, so you should plan to be alone (if that's too uncomfortable, plan to be with a friend with whom you can talk about your encounter). By all means do not have this discussion before you go to work, or at bedtime. A day when you are both off and otherwise relaxed is ideal. As I said, you will need a significant amount of time for this meeting, but there should also be a limit. When you are dealing with exhausting emotional feelings, there comes a point when talking is nonproductive. You will need to process the experience, and you can revisit the issues during an ensuing conversation.

Plan a specific time and place for your next meeting before you finish the first. Don't leave it to "we'll talk." There can be a strong temptation to avoid the discomfort you anticipate, and you may do just that. Should you not have the next discussion, the process may be incomplete, which could forfeit the closure you need.

The Purpose of the First Meeting

The primary reason you are meeting with your lover is to end the relationship you now have with him. You are creating a new boundary, a significant "before" and "after" in the chronicle of your life. And although I have already said this, it bears repeating—while he may feel the same way, while he may be in full agreement, while he may have been just about to do the same thing, this is still a *unilateral* decision in a sense. You have made this decision because the relationship can no longer work for *you*.

It's essential to communicate these facts clearly and without hesitation. You should be speaking from the "I," taking responsibility for what you have decided. It also serves no purpose to beat around the bush with long prologues and confusing messages such as "I think we need to take a break for a while." If you really think you need to take a break for a while, you are doing something different than ending a relationship. That is a legitimate option in a problematic relationship, but that means you have not concluded that your relationship is not workable. This is *not* where you are in this encounter.

Those first words are, of course, the most difficult to express. Accept the fact that no matter how you say it, these are harsh, scary words. They are not going to create happiness or serenity. They are also very serious words, so don't try to present them in any kind of joking manner. We sometimes joke as a way to take the edge off anxiety, but that is not appropriate here. Try to express this state-

ment in the most matter-of-fact manner you can, although obviously there will be emotion in your voice. Certainly, attempt to control
anger and expressions of apology or guilt. What you are about to
say is not really good, bad, moral, or immoral. It's simply what has
to be done.

Here is one way I'd recommend you say it:

> Jeff, I wanted to meet with you today to let you know that I
> have decided I can no longer remain in this relationship with
> you. I would like to take some time with you now to explain
> why I have come to this decision.

I like the above statement because of the following:

- The speaker is taking full responsibility for his decision—"I
  have decided . . ."
- The issue is expressed immediately—there is no "drumroll"
  period when anxiety builds. He tells Jeff immediately that he is
  breaking up with him.
- He is letting Jeff know that he will explain forthwith why he
  has come to this decision. This makes such a traumatic statement more palatable because the speaker is saying there will
  be an explanation for this. It also implies respect for the speaker's lover—"I owe you an explanation for something that will
  so profoundly alter your life as well as mine."
- There is no blaming. There is no bad guy.

Here are a couple of ways I *wouldn't* recommend saying it, and
why:

- "This relationship doesn't work anymore and we have to go
  our separate ways." The speaker is not taking responsibility for
  himself and is implying the relationship is not working for his lover
  as well as for him. Perhaps, as far as his lover is concerned, everything is just dandy.
- "I'm leaving you, Ross. I'm really sorry that I had to do this
  but I have to. I know how much this is going to hurt you. I know
  how much you have been hurt before, and believe me I don't want
  to give you any more pain. Please don't be angry with me, I won't
  be able to stand that." The speaker is expressing guilt on his part,

which is inappropriate. (Why should he be guilty for a decision he needs to make for himself? Sensitivity to his lover's feelings is fine. Guilt comes from doing something "wrong," and therefore it does not belong here.) He is also claiming knowledge he does not possess when he says he *knows* how much this is going to hurt Ross. He does *not* know exactly how this will hurt him. Finally, he is telling Ross not to feel a certain way not for Ross's benefit, but for his own. "Please don't be angry with me, I won't be able to stand that." There's a lot more wrong with this. It's patently absurd to tell anyone how they should feel. One cannot adjust one's feelings to satisfy another. Indeed, many of us have difficulty adjusting our feelings to satisfy ourselves! Ross also has a right to feel anything he wants, including anger. The speaker is invalidating Ross's experience of this by telling him not to feel a certain way. That is unfair and a poor way to begin the delicate, painful process of breaking up.

• "You know, as I know, Joseph, that this relationship has not been working for a long time. Don't you agree we should call it quits?" Again, in this situation, the man is assuming that his lover sees it the same way as he does. He is also dodging responsibility for the decision—he is trying to have his lover take responsibility, or at least bilateral responsibility, for a unilateral decision.

• "I need to change our relationship. I can't be your lover. I'm really not able to be in a relationship now, Cecil." That's fine if it's true. But if he's not able to be in a relationship with *Cecil*, he is lying.

• "This is not working for me, Jay. We have to call it quits. But it doesn't mean all is lost. We can still be great friends." While many men do form lasting friendships with their ex-lovers, this cannot always be accomplished. At the time you are breaking up you do not know whether this can be attained. Talking about friendship at this point is precipitous, and may be a phony way of trying to soften the blow. It's really a false reassurance (even though you may not intend that), which can sound very hollow to your lover. Furthermore, it may never be realized, which can create angry and disappointing feelings in your lover later. "Yeah, he said we'd be great friends and I don't even see him anymore. What bullshit."

While it is important to be clear that you are breaking up and not "taking a break for a while," it doesn't mean you could *never* go back together. Unforeseen occurrences, perhaps the breakup itself, may cause changes that will make a relationship with him viable once again. I will address that option later in the book. Suffice to say, however, that when you are saying good-bye this scenario is not a strong prospect. Thus, you may never want to say never, but it's not helpful to communicate false expectations.

Aside from the purpose of creating the "official change," this talk has four other major aims: it's the moment to explain why you have come to this decision, an opportunity for him to express his thoughts and opinions, an occasion for both of you to begin processing feelings, and the time for both of you to plan what comes next. Your lover may be thoroughly uncooperative, and these four other goals may never be realized. You cannot control his behavior, and to try to do that is far more damaging than to forgo this process. He may be in a state of shock, so if he needs time and space to process this on his own first, let him have it. If he never wants to talk to you again, as sad and unfinished as that will be, it is *his* choice and you must accept that.

For our purposes, let's assume that you get the opportunity I've just described. Let's take a closer look.

Explaining Your Decision

It's important to let your lover know why you reached this conclusion. This aids you because you are getting an opportunity to express important feelings and at the same time engaging in responsible behavior toward a person who has meant (and may still mean) a great deal to you. It helps your lover because it gives him an opportunity to make sense, at least from your perspective, of why this is occurring. This supports closure for both of you.

It's likely you will be expressing raw, uncomfortable feelings. For example, statements such as "I am not enjoying time with you any longer," "I no longer love you" are powerful, painful words. You do need to be direct. If you don't love him anymore you need to let him know that. The problem comes when, as described earlier, it's presented in a way that attacks and inflicts punishment. Stay far away from that. Say, "I am leaving you because . . ." with the focus remaining on you, with the account underscoring why you are doing this for *you*. It of course doesn't mean you shouldn't express negative opinions and feelings about him. If you are unhappy with him, there are obviously things about him you don't like. It's fine to make that clear. In fact, trying to avoid that would sound stilted and phony. But the conversation always needs to come back to why this is not OK for you. Personality assassination is highly counter-productive. You should never get into "I am leaving you because of so and so, and this makes you a so-and-so kind of despicable person, and you deserve such-and-such punishment for this evil you have perpetrated for so-and-so many years!" Not only can this be devastating for him, and bring about the other negative ramifications I have previously mentioned about punishing behavior, but it robs *you* of the opportunity to articulate your needs. Expressing your needs will aid your closure.

An example of an appropriate way to express your reasons for leaving could go something like this:

> Jason, I've made the decision to leave because I am very unhappy with you. You are a very needy person and I can no longer take care of those needs. We seem to have set up a parent-child form of relationship in which I take care of you and forget about me. In one way or another I lose me. In many ways this is really my problem. I have a long history with this as a child and with other men I've been involved with. But I realize this is very destructive for me. I also need to be taken care of. I want a mutually caring adult relationship where both of us can be equal partners. This has not been our relationship, Jason, and although we have talked about this many, many times, there has not been any real change. I have gone down this path for too long in my life and I can't . . . won't go down it any longer. I am leaving because I need to take care of me. I do hope you understand.

Keep in mind that expressing your reasons does not mean *justifying* your reasons. You don't need "good enough explanations"; you do not need for him to approve your rationale.

In the above example let's say Jason reacts as follows:

> You know, Kenny, I have made many changes and I will make more in the future. It takes a very long time to learn to

stand on my feet . . . you know I was always babied by my mother but I have been working on this in therapy. You are very selfish to think only of yourself, and throw out all we have . . . all we can have. Besides, you are not thinking of it accurately. I do many things for you; we can have an adult partnership. I think you are just very angry with me and you are doing this to get even. Your reasons don't make sense. This is a very big mistake you are making, and you will feel sorry someday if you do go through with this.

And a good way for Kenny to respond to this would be:

My reasons make sense to me. I am in no way doing this to hurt you, but if you want to believe that, there is nothing that I can do to change that. I also know that you have certainly tried to change but it's still not working for me. I am not happy. I have not been happy for a very long time, and this is a decision I have made for me. You are certainly entitled to your opinion, but so am I. And since I am in charge of me, I have to listen to me. It would be nice if you saw it my way, but with all due respect, I don't need you to see it my way. I still care very much about you, Jason, and I feel very sad about all of this. But I also know it's the right thing for me to do.

Notice that Kenny makes no attempt to attack Jason, even though he fully disagrees with him. It's also very healthy that Kenny is able to express caring feelings at the same time he is telling Jason that he can no longer be with him. We will explore that issue further in the section on processing feelings.

His Thoughts and Opinions

He may agree that this is the best thing you ever did, and that he was going to do the same thing also. Fine and dandy if he says that. On the other hand, as in the previous example, he may strongly disagree with you, and want you to change your mind.

He has a right to his opinion, and you should listen to it with respect. It's important for his closure for him to have an opportunity to express *his* views. It doesn't mean you have to concur with him. Kenny handles this nicely in the above vignette.

You may also see his thinking is clearly illogical, and want to go on a mission to correct him. For example, he may tell you that you can learn to love him again (if you tell him you have fallen out of love), when you know that learning has nothing to do with it. Forget about that mission to make him see the light! You are unlikely to convince him, and why expend energy on that endeavor in the first place? Nothing is going to change for you whether he sees it your way or not. Just as with Kenny and Jason, Kenny is still leaving. Your inability to love him is *your reality*, and you need to honor what you know to be true for you. Furthermore, he may need to believe what he believes right now. Perhaps this is what will help him cope. So let him. Hopefully he will see it more realistically at some later point. But even if he doesn't, it doesn't matter for you (other than gratifying your wish for him to be in agreement). Keep in mind that we can never control what someone else thinks, and we have to make peace with that fact.

Processing Feelings

During this experience, many feelings are going to be activated. Aside from being powerful, they are likely to be conflicting and emotionally draining.

In an antagonist situation, it is difficult to express feelings other than anger and disappointment. If your breaking-up discussion is very hostile you may not feel anything other than rage *on the surface*. But many other feelings are certainly there. You have loved this person, or still do. You have cared about this person's welfare, and probably still do. If he were suddenly to be hit by a car, would it really not affect you? You also have a history with him, and some of that time, perhaps lots of that time together, was very happy. You never would have stayed with him if that wasn't so.

It's important to share some of those feelings. This will facilitate closure. Talking about those feelings with your partner helps both of you psychologically integrate the fact that positive aspects were also part of the experience. People often feel they failed when they break up. But there is another way to frame this. The fact that it couldn't last forever may be a failure in a sense. On the other hand, you have had an experience that was unique and that "gave" to both of you. You can walk away with a sense of accomplishment and inner peace, although sad.

By talking about it, each of you has the opportunity to let the other one know what you have meant to each other. This doesn't work only in the sense of learning how you were valued by your partner (if he expresses this to you). It will be psychologically important for you to express to him your good feelings. In an emotional storm of anger and disconnection, these sentiments may be the furthest from your mind. But since they also exist, there could be negative consequences later on if you deny them. There could be deep regrets, and regrets are among the most painful feelings to have.

This is best illustrated when someone we care about suddenly dies. We may have been very angry with this individual at the time of his death. When we learn that he has died, few of us would lament over the missed opportunities to share even more negative sentiments. It's likely that we would be disturbed about not having let him know about the aspects of him we deeply valued and loved.

But your partner doesn't have to die. Expression of these feelings will still benefit you in the long run. After time passes and the emotional storm of a breakup is over, we do indeed remember the good times. You may feel cheated if you never got the opportunity to let him know that he gave those to you. It will interfere with your happy memories because you will feel that something is not complete. The following is an example of expressing positive sentiments in an uncoupling discussion:

(Rico speaking)

Bryan, as I said, we have grown apart over the years and you are not the person that feel I can be involved with any longer. I am very different now—very, very different from the "little boy" I was when we first met. I see the world in a whole different way and I have needs you just can't satisfy. I am not saying this is your fault—I have changed. I have been chronically frustrated with what our lives together have become. I can't live my life like this anymore. But I want you to know that I have always loved you and still love you right this very minute. Bryan, I am very, very sad that it has come to this and

I will miss you very much. Very much. This is not going to be easy for me. Baby, if I had it to do all over again, I would never change the fact that we got together. I have had some of the happiest times in my life with you. We shared stuff that, well, was just indescribably wonderful. I will never forget when we went to Europe, I will never forget all the other places we saw together, all the great times we had. I felt so special and safe with you. You did so much for me, you were always there for me when I needed you. I will always keep that with me, and you will always remain a part of me. But whatever way I look at it now, I know that it's time for me to move on. I'm very scared, Bryan . . . very, very scared.

When you are breaking up with someone, expressing feelings of vulnerability and sadness and love may be very difficult and emotionally threatening. Raging gives one a false sense of power and safety. Anger can temporarily mitigate the anguish you are feeling. Avoidance, while not as powerful a cover as rage, at least won't make you feel as uncomfortable as direct expression. But those good feelings are there and very real. Denying them is denying offerings to both yourself and your lover.

Rico is certainly taking a chance by saying this to Bryan. He may break down and cry and feel embarrassed. It may feed his ambivalence about leaving, and make it harder to let go. But months and years hence, when the pain and tears subside, it will be very good for both. If Bryan can do the same, it will add further to the closure for both of them.

If there is a lot of anger at the point of breaking up, addressing these kinds of feelings will decrease the likelihood that the discussion will turn into a fruitless blaming session. You could bring the anger level down tenfold.

You may ask, "Should I talk about all of this in that first discussion when emotions will be so intense? Isn't it better to discuss that later on?" My answer is yes and no.

Such complex and potent feelings cannot, of course, be fully addressed in one discussion. The case can also be made that the tension is so extreme that is makes such a discussion impossible. On the other hand, this may be the time both of you have best access to those feelings. In crisis, people's defenses are down and they may be much more in touch with feelings that are usually repressed. In clinical work, for example, a client in crisis is likely to be considerably less defended and more open to psychotherapeutic intervention.

Furthermore, you don't have a guarantee that you will have another chance. In the best of all circumstances, both of you will be committed to address these feelings in subsequent discussions. That may not happen, however. Since you have no control over your partner, what if he never wants to meet with you again? What if he never wants to speak with you again? This may be the only opportunity for both of you.

Planning for What Comes Next

As I mentioned before, you should plan to have another talk and set up the time and place before you leave the first meeting. I would give it a number of days at minimum to give both of you time to reflect on what has happened. It is also imperative to be clear with your partner that as of now you are no longer a couple.

Should something dramatically change in this meeting and you discover that you do not want to uncouple, then we are talking about a different story. Be aware that feelings like that may just be anxiety—you really are breaking up now and you are getting cold feet. If that is what is happening, you will just be making the process more difficult for both of you. If you do feel something very different has happened, be clear to yourself about what this is. Is this something you felt before, is this something he has promised before just when you were at the brink of dissolving as a couple? Be certain that it really is something that has never occurred, and that it has validity before you commit to trying again. Indeed, the most you should give in such a scenario is to tell your lover that you will think about it. This meeting is a highly charged emotional experience, and a major change in your thinking necessitates time and distance from ground zero. You must be certain that your brain, and not your emotions, are "speaking."

It is possible your lover will refuse to accept that you have left him, no matter how many times you tell him that it's finished for you. You are still his partner, he declares. Fine. He has the right to his thoughts. It has nothing to do with you. Remind yourself that you don't need his approval to leave him. *Your decision to leave him makes it so. Period.*

If you are living together, there are practical decisions to make. Does one of you move out? What happens to mutual belongings? You don't need to answer these questions in that first discussion; indeed that encounter is *definitely not* the time to discuss that. Dividing property and making moving arrangements have an emotional life of their own. Acknowledge that it is an issue but do not discuss it further at that time. Plan to address it in a subsequent talk.

After a discussion like this, it is a good idea to have some physical separation. Can you or him stay with a parent or a good friend? Can you make an arrangement, for the next few days, to minimize the time both of you are in the house at the same time? (This of course assumes you are living together.) Can you go away for the weekend to visit a friend in another city? Your resources will affect what you can do. But I urge you to be creative. Both of you need some distance.

If you are not living together, you should definitely not see him until your next planned meeting. There may be a desire to see him right away for a variety of reasons. Maybe you feel very guilty about what you said, and want to be around him so that in some fantasy way you can "rescue" him. The prospect that you will be going your separate ways may make you feel that you need to spend some more time with him before there is "no time left." These reasons cannot produce beneficial results if you act on them. You are not responsible for his feelings, and even if you physically attached yourself to him, you couldn't change how he will experience this. Breaking up also doesn't preclude the possibility of having some kind of relationship in the future. You may still have a lot of time together. But yes . . . life is going to change in a very significant way. Being physically together right now is not going to make that better.

Your next discussion is likely to involve some similar topics—expression of feelings, a review of your relationship, and a decision on where to go next. Hopefully, both of you will be more relaxed and able to be more objective. As with your first discussion, it is important to be clear that you are meeting to achieve closure, not to go back together.

You may need a few of these discussions, and it's up to the two of you to decide how many. (However, if it seems that he continues to want to meet with you as a way to avoid the end, you may have to make a unilateral decision to stop meeting. Likewise, he can stop at any time, even if you believe there is more to discuss.) But there does come a time when it needs to end. That is the point where it will be unclear when you will be getting together again, if ever. In a sense that can be like another breakup, and it can be extremely difficult.

CRYING AND MANIPULATION
AND FORGETTING THE WHOLE THING

The first words that signify a breakup can be as traumatic as they are sad. Your lover may have anticipated this but still be unwilling to accept it. There is also a good chance he will be caught off guard.

Prepare yourself for a very serious emotional roller coaster. Begging, crying, promising to change, bringing up old memories, holding you, kissing you, telling you this is the biggest mistake you ever made, even threatening to commit suicide if you leave him, are possible scenarios. Since you may have very ambivalent feelings yourself, and since you may care about his welfare and still love him, you may feel confused and guilty.

> [I thought] . . . maybe I made a mistake. Maybe I made this decision wrong. . . . Maybe I did something wrong. Maybe I shouldn't have instigated this whole thing. Maybe I should have stayed in this relationship or should not have brought up this topic and just let things continue. Because I was emotionally very upset. I hurt pretty bad inside. I felt guilty for what I had done. Even though I knew that it was the best thing for me.
>
> Lamont, 27, waiter
> Dallas, Texas

While I emphasize the importance of going through the process of saying good-bye, I do not mean you should let yourself become emotionally abused. If your lover is behaving in this manner and will not stop (which he really might not be able to do), I suggest you inform him that it is not appropriate to continue talking at that time. Then end the discussion forthwith. *Don't communicate that you are punishing him.* In an emotional climate of crying and begging, not much can be accomplished. You should simply communicate that fact. If you are living together you will need to separate either by going into another room or leaving the house. If you expect a very bad reaction, be proactive and, if possible, plan to stay with a friend for a day or so (or even go to a hotel if necessary). To leave the scene when your lover is extremely upset will take a lot of discipline. If you anticipate this possibility, it's crucial to be mentally prepared. One way is to visualize the scene before it happens (before you meet with your lover for this discussion). Visualize yourself calmly but firmly and *quickly* ending the discussion.

DRINKING, OTHER CHEMICALS, AND YOUR PHYSICAL STAMINA

Drugs (including alcohol, of course) that alter thinking and mood can be absolute poison in a situation like this. Emotions will be raw enough, and such chemicals could accentuate problems. If you are taking prescription drugs (as I am not medically trained, I am not qualified to give you any medical advice and please note that no attempt is being made here to do that), you should check with your doctor as to what effect they may have on you in an emotionally stressful situation. Indeed, if you are taking any street drugs or drinking excessively, you should consult a medical doctor.

It is common sense that you should be in the best possible physical shape before you undertake anything that requires significant emotional energy. Eating well, getting plenty of rest, avoiding other stressors, and so on, will aid you in this task. Of course, you may be very stressed just from the fact that your relationship has fallen apart. *Do the best you can, and be creative about what you can accomplish to this end.* For example, you may not be able to sleep the night before your planned meeting. But if you haven't been sleeping all week, and you have had a particularly stressful time at work, it makes perfect sense to postpone the discussion for a week or so.

VIOLENCE

You may be in a physically abusive relationship, and to inform your lover that you are leaving him could put your physical safety, even perhaps your life, in danger. Obviously, in such a situation your safety is the priority. This may mean no meeting with him face to face. It may mean meeting in a public place and possibly with a friend. The "rules" I have mentioned can indeed go out the window when violence is in the equation. Keep in mind that if you are being abused, your judgment may be impaired, and you could underestimate danger. I suggest you consult with a professional counselor trained in domestic violence with gay men before you have this talk with your lover. If you don't know where to find help in your community, please consult the Appendix in this book for information on receiving help in a situation involving potential violence. *I want to emphasize that as important as it is to achieve closure when uncoupling, you should never risk your safety. Some relationships are so toxic and dangerous that leaving means no talking and literally running away and hiding!*

It is also important to acknowledge that the act of leaving itself is often very difficult for victims of domestic violence. I am not referring just to psychological factors—leaving, as with staying, can be very dangerous. Other factors also impede this option. It's imperative that you seek outside help from those trained in handling gay domestic violence if you are being battered.

WHAT AND WHAT NOT TO SAY

What you say to your lover at a time like this should not sound like a script. It's imperative to be yourself, but equally significant to be aware of the impact of your words. Saying the wrong things can block communication and turn the discussion into a fruitless blaming session. Since there is a good chance that the two of you have not been communicating very well, it's judicious to put extra effort into how you will speak at this time.

When you are in a calm, quiet place, think of the kind of statements you make that often result in bickering with him. As seductive as it may feel to say those kinds of things, especially if you are angry, make an agreement with yourself that you will stay away from that. Create Plan B in that calm quiet place in the event you end up approaching the point where you will not be able to resist. Plan B should be ending the discussion before you drop the bombs. It's a good idea to state this condition in the beginning of the discussion. "I am interested in having a constructive discussion with you, Bob, and if I get too upset I will need to take a break." It's material that you take responsibility for this—"if I get too upset," not "if you piss me off." Set up a mental scale from one to ten so that you can check on how close you are to blowing up. If you get to seven it's probably time to leave.

This endeavor will not be effortless. It's easy to dive into a familiar pattern such as verbal attacking if you have been very angry with him. But if you keep in mind that the usual pattern is not going to serve your purposes, you will be motivated to control your impulses. Planning this out in advance, away from ground zero, will prepare you. Monitoring yourself while you are in the middle of it can move you away from *acting* into *thinking before acting.*

It's not productive to precipitously terminate a breaking-up discussion. But it is better than an orgy of attacks and counterattacks.

Not to confuse you, but be on guard that if you decide to stop the discussion, your decision is not a form of avoidance. Significant emotional discomfort comes with this process, and you will not be able to escape that. It is crucial to ascertain what you really can and cannot tolerate.

Now what about what he says? What if he symbolically goes after your jugular vein with that special attack talent of his? Not fair, right?

Correct. *But this is not a contest to see who comes out being "more fair."* You can state a ground rule at the beginning that no one "pushes buttons." But you can't force him to comply. And remember, you have the advantage of preparation. He may have the added disadvantage of being surprised about the breakup altogether. He may feel backed into a corner.

It's best to anticipate the worst-case scenario and prepare for your reaction. Again, in comfort and privacy away from him, plan your strategy. Visualize the scene. Think of the kind of things he says that aggravate you the most. Imagine him doing that during this discussion. Question in your mind how accurate his accusations are. Tell yourself silently that just because he says it does not make it so; *it's his reality and there is no need to "correct" his reality.* Imagine yourself in the scene remaining calm and focused. Here is an example:

> **Peter:** This simply isn't working for me and I need to let go. I have not been happy for a long time. I have decided to call it quits.

> **Jeffrey:** So this is what you have been planning? But I shouldn't be surprised. You never gave a shit about us . . . I always knew it. And how could I expect you to hang in there? You *never* hang in when it gets tough. It's *always* too hard for you. That's why you *never finished college, why you never stay with a job, why you never finish anything. You always cop out. You're a quitter and a loser.*

> **Peter:** I am sorry you see it that way. I do not. I'm not happy with our relationship, and I am leaving you.

Of course, he may continue to hurl insults, and you shouldn't permit him to abuse you. You have the option to leave if he is out of control, just as you can and should if you feel you are getting out of control. If possible, warn him (in a nonattacking way) about this:

> Jeffrey, I feel attacked by you and I will not accept that. Let's stick to the issues at hand and not bring up all the wrongs that we feel we have both committed against one another, and all the "deficiencies" we both have. If you continue to attack me, I will need to end this conversation. I'm here to talk with you, not to fight.

MOVING OUT

Some people break up but continue to live together as roommates. I strongly discourage this. Breaking up means letting go, developing a new identity, and starting a new life.

Often, people remain together because of finances. In many big cities such as San Francisco and New York, it is very difficult to go from sharing expenses to living on one's own. Although this may be a very real problem, I still strongly urge you to live in separate residences as soon as it is humanly possible. Be aware that the fear of change and letting go can coexist with financial concerns. Money concerns can mask emotional issues. Poverty is much easier to address than sadness and guilt. Remaining physically together can cause other unforeseen problems. Lamont describes this quite graphically:

> I showed up [I had returned home] about twenty-five to two and opened the garage door and there is a strange car there. It wasn't his car. I come into the house. . . . and I knew. I knew he was upstairs with somebody. I'm not stupid. I just kind of stayed downstairs, waited for a while. I didn't know what to do. It really still bothers me a lot. Only happened last week . . . I came upstairs and I did my stuff. And then they came out of the bedroom. I thought, "Well, let's be the bigger man; let's try and say hello to this person." So I went to go shake hands with this guy and say, "Hi, my name is Lamont. Nice to meet you." He walked right past me, went down the fuckin' stairs and at the bottom of the stairs he looks up and says, "Oh, by the way, my name is Mario." It bothered me a lot. It bothered me a whole lot. . . . It hurt to see that happen in my house. I was with him for nine years—never had that feeling of loss. Maybe I finally realized it was over even though I was the one who started it all. I just felt more distant, more alone, than I had before.
>
> Lamont, 27, waiter
> Dallas, Texas

Who moves out, or if both of you do, is a decision you and your lover will need to reach. Even in the most harmonious divorce, this is likely to be extremely painful for both of you. Aside from the practical difficulties of changing a residence (or remaining alone in a place you have shared), moving out has tremendous symbolic meaning. It is likely to trigger feelings of failure, loss, broken dreams, and profound sadness. It's important to prepare for this.

One thing to do is to have a trusted friend come with you when you take your belongings. It may be helpful to arrange with your ex for him not to be there when you move out. The first night in your new home (or with your lover no longer living in the apartment) can be agonizing.

> . . . our bed was gone . . . that was probably the thing I focused on first. I think that was kind of a little bit of a reality slap for me, to see the room empty of all his stuff. It was really empty . . . I freaked out. I was crying. It was a scene. . . . I suddenly had this feeling, "Jesus, this is it. I'm by myself." It was weird.

> Jason, 24, fitness instructor
> Atlanta, Georgia

I just wasn't sure how I was going to exist.

> George, 32, automotive mechanic
> West Hollywood, California

You may want to prolong the time before moving out because it's so distressing. Procrastination will only amplify the pain. Of course it is usually difficult to find a nice place to live on short notice. So get busy right away. It's a good idea to set up a deadline; more than a month is probably too long. If you can stay with friends for at least part of the time during your or your ex's apartment search, do that. If a good place to live is not forthcoming, consider a temporary residence or even a hotel. These may sound like drastic measures, and indeed they are. But consider the emotional price you are paying by continuing to live together.

Breakups, without a doubt, are not all harmonious, and choosing who moves out may be fertile ground for conflict. Certainly you should not abdicate your rights, and it may come to consulting with an attorney. If you are embroiled in a battle, though, be honest with yourself about what are you fighting about. Is it really important for you to keep the apartment, or do you feel that this is just another thing that he is trying to take from you, and this time you won't let him? Are you so angry with him that you want to punish him, and making sure that he doesn't get the apartment he loves is an excellent way to hurt him? You are going to need a lot of energy to handle all of the changes that will be happening to you. Investing energy in "getting even" is a not a wise use of that energy. When you are calm and away from him, look at yourself in the mirror and ask yourself what is going on. What is it costing you emotionally? Perhaps the apartment should legitimately go to you, but maybe you will gain much more by letting it go to him.

GETTING YOUR STUFF BACK

If you don't share a home with your lover, it's likely you keep some belongings in his place (and vice versa). The obvious reason is convenience, if you are spending a lot of time there (clothing, your favorite CDs, etc.). But there is symbolic meaning to this also. Leaving clothes at your lover's house, for example, also says that you are connected with him. For those reasons it's important to settle the issue of possessions in a timely manner. Sometimes we leave belongings at an ex's house for months. I believe that is a way of symbolically avoiding the end—as long as part of you is still there, as long as you still have something to take care of, it has not ended. But indeed it has ended. This can negatively affect your ability to move on.

Set up a time with him, and remove all of your possessions on that day. As with moving out, it may make sense to go with a friend and possibly even request that your ex not be there (perhaps one of his friends can be there instead). This needs to be discussed and worked out sensibly, depending on the nature of your relationship and your relationship with his friends. Another option is for him to bring your belongings to your house, or for you to pick them up at a neutral place. Naturally, all of this works the same in reverse—if his belongings are in your house.

If he will not cooperate, it's still imperative that you bring closure for yourself. Perhaps the items you left at his house are relatively inexpensive, and it may be better to simply "write them off." Make this clear to your ex—if you can't come to his place by such and such a time, or he can't bring them to you (within reason), he might as well dispose of your things. If you decide this, stick by it, and don't agree to pick them up at a later time when he calls you. That may be a conscious or unconscious setup on his part—you agree to come, he cancels again, and you are back to square one.

If he has left his belongings in your house, give him a reasonable deadline to retrieve them. If he won't pick them up, dispose of them (without a doubt, give him ample warning that this will occur). Holding on to his property keeps your breakup in the same state of unfinished business.

Significant Mutual Property

Perhaps you and your lover have been together many years, and you own a house and other property together. Significant assets usually mean lawyers and other forms of royal aggravation.

The worst-case scenario is when sizable assets are at stake, and you have an acrimonious breakup. You are then apt to be involved in a protracted legal battle. Legal conflicts are bad enough, but your pain will be worsened by the fact that you are battling a former lover. I am not suggesting that you give up the farm, but I encourage you, again, to address the emotional cost alongside the material expense. Such a battle can have serious psychological ramifications for you. Sometimes it makes more sense to walk away, even if it means losing a lot of money.

If you don't want to walk away, you can try to minimize direct battling with your ex. Speak to your attorney about what can be accomplished without contact with him. If you have to negotiate directly with him, and it is extremely difficult to do this, ask your attorney to be present during this conversation (have your attorney arrange the meeting with your ex and his attorney). Keep focused on the monetary/property issues during this meeting without using the discussion to address emotional issues.

Keys

This section is not going to take very long. On the day that you have the initial breaking-up discussion, it is imperative to return keys to each other. Nothing is more symbolic of remaining connected than to have keys to each others' homes. If your ex will not cooperate, I suggest that you change the lock in your home and *inform* him of this. But you may say, "That's silly and a waste of money. He wouldn't use the key anymore." I am not suggesting you do this because of a security issue. It's important for the closure process, and it's consequential for *you* that he no longer has access to your home. If he tells you to keep his keys, do not, and inform him that you have disposed of them. The same rationale applies.

A WORD ON BEHAVIOR
AND THOUGHTS AND FEELINGS

Thoughts and feelings certainly affect behavior. But it also works the other way around. Behavior affects thinking (we "watch" ourselves) which subsequently changes feelings. Certain behaviors also "stand for" or are symbolic of something else. The symbolic nature of these behaviors can have a significant psychological effect in addition to or in the absence of what the actual behavior accomplishes.

The ceremonial behavior of a funeral, for example, has no actual real-world impact on the deceased, and we the living know that. From the perspective of pragmatism, what this does for the deceased and the living is meaningless. But the symbolic nature of the behavior, which is expressing respect for the deceased, saying good-bye, and accepting that the person is indeed dead, profoundly affects the living, and are material elements in the grieving process. Thus, even though the behavior of returning keys or removing belongings may have no powerful "reality" consequence in themselves, the psychological impact of that in relation to an uncoupled identity can be very powerful.

Endings are very hard in our culture, especially breakups. I have found in my practice that most couples who do not break up mutually/amicably (and even some who do) require a complete separation period for a while in order to truly separate. This includes removing absolutely all traces of the other, at least for a while.

Thomas J. Caldarola, MFCC
psychotherapist, private practice/CAMFT
San Francisco, California

NOW THAT YOU ARE SINGLE

Breaking up with your partner has been a formidable task, but it has been accomplished. As with all significant changes, relief usually occurs when the first step has been taken. However, a major life transition presents innumerable challenges, so the sigh of relief may be short-lived.

Recognizing that the road ahead is rocky will prepare you to navigate. There will be sadness and anxiety. You may feel guilt, confusion, and depression. You may even question your judgment, and wonder why on earth you ever went through with this in the first place.

In the next chapter we will examine some of the major psychological consequences of uncoupling. Experiencing profound loss, letting go, and starting over is not easy. But "not easy" doesn't mean ghastly or annihilative. In fact, your breakup may be one of the best growing experiences you ever have. Change that nourishes the self renders boundless gains.

Chapter 4

A Time of Pain:
Dealing with the Emotional Aftermath
of a Gay Divorce

You did not break up with your lover so that you could feel more unhappy than when you were together. However, in the early aftermath of uncoupling, it may feel like just that. Ironically, this can be worsened by initial feelings of euphoria.

The first week after you leave him, you may want to go out partying. If you do that, you may, at first, discover that you love all the attention you are getting. Your newfound freedom may be very exciting, and you may feel terribly confident. You may declare to yourself, "This is not so hard. What the hell took me so long?"

Your partying will be, more than likely, an attempt to cover up the hurt you are experiencing. When it hits you that it's not all roses out there, the magnitude of your situation will feel all the more crushing. That euphoria is false, so coming down from it will make you feel worse. Therefore, my best advice is to take it very slow in the early days and weeks following your breakup. Heavy partying, and *especially the use of chemicals* is not in your best interest (indeed, the use of chemicals is *never* in your best interest). In fact, such behavior can be exceedingly destructive. Sitting home and taking it easy will make it difficult to avoid painful feelings of loss, and that's OK. In fact, it's better than OK.

Ending your relationship, by definition, will create much uneasiness. There is simply no getting around this. If he meant anything to you, the loss of him will matter a great deal. Loss of people who matter to us can be agonizing, no matter how much misery their presence also caused us.

It was really difficult for me sort of believing that it was going to end, that I had to let go. . . . It was horrible, I don't even think I can describe it.

> Jason, 24, fitness instructor
> Atlanta, Georgia

As reality set in, I freaked out . . . I just walked around stunned and in tears.

> George, 32, automotive mechanic
> West Hollywood, California

The most fundamental way to cope with this is to recognize that you will experience this, and do everything in your power to embrace those feelings. *Yes, embrace pain and reject denial.*

And why do this? Because that which we dread has a remarkable way of losing domination over us the moment we stop running and hiding. Furthermore, it's the only way you will be able to work through those feelings and get on with your life. You can't resolve something you avoid.

In fact, I would swing my apartment/house door wide open (make sure your neighbors are not watching!) and declare in a powerful, clear voice: "Come on pain. Come on in, baby, I've been waiting for you!"

Now let's take a closer look at some of these difficult feelings I'm referring to, and how you can manage them.

ABRUPT LOSS AND SADNESS

The most obvious change in your life is that you no longer have a lover. He may have not been there psychologically for years, but an actual breakup is still very different. Dinner, sleeping, what you'll do next weekend, your normal five o'clock call from work, the message you expect on your answering machine, will all change. Losing a person who has been significant to you can create profound feelings of sadness.

> Well, it's like experiencing a death. . . . I just went over there three days ago 'cause he's gone on vacation. I picked up

a CD player because I was renting a car. I started crying. I just bawled. I just was very, very sad. I look at the house, I think about the memories, I think about our dreams, what we were hoping to do, and then, I've thrown that away, in a way. That's really, really sad. The house definitely represents that 'cause it's so sad to see it; it's such an empty house. And he still has pictures of me up there. Drawings I did. I know he cares about me, he still says he loves me, but he has a lot of work to do. I don't want to be there. I don't want to go with him down that path.

Antonio, 29, management consultant
Boston, Massachusetts

Initially, it was horrible. I hated it. It was scary, and it was very lonely, and even though at the time I knew that being away from Fred was the right thing for me, that wasn't a consolation to just feeling sad and alone.

Michael, 47, attorney
Washington, DC

Part of working through sadness is to let yourself feel it in all its gory. It's OK to remember the good times and *feel* the pain of their loss. It's OK to take out pictures, put on some sad music, and cry about the past and about broken dreams. Crying from the depths of your soul is difficult, but guess what happens when you go through that? You *emotionally learn* that it is difficult but not *devastating*. Not infrequently we are terrified when we find ourselves, or some- one we care about, crying. Crying is not dangerous, and you may feel better afterward.

During the early days and weeks of your breakup, if you don't feel like socializing much, I wouldn't push it. It's not going to harm you to withdraw *for a while*. It's even OK to be self-indulgent. Take yourself out to a nice dinner or go out and buy yourself a few things. Obviously, don't go overboard.

Withdrawal doesn't mean cessation of contact with friends. (There is the telephone!) Indeed, friends can play a very important role in helping you get through this. You will need them now to talk about what has happened.

And I mean talk. You will want to talk about the past, talk about your feelings, and talk about him. You will curse him, tell them how much you miss him, and then tell them how glad you are that he is out of your life. You will ask them for their advice, and then tell them why you can't follow it. And after you are finished, you will want to talk about it all over again!

This is not verbal diarrhea. On the contrary, expressing what is troubling you can serve as an important coping strategy. People who have difficulty sharing their emotions are the ones most likely to run into trouble. By talking, you ventilate feelings, gain insight, see options, and gradually let go. Of course this will not be easy on them, but real friends make sacrifices for friends. I am not saying you should abdicate responsibility and abuse them. But you are needy now, which means you *need* emotional support. That, indeed, is what friends are for.

> . . . just the process of saying and reiterating and talking about all the things that had happened . . . I was able to relive the experience, and as I relived the experience, some of these experiences two or three times until my friends were tired of hearing them, I was able to finally get the emotions out of my body and gone with.
>
> Edward, 44, clerk
> New Orleans, Louisiana

DEPRESSION IS NOT SADNESS

There is a vast difference between sadness and depression. As I mentioned above, it's OK to remain inactive and sad for a while. But if your change in functioning becomes severe or unrelenting, then you need to be concerned.

No one should self-diagnose depression, let alone from a book. But I want you to be aware of some of the signs that can indicate serious trouble. What will follow is a list of warnings that may mean you are clinically depressed. If you have any concern, that's reason enough to consult a mental health professional. If you are depressed and it is left untreated, you may not only suffer needlessly—you could *die*. Depression can lead to suicide. A depressed person may not even intend to die, but accidentally perish nonetheless. Example: A man takes an overdose, believing his roommate will come home at 5 p.m. (as he usually does), find him, and call 911. But his roommate's car breaks down, and he gets home three hours later. You may say "that isn't using very good judgment," and that is precisely the point! Depressed people have impaired judgment. They may make a suicide "gesture" out of desperation, but because of their impoverished judgment, they die by accident.

Depression may lead to death in even more insidious ways. A person may simply neglect himself by, for example, drinking excessively and not eating. Or he may be very careless, walking in a dangerous part of town late at night, or driving his car while intoxicated or very tired. An accidental death may actually be a form of suicide.

The signs I will list are not meant to be an exhaustive description of the symptomatology of clinical depression. It's also important to note that some of these signs may indicate other problems. Some symptoms of depression are physical, and it is imperative to be evaluated by a medical doctor if you have physical symptoms. You can consult the list of resources in this book for help.

Some of the signs you should be concerned about include the following:

- Excessive self-blame
- Inability to find pleasure in any activity
- Difficulty with concentration
- Excessive sleep or insomnia
- Loss of interest in sex
- Depressed mood for a period that is excessive (it may appear excessive to your friends and not to you)
- Lack of energy
- Isolation
- Thoughts of self-harm
- difficulty with remembering pleasurable events in your life— it seems that life has always been horrible and that is all you can expect for the future
- Not tending to your hygienic needs
- Decreased appetite, loss of weight

While depression may not be avoidable, certain behaviors and patterns of thinking can make it more likely to occur and/or intensify it. This can be tricky because the destructive thoughts and behaviors may seem to be helping you (and may do so for a while).

Behavior

For example, I indicated above that it's OK to stay out of circulation for a while. Staying home may feel good and it may give you time to think. Be aware of how long you are doing this, however, and especially how you feel when you are at home. Has this been for a couple of days, or has this gone on for a couple of weeks? Is it relaxing, are you processing what happened and feel you are getting a better handle on your life? Or do you feel increasingly depressed and angry, ruminating over the past, and experiencing a sense of being out of control? If the latter is happening, it's time to force yourself to get out. One of the maddening aspects of depression is that you often don't feel like doing that which can, ultimately, make you feel better. In the short term it takes a lot of energy to socialize when you'd rather be pulling blankets over your face. But getting out can distract you from painful thoughts, which may improve your mood.

Thinking Patterns

You may have made a lot of mistakes in the relationship that just ended. Perhaps you behaved very childishly. Maybe you did things that were downright vicious. To heal you will have to take responsibility for your actions. That will mean making an agreement with yourself to avoid that kind of behavior in the future. You may even need to apologize to your ex at some point.

There is a great difference however, between taking responsibility and attacking yourself for your misdeeds. When you cross into "I am a bad person deserving punishment for what I did" you are on your way to being depressed.

People at times confuse self-attack with taking responsibility. You may believe that if you hurt badly enough, it means you are "taking responsibility." You may tell yourself that a commitment to change is not enough, that you must pay for your misdeeds with pain. Unfortunately, that will only deplete your energy and self-esteem, and may not prevent you from repeating your actions in the future. When you are feeling lousy about yourself, you are actually more likely to repeat negative behavior.

How you interpret events also plays a major role in your mood. A positive change in thinking can positively affect your mood. This is one of the major tenets of cognitive behavior therapy. Our interpretation of an event, our thoughts about it, materially affect our feelings, not just the event itself. In this model thoughts are seen not as reality in themselves, but as subjective interpretations of reality.

Let's explore a simple example: Jerry and Seymore are both late for work because the subway has broken down. They don't know each other, they do not speak to each other, but they are on the same subway platform waiting for the train. We will assume that neither man is late often, and neither is in any realistic danger of being disciplined. Jerry tells himself that being late is not desirable, but it's no big deal. He knows his boss will be angry, but he tells himself that his tardiness is unavoidable and his boss will just have to get over it. He concludes that he will stay a little late to catch up even though he'd rather be home watching a particular show on television. Seymore tells himself, on the other hand, that no genuinely good employee should come in late and he will just *die* when he sees his boss frown. He knows that lateness is an example of how he always screws thing up, and he asks himself why on earth he didn't leave half an hour earlier—he's stupid to boot! And of course he can't stay late today because he enjoys watching that same television show and it would just be *terrible* to miss it. Remember, both men are affected by the same event; the train is late, making them late for work. Who do you think will be calmly reading the newspaper, and who will be pacing the platform like a madman?

One of the sad facts about what I call "self-destroying thinking" is that it's not only toxic for you. *It's not true.* Seymore will not die from his boss's frown. The most responsible employee in the world will come in late if the train that takes him to work is late. With thoughts that trigger depression, the same principle operates. You can make yourself miserable or even kill yourself because of something *that isn't true!*

Now you may say to yourself, "Oh, these theories are nice but this Neil Kaminsky, LCSW, doesn't really know me. He doesn't know what I did to my ex. How does he know that I am not really rotten to the core?"

Well, I don't know it, but you do!

Thinking that destroys self-esteem distorts information into global pejorative interpretations of the self. This can happen because evidence that contradicts the interpretation is ignored.

Since thoughts and images go through our minds at lightning speeds, it may be difficult to catch the contradictory evidence, that is, information that would call into question your conclusion of how very "bad" you are. If you talk to yourself in this manner without challenging the logic of your thinking, it will be very easy to wind up with a self-perception that is terribly negative and very inaccurate.

This doesn't have to happen, however. You can slow down your thinking, so to speak, and be more objective about your conclusions.

I am not trying to soften what you may be responsible for. Perhaps you treated your ex-lover poorly a good deal of the time and did some very bad things to him. But did you do *only* bad to him? Do you do only bad to *everybody, all the time, all of your life?* Do you really have evidence that as a person you are intrinsically evil and deserve dire punishment for that?

One way to get a handle on this kind of thinking is to write down your thoughts when you are feeling unhappy. As you note your depressed mood, ask yourself, "What was I thinking just now?" (It can also be an image—"What did I see just now in my mind's eye?") Write down the thought or the thought derived from the image. On the next line, write down the evidence you have *for* the thought. On the following line write down the evidence *against* that thought. This may take a little work, but scour your memory. Then on the last line, see if you can come up with a conclusion that more accurately describes the reality—you may call it a more balanced thought. Here is an example:

> **Thought:** I was a totally horrible lover to James. I hurt him all the time.

Evidence For: I cheated on him numerous times. I lied to him. I took him for granted. His friends always told him what a shit I was and they were right.

Evidence Against: I cared about his welfare at times. When his mom died, I was there for him all the way. I remember how I used to pick him up when he came home late at night from work because I wanted him to be safe.

More Balanced Thought: I did some very horrible things to James, and they are not excusable. I really wasn't the right man for him. But there were times, perhaps a lot fewer times, when I also was good to him, when I was there for him. I was not always bad, and I did not always hurt him.

You may ask yourself, "So what if this man realized that he did some good things? He still behaved atrociously, and he's not going to feel better about what he did to James."

My response to that would be that, first of all, I'm not so sure that he wouldn't feel a little bit different. But even if he didn't feel significantly changed in this instance, there is a more important issue to consider. People feel depressed because these kinds of thoughts are circulating in their heads hundreds, maybe thousands of times a day. This will have a very profound cumulative depressing effect. Negative thoughts are fuel for an interpretation of oneself as a horrible human being. People who are depressed feel like horrible/worthless human beings. By engaging in this exercise, you not only challenge a particular thought at a particular time; eventually, you get into the habit of doing this mentally and automatically whenever you are feeling bad. You may sense your foul mood, catch what you are thinking, catch the distortion, and change your thought and feeling. Or you may find yourself beginning to think negatively, and short-circuit it before you even feel bad. Hopefully, the cumulative effect of doing this will be to help you change your mind about how "bad" you are, or help you avoid feeling like that in the first place.

IDENTITY DISRUPTION

Identity, how we view ourselves, is substantially shaped by the major roles we play in life. When you are involved in a serious relationship, the fact that you have a partner is a material description of how you define yourself to the world. It's also the way the world defines you. Homophobic delegitimization of our relationships aside, this still holds true for gay lovers. You are no longer just John. You are John of John and Ted.

Breaking up causes a major transformation. Although your identity as being married may have been fracturing as you grew discontented with your partner, "single" creates a materially different identity than "coupled and unhappy."

This can affect you in a variety of ways. Being single may give you a sense of freedom that you have yearned for. You no longer have to answer to him. You no longer have to get his OK if you want to buy something for the house. But "freedom" can also create anxiety because where there was once structure there is now nothing. Structure, as I am defining it here, is a form of grounding, a home base of sorts. This is one of the reasons why we get into relationships in the first place. We want to belong to someone; in a sense we do want to be accountable to another human being. The structure in your relationship may have felt like a prison and you longed to break free of that control. But when the baby goes out with the bathwater, you are likely to miss the baby. No longer do you have to call him when you stay out late, for example, but it will feel strange to know that there is no one to call.

After you break up you may have "thought slips"; you may find yourself thinking as though you were still in the relationship, only to catch yourself. For example, you could find yourself laughing during a movie and thinking, "John will love this . . . gotta tell him this . . ." only to realize that you don't do that anymore. When you have thought slips about positive experiences, it can be quite painful.

> . . . we used to go out a lot to different restaurants. . . . If I was reading the Sunday paper and there was a write-up about a great restaurant the thought that would come to my mind immediately was "Joe and I," and then I would realize there is no Joe. And that was very, very sad for me.
>
> Juan, 44, research psychologist
> New York City

... it calls attention to the fact that you are no longer with this person. You can go your whole day and kind of put it out of your mind . . . then you make that slip of the "we" and then you consciously correct yourself that it's not the "we," it's the "I," or it's not "our" place, it's "his" place . . .

Michael, 47, attorney
Washington, DC

Part of coping with the loss of your coupled identity is remembering that there was a "you" before there was a "we." You may have had some wonderful experiences with your lover, and your primary enjoyment of experiences may be with a lover. But that does not mean that you can't have enjoyable experiences with yourself. In fact, if you look back at your relationship closely, you'll probably remember times when you really would have preferred to do something by yourself or for yourself, but decided to forgo your preference because of him.

So start making yourself remember those times! When you are in a state of sadness, thought slips, and selective memory, it may be a little hard. But confront yourself and *confront yourself the most when you are feeling the weakest.* Misery created by misery-making thoughts has a tendency to dissipate if you mobilize yourself! If you fight painful thoughts with balanced thoughts that more accurately reflect reality, it's hard to stay miserable! For example, you could be walking through a store having a thought slip about what he would think about a bed you'd like to buy. That may set off memories about how you used to shop together for the apartment. Those *are* sweet memories, and I don't suggest that you deny them. But do you *also* remember wanting to buy something that he didn't want? Do you remember compromising when you really didn't want to? Those memories are true too, and if you give them their proper weight, they can neutralize somewhat the loss you are feeling. Why? Because those kinds of experiences, hence part of your ex-relationship, *actually caused loss in your life.* When you have to deny what you want, you are in a sense creating loss. *The end of your relationship means the end of those kinds of losses.*

Another way of coping with identity disruption, which is related to the above issue, is to systematically create a new relationship with yourself. You may have done a lot of neglecting of yourself throughout the years.

Get out a pen and paper and describe yourself as if you were another person. Describe your needs, preferences, how you like to spend free time, what gives you pleasure, and so on. Then make a plan to do some of those things.

This may feel very silly, but there is a serious issue underlying it. Part of the pain you are feeling with identity disruption can be caused by ignoring the fact that you can really be OK with yourself. If you have just come out of a long-term relationship, or have been in many relationships (you consider yourself "the relationship type") you may have "forgotten," or never really recognized, that pleasure in life does not have to revolve around another person. This kind of an exercise can compel you to look at how *you* can make you happy.

Again, I'm not advocating denial. Loss of a relationship, no matter how dysfunctional it was, is loss. Nor do I dispute that you can feel immense gratification when you share an experience with a lover. But having experiences alone does not have to be the dictionary definition of misery.

It may feel strange planning fun activities with yourself. You may have never gone to a movie by yourself and "just can't imagine" doing that. *Order your feet to move and just go!* Stretch yourself. Enjoy a nice sunset by yourself. Take a ride in the country. Go out to a nice dinner. As I mentioned earlier in the book, we have many societal pressures against this. But societal pressures do not have to dictate your life. You can take the power out of "what they will think" by simply refusing to go along with "their" prescription for your life. You may be surprised to find out how much pleasure you can give to yourself by yourself. I will address the issue of being alone in greater detail in a subsequent chapter.

CONFUSION AND UNREALITY

You must have heard the expression that humans are "creatures of habit." This is certainly true. While change and risk feed the human appetite, and we may grow very dull without it, habit facilitates our organization of the world. Habits make life streamlined, predictable, and safe. When we are uprooted from our habits we can suffer considerable stress.

Let me give you a personal example of this to illustrate my point. Recently, I visited a very good friend of mine in Miami Beach, Florida. I arrived from San Francisco about 10 p.m., and we had to get up about 4:30 the next morning to go to Key West. My friend is a tour guide, so besides driving for hours to get to Key West, he had to pick up the tour bus, pick up various passengers in different hotels, and then drop everybody off when we returned to Miami during the evening. I was with him throughout all of this. We were probably out about seventeen hours in total that day, and this, on top of my jet lag, made this writer a pretty grumpy guy by midnight. We slept for about nine hours after this. When I woke up, I was still tired and very much in need of a cup of coffee. In fact I wanted a cup of coffee, a bagel, and a newspaper. This is often what I like in the morning, particularly when I am on vacation. It's a habit that makes me feel relaxed. Well, my friend DC doesn't drink coffee, so out in the street we went in search of a diner. One problem—this was Saturday, he lives in an Orthodox Jewish neighborhood, and everything was closed. DC has boundless energy, and he was calmly saying to me, "Oh, let's go up this street" or "Let's take the bicycles to find a place" (he doesn't like to drive, understandably, on his days off) and I was looking at him as if I was going to need a good lawyer after I killed him! "No, DC," I am thinking, "I don't want to walk around Miami Beach or get on a bicycle now!! All I want is coffee, a bagel, and a newspaper!!" I began repeating this to him like an insane person, and although we can laugh about it now, I was becoming increasingly annoyed rather rapidly. Lucky for both of us, we soon found a diner (and a nearby newspaper machine) that had superb coffee, and although no bagels, it had a fantastic turkey sandwich. (I have some flexibility in my habits!) I soon turned back into the lovable friend I am, but it did strike me how significantly my mood was affected when I was denied a habitual behavior. Lucky for me, of course, that I have a friend as tolerant as DC!

We all, of course, react to change in habitual patterns differently, and the kind of situation I described about myself would not, perhaps, have had a significant effect on you. However, when we are in a relationship, particularly if it has been of long duration, we develop hundreds, conceivably thousands of habitual patterns that abruptly terminate when the relationship ends. So many simultaneous changes will create significant stress.

Numerous habitual patterns of behavior are formed in relationships. Take a look at the following list and see how many apply to you. Think about what is not there that applies to you, and add it.

- Calls during the day at work just to say he's thinking about you
- Shopping together for food
- Buying something for him (such as a shirt) when you are buying items for yourself
- He has dinner ready for you when you come home
- Preparing dinner for him
- Sharing the highs and lows of your work days with him during the evening
- Waking up next to him in the morning
- Holding him and being comforted by him when you wake up in the middle of the night from a nightmare
- Spending Sunday afternoons with him
- Calling him when you are away on a business trip
- Sharing holidays with him
- Wearing his clothes, sharing different possessions (such as a camera)
- Watching certain television programs together (it can be particularly uncomfortable to watch them alone now)
- Eating together in a particular restaurant where the employees are used to seeing both of you come in
- Writing cards to each other
- Planning vacations together
- Visiting your parents with him
- Visiting his family

Breaking up may also cause you to lose, temporarily, confidence in yourself because your habitual behavioral repertoire is not at your disposal. For example, you may have been accustomed to going to parties with your lover and did not have to deal much with "being on the prowl" pressure. Perhaps you even flirted a lot, but you always knew you could find him in another room at the party when it was time to be "safe" again. Now, however, you are there all by yourself and this "flirting thing" may feel rusty to you. You may feel awkward and downright frightened.

Relationships create certain divisions of labor. One man may write the checks for household expenses while the other one is handy with toilets and sinks. Now that you are single you have to handle everything and that can feel daunting.

These numerous transformations occurring at the same time may cause you to feel ungrounded, confused, beleaguered, and generally weird. It's not likely that you are losing your mind. You are on emotional overload.

The first step in effectively coping with this is to recognize that it is to be expected. You may feel happy about the breakup and yet feel terribly stressed. This is probably one major reason why. The understanding that you are having a comprehensible reaction to what is unfolding in your life may decrease that stress.

Another mode of effective coping is to monitor the changes and challenges taking place in other parts of your life. You need to do your best to minimize them right now. This is *not* a good time to relocate to another part of the country or start a home-based business. Lay low for a while and let yourself recoup.

Another coping tool is to keep a journal. By writing about what is happening, you can give yourself a different perspective, almost like an outside observer watching you. This can provide new insights and give you more of a sense of control over what is taking place.

When you begin to feel unhappy in relation to your breakup, get yourself into a quiet space and begin writing. First ask yourself, "What am I *feeling* now?" "Rotten" is not good enough. Be more specific. After you have determined what you feel (take your time—you can do it) then become aware of your thoughts—"What am I telling myself right now?" Pull yourself back from your thoughts like an impartial observer attempting to learn something. Avoid pejorative self-judgments about the thoughts. (The last thing you need to do is attack yourself for "bad thinking!") Watch those sentences and be on the lookout for distortions and selective memory. Then respond to what may be distortions and half truths. It's also important to ask yourself, "What is the potential benefit of this pain I am going through now?" "Where is the silver lining in all of this?" Let me give you an example to illustrate my point.

Kevin is sitting alone on a Sunday afternoon in Cafe Flor, a cafe in the heart of the gay district in San Francisco. He uncoupled with his lover of three years, Blake, two weeks previously. Many attractive gay men are talking and laughing in this cafe, and Kevin begins to feel awful. He pulls out his journal and writes:

> OK, what I am feeling right now? I feel fucked up . . . empty . . . depressed . . . lonely . . . Look at how everybody is here with their friends. Look at those two guys holding hands at that table in the corner. I feel very much on the outside . . . like I'm watching a couple eat a meal in a warm restaurant on a cold night as I stick my face in the window from the outside. I am all by myself; what a pathetic ass I am. I am all alone in the world while everybody else is having a great time. So I guess I am feeling *very lonely* . . . that's the main feeling now . . . that's making me feel so bad. Now I should look at what I am telling myself. What are my thoughts?
>
> OK . . . Everybody is having a good time. I never have a good time. I am alone in this world. Sunday shouldn't be spent like this . . . you shouldn't spend Sunday alone . . . that's the day to be with your lover. Me and Blake always spent Sundays together. How I miss those Sundays with Blake. OK, Kevin . . . take a deep breath. What is going on here? How accurate is all of this? *Everybody* is having a good time? What about that guy reading the book? How do you know how he feels? And those guys near the door are having a quiet, serious-looking conversation. How do you know how they are feeling? Yeah, there are people having a good time and right now I am not. But what's the catastrophe about this? I am not having a good time because I just broke up with my lover. My world is all very different now. I got lots of changes going on all at once—lots of things that are no longer familiar. It's going to take time to reestablish my life. But it will get reestablished and it will be better. You were unhappy with Blake for a long time. He was emotionally dead, he did not respect you, he lied. You did this breakup to end that. The uncomfortable feelings you have now

are not going to last forever. This is part of that process—to get to a better place in life—to be with a guy who can love you the way you need to be loved. And how accurate are some of these things you are telling yourself? . . . Let's see . . . hmm . . . "You are miserable and all alone in the world?" Really now? Excuse me! Your best buddy Nester is in Paris. But he's coming back next week. He's always there for you . . . you are far from alone. And you just got off the phone about an hour ago with Jack in Washington, DC. You know Jack is always there day and night even though he lives three thousand miles away. Kevin, you got a lot a friends—they are just not sitting in Cafe Flor right now. And where is it written "Sundays are supposed to be with your lover?" Yeah, it is definitely desirable. For me . . . it's something I used to do. I would love to be with someone right now. But it doesn't mean I have to. And that I have to be outrageously miserable because I am not getting what I desire right now. . . .

DISAPPOINTMENT

We enter relationships with the hope and plan that it will work. "That it will work" means that it's not going to end. Although as gay men we are told that our relationships are bound to fail, we still don't intend for that to occur. We want him to be the right one, the one who won't slip away. This may have been your expectation, even if you never articulated it.

A relationship is also a major life undertaking. To be with a lover means you must expend a vast measure of time and emotional energy. When it doesn't work, when it comes apart, you may feel that you have wasted a great deal. You may even feel cheated. If you were with him for many years, you may believe that you "threw out" part of your life.

Thus, uncoupling is disappointing. But how do you prevent disappointment from becoming catastrophic?

I believe the answer lies, to a large degree, in what we tell ourselves is *supposed* to happen. People often get very emotionally distraught when they confuse a preference with the belief that their desire is a doctrine of nature intrinsic to the cosmos. Let me explain.

Often, when something goes wrong in life, we perceive this as an aberration of the natural order of things. We understand it as a violation of what is *supposed to be*, not as *a denial of what we want*. This has profound psychological implications. If you are denied what you are entitled to, you are likely to have significant difficulty accepting it. You will feel it is iniquitous, unfair, and probably *awful*. If, on the other hand, you see it as an impediment to your desire but *not as a breach of the Torah*, you are likely to suffer less emotional pain.

If I asked you whether the universe made a deal with you that your relationship would work out, you'd probably think I was asking a ridiculous question. But if you listen closely to your inner voice, you may find that that is exactly what you are telling yourself.

Let me give you an example of this by peering into the mind of a man named Armando. He broke up with his lover, Brendan, after a seven-year relationship. Armando is very distraught and his thinking goes something like this: "I shouldn't be alone after all that work I put into it, after all those years. This is totally horrible. My life is now fucked up and he fucked it up. We shouldn't have had to break up but he was so impossible."

Those kinds of thoughts express and reinforce the belief that the relationship was *supposed* to succeed. But imagine that Armando thought about it in the following manner: "Brendan was extremely difficult to be with. It created an intolerable situation for me, and I had to save myself by leaving him. Sometimes relationships don't work, and unfortunately it didn't for me and Brendan. I really wish it could have." This second set of thoughts are not just less painful. *They more accurately reflect reality.* Armando would have preferred for it to work for him and Brendan, but there was never a guarantee by some cosmic force that it would.

This may appear, at first glance, to be a meaningless word game. It is not. There was no reason that the relationship should have worked. There was no natural law that said Armando shouldn't be alone after all those years together. He didn't want to be after putting all that effort into their relationship. It would have been preferable that it worked out. This difference in perception can really make a material difference in the emotional experience of the event.

Certainly, Armando is not happy about the breakup in either scenario. But there are degrees of unhappiness. "Should have," "supposed to be," tends to intensify that uncomfortable emotion for the reasons I described above.

There is also something much more *empowering* and *hopeful* when you dispense with the "shoulds." If you prefer something and you don't get it, there is an implication that you have a role and power in creating that which you prefer. *Preference means choice.* In the second scenario, Armando can now think about what he can do differently the next time around to lessen the likelihood that he will have an unhappy relationship. If his energy is focused on "it was supposed to work except for what Brendan did," he may spend a lifetime blaming the Brendans of the world for interfering with the cosmic plan for him. And even if he applied the "supposed to" to himself ("It should have worked except that I am such a screwup"), he is still working against himself and reality. If he sees himself as upsetting an order, he is more likely to see himself as intrinsically flawed, not making a mistake that is redeemable. The "supposed to" and "shoulds" tend to obscure the responsibility and power of the individual in creating unfavorable and favorable circumstances for himself.

FAILURE AND HOMOPHOBIC FAILURE MESSAGES

If we work hard at something we want, and we don't achieve it, there is likely to be a sense of failure. Despite all our knowledge about the toxicity of dysfunctional relationships, as a society we still place a high premium on the longevity of a relationship. It's difficult for all of us, including heterosexuals, to avoid equating a breakup with defeat.

As gay men, this is an especially disturbing issue for us. We have always been told that the hallmark of a gay relationship is its inability to sustain. Our relationships are expected to fail, and they fail, according to the pervasive societal message, because our love is not real love at all; it's an inherently defective imitation of real, mature heterosexual love.

Many of us, at least consciously, will ascribe that kind of thinking to homophobically bigoted stereotyping devoid of any meaning. But not all of us. It might not be politically correct to admit it, but some gay men, especially if they have had a number of relationships that did not work out, may wonder if indeed there isn't some truth to that notion.

It's really not so difficult to slip into that kind of thinking. Consider the hundreds of thousands of messages that you have been exposed to during your lifetime that conveyed that supposition. We know that messages conveyed early in childhood are formative and resist change despite conscious, logical thinking. I have spent countless hours as a psychotherapist trying to help clients free themselves of destructive self-images created by early parental messages. Even though the messages really said much about their parents' psychopathology and nothing about my clients' self-worth, it was very hard for them to shake those beliefs. When you have the pressure of yet another breakup in your life, it may feel very easy to shift into major internalized homophobic meltdown.

Of course you can fight that. *And you can start by giving yourself permission to feel that way. Embrace your internalized homophobic beliefs!* As I have said previously, you cannot resolve something by avoiding it.

Messages that are drummed into you from early childhood are likely to resurface when you are under emotional pressure. You are not screwed up, immoral, or a disgrace to your gay community. You are a human being who has been exposed to pervasive societal misinformation, and under pressure you are having a reaction to those old messages. If you have a close friend who is comfortable with being gay, and who will not judge you, he may be a good person to discuss these feelings with. He may be able to gently confront some of the irrationality of your thinking and help you *emotionally understand* that this notion of inferior love has no basis in reality. You may come away thinking, "But of course, I was just feeling weird with all the changes and kind of slipped into that old way of thinking. I feel better now." Think of speaking to your friend as going for a tune-up, and go back again if you need another one!

Another way to procure help is by going to a gay men's group. If there is a group in your community that is addressing breaking up, that could be superb. There may be groups that deal with general gay men's issues that will also work. Of course, it's imperative that the group be a safe place where no one is personally attacked for what he says. The group members can provide support for you, and as with a friend, help you *feel* that being gay doesn't mean you can never succeed in a relationship.

You can, of course, start a group if there is none in your community. My only concern is that the group must be a nurturing, supportive environment for all of its members. A trained group leader can help ensure that. If you don't have a trained facilitator, I suggest that the group members mutually agree to ground rules including no personality attacking, confidentiality, and a mission of mutual support.

If you begin such a group (or go to an established group) you should feel supported. The bottom line is that if the group doesn't feel supportive and/or if you even feel worse, stop going. Whether it's professionally run or not!

It's possible that neither of the above options will help significantly, and that you need professional one-on-one counseling. Perhaps you have always had deep-seated internalized homophobic feelings, and your breakup has ignited them to a point where you are very uncomfortable.

If you seek therapy and prefer a gay male therapist, honor your feelings and see a gay man. The psychotherapeutic relationship is like any relationship; a certain "chemistry" between the individuals is necessary for it to work. A heterosexual woman may be a superb therapist, but if she is not what *you want*, it may not work for you. I do, however, want to caution you about one material issue. The mental health community does not have a proud history in relation to the gay community. In fact, it's quite appalling. For a very long time gay people were considered mentally disturbed because of their homosexuality. It may feel strange for the younger people reading this book to realize that some therapists would try to change gays into heterosexuals. The damage perpetrated on lesbians and gay men and their parents is astonishing. Today, of course, most mental heath professionals wouldn't state publicly that homosexuality is a mental illness (and it is not listed in the *Diagnostic and Statistical Manual of Mental Disorders,* DSM-IV—the psychiatric "bible"). They would be even more reluctant to talk about conversion. I am not convinced, however, that all of this is dead, and you could come face to face with a homophobic therapist. A homophobic therapist can also be a *gay man.*

The last thing you need, of course, is to run into a therapist who will exacerbate your confusion and pain. Thus, when you walk into his or her office, ask that person some unambiguous questions. The following is a list of questions I think is imperative to pose to a prospective therapist. Feel free to add your own. You are the consumer, and you have a right and a responsibility to yourself to know this person's attitudes toward gay people:

- Do you believe homosexuality is a mental illness? If not, why not?
- Are you comfortable with gay people? If yes, why? Given that we have a homophobic society, what kind of process did you go through to bring you to this change? If the therapist is gay (you have every right to ask about his sexual orientation), ask him about his internalized homophobic feelings, and how he did address/does address them.
- Ask the person if he has had experience working with gay people. If so, how much experience?
- Ask the therapist if he has gay friends. Ask him if he has an awareness of gay community issues.

If you don't like the way he answers the questions, or if he answers your questions with questions (that's an old shrink game that should have gone out with the dinosaurs—answering consumer-oriented questions in an initial consultation with questions is extremely inappropriate) look for another therapist. In a small town your choices may be limited, but a homophobic therapist is worse than no therapist at all. Please consult the Appendix in this book if you need help finding a therapist.

We have focused on some of the painful psychological effects of breaking up. You did not, of course, break up to feel more pain, but discomfort is inevitable when one makes a dramatic life change that involves leaving a person you have loved (or still love). We have also seen that the psychological uneasiness can be bearable. There are many ways to effectively cope and successfully transcend this period of your life. The key is to accept being a little shaky and vulnerable, and to be open to accepting support. Since you may, in fact, be very happy on many levels about your choice to end your relationship, there can be a tendency to discount the less-than-mirthful feelings. That is where you can run into a problem. If you don't acknowledge and work though the loss, it is likely to remain as unfinished business, and negatively affect you in ways you never would have imagined. By working through, you gradually let go and enable yourself to move on.

Uncoupling brings about numerous real life transformations also. Your home, your daily routine, the goals you work toward, how you spend free time, who you remain friends with and make friends with, are likely to change. Much of this will be welcomed. Many of these transitions, however, will also present challenges. In the next chapter we will concentrate on some of these environmental changes. Handled in a planful and appropriate manner, you will not only meet the challenges successfully, but may look back on this time as a positive turning point in your life.

Chapter 5

You No Longer Live Here: Social and Other Life Changes of Breaking Up

It's just awkward with him being there at a party where I am supposed to be single. . . . Do I go up there and say "hi" or do I just dance and ignore him and hopefully he'll go away? You know it's kind of weird.

Antonio, 29, management consultant
Boston, Massachusetts

I ran into him a few times in the bars and when I saw him I would leave.

Jack, 56, pet store owner
Miami Beach, Florida

. . . my friends and I would go out and one of them would run back . . . and would tell me, "Joe is here. Do you want to leave?" And I would say, "Yes, let's go."

Juan, 44, research psychologist
New York City

If you moved clear across the country the day after you uncoupled, you could probably avoid many of the awkward social dilemmas that will now come your way. But you probably didn't move further than across town, if at all. The same bars, the same cafes, and the same people that knew you and him are still there. So how are you going to deal with all of this?

RUNNING INTO YOUR EX
ON THE STREET AND IN OTHER PLACES

I will begin with an anecdote that involves the experience of encountering an ex in a public environment. Lavar separated from his lover of five years, Stan, one year ago. He and Stan both continue to live in the same neighborhood in Washington, DC (Dupont Circle). In the past year he has run into Stan probably twenty times; in the Circle and Fireplace bars, on the street, at Kramer Books and Afterwards (a cafe/book store), and in the mall in Georgetown. Although Lavar is popular and has many friends, he has had the uncanny luck of always being alone when he sees Stan, and Stan has always been with someone! This has irked Lavar to the point that he feels anxious when he is out in public by himself. He feels that Stan will think he is "all alone" since they broke up. He also feels threatened by seeing people he does not know with Stan. He wonders if they are having sex, and although he tells himself that it should not matter, he can get very upset. A friend tried to make light of the whole situation by saying to him, "Don't you know the rule about running into an ex?" "What?" Lavar asked. "Grab the guy closest to you and start laughing."

After a breakup, we continue to have emotional ties with our exes. It's one thing to have those feelings while he is not in your view. It's quite another thing to see him and *see him in this new context of no longer being your lover.* If you have just uncoupled, those ties are likely to be very powerful. The experience of running into him can ignite those feelings into potent emotional pain. Let's take a look at Jimmy and Ernesto, who had a very unfortunate run-in.

Jimmy and Ernesto lived together for seven years in Boston. The decision to break up was mutual, although Ernesto was very dependent on Jimmy, and he felt that Jimmy would have an easier time with their separation than he would. It had been six months since their breakup when Ernesto stopped for a pizza on his way home from work. They had not seen each other at that time in about two months.

Ernesto is a customer service representative for a large corporation. On that particular day, a number of people he spoke with on the telephone were difficult. His boss was in a nasty mood and yelled at him for misfiling a document. He stayed two hours late to catch up with some work so as to avoid further wrath from his boss. Ernesto was feeling tired and emotionally drained that evening. He wanted nothing more than to buy the pizza, eat it in his bed as he drank a beer, and then go to sleep. As he was waiting in line to order, his mind drifted to Jimmy. He remembered in a bittersweet way evenings like this when Jimmy would hold him and tell him it was all going to be OK. Then, just like a bad movie, or more accurately, just like a nightmare, in walked Jimmy with another man. He and the man were holding hands and laughing. They were both dressed as if they were going out for the evening. It took about twenty seconds before Jimmy's eyes met Ernesto's, and it was probably the longest twenty seconds in Ernesto's life. Sure enough, the smile was literally wiped off Jimmy's face, and he looked stunned. This was no consolation for Ernesto, who lost control and began weeping openly. He then darted out of the pizza place without ordering, horrified and humiliated, and walked for about ten blocks openly crying.

Who you are, and the circumstances of your encounter with an ex, are certain to affect how you feel. But there is likely to be some emotional uneasiness. Although many of us strive not to feel possessive with a lover, to a certain degree that feeling is unavoidable. *A relationship, by definition, implies a certain amount of "possession."* It may be very politically incorrect to acknowledge this, and certainly destructive if you treat your lover like you own him. But this feeling, on some level, is an undercurrent in all romantic relationships. He is your lover; and much of what he does in his life is negotiated with you. When you break up, all relationship rules are canceled, and he can do what he wants, when he wants, with whomever he wants. Although you may know this on an intellectual level, your emotional system needs time to process this and accept it.

It's a good idea to do your best in the early weeks and months after your breakup to avoid your ex. Running into him in a pizza place as Ernesto did is unavoidable. But if you know he frequents a certain bar, or if you know he is going to be at a party, I would consider not going there. You may ask, "Well, isn't that just postponing the problems? And why should I let him dictate where I can go?"

I don't think it's a postponement, because at a later time you may be more psychologically able to handle it. In terms of whether he is dictating your freedom, you will feel that way only if you frame it in that manner. It is true you may be limiting your freedom somewhat.

But *you* will be doing it *to take care of you*. That puts the power back in your hands. He really has nothing to do with it.

Some men may also see running into an ex as a challenge and a test. "I should grow up; I should be able to handle it." "If I avoid him, he wins." This has nothing to do with maturity, or mental prowess, or some kind of a contest. Emotional pain is a reality, and emotional pain is an expectable reaction to seeing an ex-lover. Honor your humanity and cut yourself a break!

If you run into him unexpectedly, you don't need to panic. Indeed, if you both participate in the same gay community, it is likely that you will see him at times. You can prepare for this by accepting in advance that this will happen. That may make the experience less abrupt and less shocking.

You will nonetheless feel uncomfortable. The best way to cope is simply to go with the feeling. It is quite normal to feel this, *so don't fight it.* You could say something to yourself such as, "Oh boy . . . I'm feeling really terrible right now but that's exactly how I should feel. Jack is standing ten feet from me with who knows who . . . what else should I be feeling? I'll be OK; this won't last forever."

If the two of you communicate, do your best to keep it short, sweet, and *superficial.* You don't want to get pulled into any discussion that will stir you up emotionally. The encounter itself will do ample rousing. You are likely to feel very awkward and you may behave in a bumbling manner. Go with this also. It is an awkward situation. What's the worst that can happen anyway? He'll realize you were uncomfortable? He's going to laugh about it? He's going to tell someone? *So what?* What lasting impact will that have on your life? If you try to fight it you may appear more clumsy and feel even more frustrated.

As I mentioned earlier, you didn't want to run into him in the first place, but now that it has happened, the question is, "What should I do with this situation?" You have to use your judgment with this. If you run into him at a play, you may not want to walk out before the curtain goes up (although you may, if you feel very uneasy). If you are at a party, you could leave. Assess how you feel. Are there many people in a big house, and he's lost in the crowd? Is it as if he's not there? If so, great. Stay and have a ball. On the other hand, are you staring at him every five seconds, and feeling increasingly uncomfortable? In that predicament you may want to leave but think, "If I go now he and everyone else will know why." To which my response is, *"So what?"* Your job is to take care of you. If you are feeling distressed in his presence, utilize your power and get the hell out of there!

EXPLAINING YOUR NEW STATUS TO THE WORLD

If you have been together for a considerable amount of time, people associate the two of you together. It's to be expected that people who don't know what happened will automatically ask you, "And how is so and so?"

This can be uncomfortable for a number of reasons. Each time it happens, it's another reminder of a painful fact—your breakup. There is also a possibility that the person will communicate a message of failure even though he has no intention to. "You two broke up? Wow, I thought you got along so well together." There may also be a feeling on your part that you owe an explanation. This can mean describing the whole long unhappy story again, chapter and verse.

The first two problems are probably unavoidable, although you can remind yourself that the sense of failure he may feel does not have to be your feeling.

As far as telling the whole long story over again, you really don't have to do that. I mean that you have no *obligation*. You may want to vent and that is fine. But if you feel you owe the public details, you don't.

Rehashing the story once again can cause an unnecessary reexperience of all of the pain. Working through a separation does require thinking and talking about what happened. But healthy letting go also means concentrating on the present. Sometimes it's important *not* to think and talk about him.

People are naturally curious, or just may be missing a life, and you will be prodded to explain. Keep in mind that you are not obligated to satisfy a person's "nosy needs." Gently, calmly, but firmly inform the person that you don't want to discuss it. Your conversation may go something like this:

Andre: You and Jeff broke up? Oh my god! What in the world happened?

You: I'd rather not talk about it.

Andre: Oh, I know it must have been real bad and it must be very difficult for you. But you guys seemed like the model couple. What happened? Was it another guy?

You: I really don't want to talk about it.

Andre: Come on, I know you guys. You got to tell me what happened. I am not going to blab this to anyone. I am just worried about you and real surprised. I mean this is a shock. What happened?

You: If you are really concerned about me, you'd respect my feelings when I tell you that I do not want to, and *will not,* talk about it. Please, Andre . . . back off.

RELATIONSHIP SECRETS BECOMING PUBLIC

If there was intimacy, you know each other in ways that no one else does. Each of you, thus, has knowledge of the other's flaws and weaknesses. Some of that information could be very embarrassing were it to become public.

Occasionally ex-lovers express anger by revealing these kinds of secrets. This is obviously an immature and useless mode of addressing anger. From the perspective of your self-development (aside from the importance of behaving appropriately toward your ex), you should not engage in this kind of behavior. You may get some immediate gratification by "sticking it" to him. But it's not going to really make you feel better, and you may come to regret what you did later on. When we behave in a way that is not appropriate, our "self" notices it and doesn't forget. Engaging in vindictive behavior can be damaging to your self-image and self-esteem in the long run. Moreover, this can create other problems should you want to reestablish a friendship with him at some future point.

But what if he does it to you? What if he's unloading every secret you had between you to anyone who will listen? What if some people drop the fact that they know information about you which embarrasses you? Shouldn't you get out the "big guns" and retaliate? Are you just supposed to sit there and do nothing? Well, you don't have to continue sitting there. But, yes . . . *you should do absolutely nothing.*

Why?

Sharing secrets, letting him inside, is one of the risks and gifts of intimacy. You let down the mask and became vulnerable with him. It's actually a beautiful experience, and it is indeed unfortunate if he violates your trust. But fighting back on the same low road just debases that wonderful experience even further. And it won't put the toothpaste back in the tube. There is also another reason to resist the temptation to react. There are reprehensible people in all communities, and anyone who is letting you know that he knows your secrets is probably up to no good. You'll feed his malfeasance by responding to it. Conversely, you'll short-circuit his fun if you act as though you couldn't care what he knows.

This is not to say you treat your ex-relationship like a classified secret. You may have a legitimate need to burn off steam with a close, *trustworthy* friend. That is quite different from informing people of your ex's shortcomings in an attempt to hurt him.

UNSOLICITED AND SOLICITED
INFORMATION ABOUT HIM

It may be very tempting to "keep tabs on him," if you are no longer in contact. Is he miserable without you? Is he having a great time? *Is he involved with someone?*

In the early phase of uncoupling, you need physical and mental separation to successfully let go. If you keep up with what he's up to, it may be difficult to achieve that. It can also be very uncomfortable. If he gets involved with someone, do you really want to know that? If he's been frequenting the clubs and seems to be having the time of his life without you, are you sure you want to know this? Hopefully you wish him well, but there is always ambivalence when we end a relationship. That kind of information could stir up feelings of jealousy, anger, sadness, and so on.

In a close-knit community, you may learn information from others even if you don't want to. Sometimes there is no hurtful intention. People talk and you happen to be there. Sometimes, however, there is a malevolent agenda.

Sadly, there really are some people who thrive on trying to make others miserable. When they see you coming, they drool with anticipation. Within seconds they are informing you that he has a new boyfriend, or that they saw him with so-and-so, or imply that he is happy that he is rid of you.

You should keep in mind that you don't even know if any of this information is true. You can end this person's fun and preserve your sanity by informing him that you have no interest in hearing *anything* about your ex from him. If he is particularly vicious, you may need to cut him off as he starts talking. This can stop the flow of information and stop the damage before it begins. If this person insists on telling you, insist on not listening, and walk away.

I want to repeat this—walk away if you can't otherwise stop him (or even if you can but just don't want to be in this person's presence). You really have that option, and it is a very powerful act. You do not have to remain there and be psychologically abused.

Legitimate Concern About Your Ex-Lover's Welfare

Of course you may want to know something about your ex. You may want to know that he is OK. This is certainly an appropriate concern. But it may not be a simple endeavor. If you start asking around, or if you do call him, it's very easy to learn other information about him that you may not want to know. One way to handle this is to be clear, to the point, and brief if you call him. Another way is to speak to a friend who may talk to your ex. Tell your friend that, at times, you will ask him about your ex. Make your intentions unambiguous: you don't want unsolicited information; you would only want to know whether he is doing OK.

The above circumstances imply that your ex-lover is in fact OK. But what if he is not? Perhaps he is not physically well. Maybe he is having financial problems. Perchance he is depressed. When it comes to trouble, the possibilities are infinite.

Of course you do need to know a lot more if your ex is having serious difficulties. Breakup or not, if you still care about him, you are not about to let him fall into harm's way. You would probably want to support him emotionally if he really needs you. Getting involved in this way soon after your breakup can be very tricky, however.

An ex-lover's needs can be a vehicle for getting you back into your former role with him. He may consciously create this in order to achieve that. It can also happen unconsciously. Or it may have nothing to do with intention—bad things do happen that could create a need (let's say one of his parents died). Rightfully, you would want to be there for him. But how do you do this without compromising your need to separate and let go? Being there in a crisis fuels feelings of attachment. In the early stages of a breakup, this can interfere with your work toward becoming unattached.

Thus, you have a dilemma, and it is therefore imperative that you keep focused on the legitimacy of your needs. The fact that he is in trouble and you care about him doesn't change the fact that you needed to break up. Being supportive is also not synonymous with being lovers or "going back." However, this may be difficult to conceptualize emotionally.

You can weather this well by first reminding yourself that you are likely to feel confused. Then remind yourself that you care about him, that you'll do what you can, but nothing has changed about your reasons for breaking up. And breaking up means that this reinvolvement has to be temporary—you need to get back to your "space" to work through letting go (perhaps at some future point you can be good friends but not now). Therefore, put a limit on your involvement with him. Perhaps you can call him or come by a couple of times, but then you need to pull back again. If he continues to "need you," you should explain to him why you can't continue in this manner. If he's in serious emotional trouble, suggest that he seek professional help. In a grave emergency such as a potential suicide, you may have to call the police to get him help. But then you still have to take care of your life. The bottom line is that you guys are no longer together, and you need to do what's right for you to remain uncoupled and successfully grieve the loss.

All of this becomes significantly more difficult if you were raised in a family where you assumed the role of caretaker.

In my clinical practice, I have observed that people have an extremely difficult time letting go of this role. On a deep level they feel something is immoral about their needs coming first. Thus, in the situations described above, forgetting you and taking care of him may be a knee-jerk reaction. But you can't forget about you, because "you" is all you have. Yes, you do come first, and you need to make peace with this.

WHAT HAPPENS TO HIS FRIENDS AND YOU?

One of the added difficulties of uncoupling is that you may lose relationships other than the one you had with your ex. You may have become friends with his friends, only to find out that they have taken sides, and it's not your side they have taken.

If someone no longer wants to have a relationship with you, there's really nothing you can do. But what if his friends want to continue their connection with you? What should you do then?

If you would like to remain friends with them, you need to be clear about a number of things. Certainly, it is possible to develop a good bond with a friend or friends of a lover. Indeed, good relationships are precious, and I would think long and hard before I'd give one up. But remaining connected with friends of an ex is complicated and can be a challenge.

One issue to consider is how your ex will feel about this. True, it is, in a sense, none of his business. But if it makes him very upset, what effect will ultimately trickle down to you? Will this create significant tension between the two of you, and serve to maintain chronic unpleasant feelings? What is *your* agenda for maintaining involvement with his friends? Is it a way of not letting go of him? Is it a way to keep tabs on him? Is it a way to anger him? Be clear about your motivations and the ultimate effect on your peace of mind. Be certain that you want to maintain relationships with them simply because you value those relationships.

Assuming this is so, you still need to create these relationships apart from your ex in a methodical manner. As I have mentioned repeatedly, its very important to develop physical and psychological distance in the early aftermath of a separation. His friends are probably an integral part of his life, so in the beginning you will probably need some space from them also. If you have good relationships with them, there should be good communication between you, so just let them know this. Tell them that you very much desire and intend to remain friends, but for now you will need a little space. If you believe you can continue seeing them without a deleterious effect on you, certainly try it out. But if your ex-lover keeps coming up (or simply seeing them reminds you of him) and you are feeling uncomfortable, stay apart for a while until your feelings are no longer so raw.

In time, you can start reconnecting. Your relationships with them will likely (and should) change. These are now friendships in their own right.

It's unavoidable that your ex will come up in conversation, but this should not be the focus of your relationship. Indeed, you could probably get a continuous up-to-date report on him if you wanted. I suggest that you discuss two simple ground rules with these friends when you start to socialize with them again. Those rules are "Don't tell me anything about so-and-so unless I ask (and only if you want to)," and "don't share any information about me with him unless I tell you it is OK to do that (and only if you want to)." If they cannot consent to these rules, they are not respecting an important need of yours.

WHAT ABOUT YOUR FRIENDS AND HIM?

What about the people *you* knew long before you met him? What if they want to continue a relationship with him?

Don't be embarrassed if some childhood feelings are triggered. Don't be surprised if you discover that you are thinking: "Those are *my* friends and he can't have them!"

Feelings like these are not bizarre, and it doesn't make you crazy, immature, or a spoiled brat to have them. If your friends are really your friends, they will be able to listen to and understand how you feel. It doesn't mean they will (or should) change their behavior, but they will respect how you feel. You are considerably more likely to do a lot of damage to your relationships with them if you are feeling this way but keep it a secret.

Talking about how you feel gives all of you the potential to arrive at a solution. It may even mean that they do forgo relationships with him primarily because of how you feel. For that to be viable, however, it has to come from a voluntary desire on the part of your friends, not because they are reacting to demands or manipulation by you.

They may not, however, stop seeing him and while this may hurt, I don't believe it is a reason to destroy your relationships with them. Uncomfortable *feelings* are understandable; demanding that they end a relationship because of your feelings is another matter. After all, they are individuals, and if they have developed good friendships with him, it is asking a lot for them to end those friendships. It is not, however, asking a lot to respect your feelings. If you don't want to know anything about their activities with him, I believe that request should be honored.

THE EX, FRIENDS, AND SEX: CAN YOUR FRIENDS NOW DATE YOUR EX?

Benjamin and Dwayne have broken up after being together for six years. Robert, Benjamin's friend, feels Dwayne is free to date whomever he wants now. He asks him out.

This is a question about boundaries, and it's true that societal boundaries sometimes limit people in ways that are unnecessary. Some of us in the gay community feel that we have more of a consciousness about this than heterosexuals. The argument goes something like this: Since we were never part of the acceptable heterosexual culture, we are more aware of the arbitrariness of societal dictums. We are better able to question rules about love and sex and relationships that have no real value. We are more free to develop standards that are concordant with our needs. For example, it is probably more permissible in our community (although not universal) that coupled men can have sexual experiences outside of their relationship. Those in our community in favor of this argue that monogamy creates unnecessary frustration and may lead to cheating and ultimately destruction of the relationship. By agreeing on rules that don't threaten the primacy of the relationship between the couple, these gay men can procure the best of both worlds. They can have sexual variety and at the same time reap the benefits of intimacy with a lover.

I agree that this argument is valid for some, and that we should discard social constructs that make no sense. Denying the importance of powerful emotions, however, is equally ill-considered. Frequently, the importance of feelings is denied when boundaries are presented as an irrational impediment to sexual and romantic freedom. Boundaries can certainly function like prison walls, but they can also serve to protect us. Boundaries are essential between your friends and your ex-lover, and between you and his friends. Sexual and romantic involvement is apt to culminate in disaster.

As I have previously discussed, feelings of possession are an integral part of a relationship. While we may rightfully frown upon behavior that seeks to control another human being, such behavior is not equivalent to possessive feelings. One is a behavior, and the other is an emotion. Furthermore, control is a dangerous, perverted outgrowth of what otherwise can be a relatively benign phenomenon. There is a world of difference, for example, between expecting your lover to be faithful through a mutually agreed-upon understanding (possessive feelings), and ordering him to do so (controlling behavior).

Possessive feelings are significant and deeply seated. Power needs to be respected. We all know the dangers of not respecting power in nature. Speak to someone who barely survived a hurricane because he did not heed the warning to evacuate!

Feelings do not need to correlate with logic, and these feelings often do not. You can feel possessive toward your ex even though you are no longer together and do not even want to be with him.

If your ex-lover becomes involved with another man, you may feel "taken from," "robbed," and "losing what rightfully belongs to you." Of course no one is taking anything from you, *but that does not matter. Again, I want to emphasize that these are not logical cognitions. I am talking about powerful, primal feelings.*

> I cannot stand seeing Joe with anyone else. Because I'm thinking, oh my god, that means they're having sex.

... I feel like he's mine. I don't want anyone else to be in a relationship with him.

Juan, 44, research psychologist
New York City

Feelings like these are apt to prevail if your ex-lover gets involved with someone in the early aftermath of your separation, or when you are still together. If it happens after some time has passed and you have been able to psychologically let go, it is less likely you will experience this. But that is not to say that your psyche becomes totally devoid of all remnants of these feelings, and that they could not be activated under the right conditions. A friend becoming involved with your ex could provide the ideal conditions, probably at any time.

One of the reasons for this is the emotional connection you have with your friend, and how his involvement with your ex can serve as a constant, irksome stimulus (stimulating pain related to the loss of what you "possessed"). Part of it also has to do with role conflict. Relating to him as your trustworthy buddy and the lover of your ex is confusing because they are very different roles. They have different dynamics and can be conflicting. The confusion is painful in its own right and can also set off the possessive issues.

The most significant part, however, is possessive feelings created in large part by male socialization (possessive feelings are also developed apart from male socialization, but this form of learning creates many beliefs that are at the core of possessive feelings). Male socialization imparts powerful rules about competition, dominance, and winning. It also defines potent pejorative psychological descriptions for the self when one loses, particularly when it involves losing a lover to a competitor.

As a man, you have been socialized into highly valuing the possession of things. You have been taught that the more things you have, and the bigger those things are (which is just another way of describing "more"), the better you are. Even if those things have no intrinsic value, *more is just better*. Those "things" can also be people.

You are supposed to compete fiercely with other men to get more things, and are not to lose to another man. If that happens, your self-image is diminished because it means that you are less than that man. Think of the expression, "may the better man win."

There is yet another pressure on us as gay men. Society depicts us as men who can never achieve adequate maleness. These issues may therefore be more important for you than for some heterosexual men. "Losing" can create significant emotional pain because it stimulates old psychological wounds about being intrinsically inadequate.

But you say these are absurd, frankly insane notions that you rejected long ago, or never accepted in the first place. You certainly may have (and wisely so) *consciously* rejected much of this. But a lifetime of socialization cannot be fully expunged. Many of these beliefs may still be alive unconsciously. Feelings related to them will have a way of seeping into your life, especially around emotionally charged issues. It will be bad enough to lose your ex to some creep by the name of Louie you never met. But if your good friend is now dating him, it can be a nightmare.

The effects of your socialization in such a scenario can create emotions of rage, shock, disappointment, betrayal, narcissistic wound, humiliation, and depression, to name a few. It's unlikely that you will be able to change these feelings, nor do I recommend that you make any attempt to. They are too deep and too much part of the fabric of your society and who you are. Of course this doesn't mean that the acute pain lasts forever, or that you won't eventually move on in your life.

If your friend dates your ex-lover, there is a good chance—I'd say an overwhelming chance—that your friendship with him and any potential relationship with your ex will be destroyed. You may never want to have anything to do with either of them again.

You may also be the one who is asked out by your ex's friend, or you may be the friend of someone who just broke up and are thinking about approaching his ex.

There are likely to be many other complications. This "friend" who is asking you out may have (consciously or unconsciously) a punishment or competition agenda with your ex, and is using you in his game.

You may have an agenda (conscious or unconscious) of wanting to inflict punishment on your ex and will therefore date his friend.

In the long run (and probably not that long!) it will do nothing to address your anger.

Even if there were no hidden agendas, and the people involved have real feelings for one another, the relationship they create is prone to being haunted by ghosts. Relationships are problematic enough, and this kind of a relationship is not very likely to succeed. This is a class A no-win situation, and apt to cause grave detriment to all involved. If you have any control in creating this kind of a relationship, I have some simple advice. Do not do it.

YOUR FREE TIME: ANXIETY AND NEW ACTIVITIES

A relationship requires a considerable share of your time. While you were with him, you may have complained about all the experiences and people you were missing. Perhaps you dreamed about the vast freedom you'd have if you were single. Now that you are, however, it doesn't seem as good as the dream. You feel unfocused, worried, out of sorts. You feel, in a word, lost.

It's not peculiar to feel uneasy when, abruptly, you have abundant free time. A routine provides psychological structure. Life with your lover provided such a structure. While some, or even much, of it may not have been pleasurable, it kept you from the anxiety you have now. Structure provides clarity and predictability and therefore comfort. You knew what to do, when, and the likely outcome. Christmas was with him and his doting mom in Topeka. Saturday was chore day and then off to the movies. Thursday nights you watched *ER* together.

Your anxiety is on two levels. One is derived from the new freedom and the loss of your routine. There is a void now. A void, in itself, is frightening. The other level comes from the process of filling the void. This process will involve developing a new structure in your life. This will include new experiences, new behaviors, new people, and therefore psychological risk taking.

Anxiety can be very subtle. You may not be consciously aware of it, but it can be devastating nevertheless. You may find yourself developing a new relationship with your television set, for example! You may be spending an increasing number of hours in front of it without realizing you are doing that. Or you may find yourself having vague plans about making changes in your life but for some reason not getting to step one. You may want to take a class, and the school is right around the corner. However, you never seem to walk in the front door to register. You "don't have the time," or you just never seem to "get around to it."

Passivity is counterproductive, but it's "safe." When you veg out in front of the TV or remain disorganized, you don't have to realistically address your changed life and the new choices you need to make. You don't have to be reminded of your painful breakup, that you are indeed by yourself right now, and that you can no longer rely on the old routines.

The way to overcome this is to get very serious about developing new activities that will help you grow. This means making very specific plans, which includes specific times by which you will accomplish goals, and a commitment to yourself to carry this out. It may be very helpful to enlist a friend as a sort of coach. Discuss your different plans with him, and make a commitment with him to carry these plans to fruition.

You could decide to accomplish a specific goal per week. For example, if you want to register for a class, you can start very simply (I recommend going slowly to avoid overwhelming yourself) and commit to obtaining the school catalog by the end of the week. Each week you should have a "check in" with your friend, in which you discuss whether you achieved the goal planned for that week.

This may sound very simple and easy. In a sense it is. But change is scary for most people, and it is truly amazing (and sad) how we can forgo tremendous opportunities because we were frightened to take that first step. Anxiety, and often anxiety we are not in touch with, is our biggest enemy. By being specific and committed to both yourself and a close friend, you could force yourself to move despite your anxiety. It's also helpful to acknowledge your anxiety and make a conscious commitment to overcome it.

You may say, "That sounds nice, I should acknowledge my anxiety, but what if I don't feel frightened?" You can try to get in touch with this by thinking in detail about a new activity that you plan to undertake. Note the different thoughts and images that spontaneously pass through your mind as you think about the steps involved in the activity. Also ask yourself how you are feeling as you experience this.

Let's say, for example, that you decide you want to go on vacation by yourself. Let's assume that all of your vacations during the past few years were with your ex-lover. Imagine the steps involved in that plan. Picture packing by yourself. Imagine yourself getting on the plane alone. Think about checking into the hotel by yourself. Contemplate how you spend your days (going to museums, eating in restaurants, going to the beach, etc.) during the vacation.

This may get you in touch with anxiety because you will be confronting the unfamiliar, and will be imagining stimuli that will trigger feelings of loss. Your thoughts (and mental images) could go something like this: You dislike packing (your ex-lover would do all of the packing) and you leave behind half of what you need. You almost miss the plane because you are anxious and disorganized (you can't find your keys as you are trying to leave your house). You are seated next to a rude woman with a crying infant (he always sat next to you). When you reach your destination, you are confronted with one disaster after another. You are terribly lonely in this faraway place, and you get sick (you get a twenty-four-hour bug). He is not there to comfort you as he normally would. Everyone is unfriendly and no one seems to be interested in talking with you. You find eating alone in the restaurants particularly uncomfortable because you are accustomed to dining with him. You finally decide to cut your vacation short and wonder why you ever went in the first place (which may persuade you to cancel your trip).

If this happens, simply tell yourself that this is your anxiety "talking," and this is what happens when you are going through the changes of a breakup. Remind yourself, also, that it is not real, and it is not going to stop you. Thus, you are getting in touch with your anxiety, and accomplishing a pivotal step in overcoming it.

You can also help decrease anxiety associated with a new activity by producing a positive "mental video" (visualization). You will have to create very specific positive images for each step. In the case of going on vacation, you will need to force yourself to visualize a wonderful vacation.

It's important to create lots of details to make it feel real. For example, you can imagine your hotel room as large and airy, with a wonderful view of the ocean. There is ornate, antique furniture. The walls are a pale green, with an attractive rug in the middle of a polished wood floor. A faint scent of roses comes from outside your window. (This is what I like; obviously, create what you like. It should also be even more detailed. For reasons of brevity, I haven't included more.)

Each step of the vacation should be visualized, creating an extremely pleasurable experience in your imagination. If you find negative images seeping in, imagine yourself launching a nuclear missile at the negative image. Watch it vaporize! Then return to the pleasurable image.

I will summarize a positive vacation visualization so you can get the overall idea. However, you will need to create detailed scenes for each part or step. Give yourself a lot of time for this. Do it when you are relaxed and alone. Avoid interruptions such as the telephone. Close your eyes during the experience. Keep in mind that you can use your other senses in your visualizations. Smell the flowers, touch the soft rug, feel the warm tropical sunshine, and so on.

The vacation story could unfold as follows: You get to the airport in plenty of time, and you have a very relaxing, smooth flight. The hotel is wonderful; the city is clean and beautiful. The people are friendly, exotic, and very interesting. You love being in complete charge of your schedule, and you adore your freedom and spontaneity. One afternoon, you are visiting a museum, the next day you are exploring an enchanting boulevard. You discover a quaint cafe and each morning you flirt with a waiter who is very cute. You learn a lot about this part of the world, and you exchange e-mail addresses with a guy who works in the hotel. He is very interesting to talk with. Now you have a pen pal in this country. You are impressed with your ability to enjoy this experience by yourself. You return home relaxed and invigorated, with a new sense of confidence in yourself.

Creating this visualization doesn't mean you should expect everything to go perfectly, and then be disappointed when it does not. Use this simply to decrease your anxiety.

Perhaps you feel no anxiety when you visualize a new activity. Perhaps it is not there. Just make certain you don't forgo the activity unless there is a very clear, real reason to do so. (You plan to go on vacation and you lose your job. You really do not have the money.) Remember, anxiety can be very sneaky.

Perhaps you will not be able to create a positive visualization. Maybe you will feel very anxious as you contemplate any new activity. You may say to yourself, "I can't do that; I will fail." It's very important *not* to give in to that. If you do, you are likely to convince yourself of your powerlessness and incompetence, while the opposite is likely to happen if you try. And even if your endeavor proves less fulfilling than you would have liked (you go on vacation and have a mediocre time), you will still be better off than if you had avoided doing it. You will at least have proven to yourself that you were able to accomplish something you were not accustomed to doing.

Keep in mind, also, that there *really* is a very positive, reinforcing side to the activities you will now undertake (not just in your visualizations!). Growing and having new experiences can be very rewarding and exciting. Seeing yourself in a different and more competent light can be exceedingly pleasurable and empowering. You may have also wanted to pursue these enterprises for a long time. Perhaps your relationship got in the way. Perchance you had to forgo these experiences for the sake of compromise. *Now you really do have the chance to do all of what you could not do then!*

What activities will you do? Decide by making a written list. Who are the people you would like to get together with more often? Who are the people you thought could be friends but you just never got around to calling? Perhaps you can go to dinner or see a movie with them. What kinds of social activities do you truly enjoy? Do you want to try tennis, skiing, hiking, square dancing? What activities will put you in situations where you can meet people in a pleasant environment? Are you interested in doing some volunteer work? What was that class you wanted to take? Haven't you been interested in photography for a long time? Is there a gay photography group in your area? Can you take a class in that? Is it time to visit that buddy of yours in Seattle?

Your list will probably be vast. I suggest you first brainstorm—put down everything you can think of that you may find fun to experience. After that, you can narrow it down in terms of desire, time, money resources, and so on. Don't throw the list away, however. At a later time you can come back to it, and pick out activities that you currently feel are impractical, or that you are not particularly enthusiastic about right now. When you make the list, also rate the level of anxiety that goes with each new activity. Plan to do the activities that have the lowest anxiety rates (use a scale from one to ten).

There is a comforting thought to consider when anxiety is intimidating you. Anxiety, a good deal of the time, is *the biggest liar in the world*. It's like a bully. It presents itself as awesome and almighty but will run with its tail between its legs when you confront it. It also warns of dire consequences but its threats are rather empty. Often, there is really no danger. Think about it. This feeling can control you. It can impede your ability to move ahead. And all the time there is no real danger.

There is also a paradoxical characteristic of anxiety. This you should pay very close attention to. You can be in real danger if you "listen" to your anxiety. The danger comes in missed opportunities. *Missing out in life is a profound loss and you should be very scared of that indeed!*

Anxiety does have a biological purpose and will protect us at times. Fear of something that presents a real-life danger is appropriate. Being fearful of standing on the ledge of a tall building, for example, protects your survival. The problem with fear is that it often becomes connected to stimuli that are not dangerous. It's easiest to observe this with a phobia. A person who has fear of public speaking, for example, will be terrified of addressing an audience. He will feel that he will "just die" as he begins to speak. But how does making a speech cause someone to "just die"? In reality, standing before an audience *presents no survival danger*. Discomfort yes, embarrassment perhaps, danger no. A phobic person, however, may experience making a speech (emotionally) as if it were life-threatening.

When you realize you are fearful, ask yourself a simple question: What, in actuality (repeat, *in actuality*) is the *worst* thing that can happen to me if I do such and such?

If you go to a party, and people look at you as though you are from Mars, so what? You have an uncomfortable two hours. Or if you take a class and the teacher turns out to be awful, so what?

Again, there is discomfort and perhaps some wasted money, but no catastrophe. You can significantly diminish the control anxiety has over you by recognizing the difference between discomfort and danger, *and be willing to accept discomfort.*

Although it's imperative to confront anxiety, it doesn't mean you try to instantly obliterate all of your fears. Don't overwhelm yourself with too many things to do all at once. Respect the level of your anxiety as a strategy to control it.

Novelty brings mistakes and awkwardness. If you can give yourself permission to flounder, it will make the experience much easier. Also keep in mind that that the discomfort won't last forever.

In the past two chapters, I have discussed the various social and psychological changes that come with uncoupling. All present various challenges. All are part of the process of disengaging from a former relationship. They are, furthermore, opportunities for growth.

Perhaps some time has passed and these changes have been integrated into your life. You have not seen your ex-lover for a while, but he certainly hasn't disappeared from your mind. He was a very important part of your life, and you now wonder if conceivably you should reconnect with him in a different kind of relationship. But why now, you think? Do you really want to go back with him, you wonder? Many other questions flood your mind. How are you going to feel when you see or speak to him for the first time? What if he doesn't want anything to do with you? How will you react if he has a new lover? Will this destroy all the progress you made? If you are going to initiate contact, how do you go about taking that first step?

I will address reestablishing communication in the next chapter. Much is at stake in the decision you make. Perhaps there is potential for a lifelong, gratifying friendship. It would be foolhardy to pass that up. On the other hand, the distance between you may be exceedingly great. Conceivably, nothing is really there any longer. Clarity of thought and control of your emotions will be your best guides. You need to know yourself, know what you want and can tolerate, and be able to separate illusion from fact.

So how do you decide whether to attempt to resume contact, or simply leave him in your past?

Chapter 6

Creating the Ex-Relationship: Developing the Kind of Contact You Want

Breaking up doesn't have to mean never coming together again. It may feel that way in the beginning because you are so angry and because any thought of involvement may feel too painful. Having sustained a relationship with a lover over a period of time, however, is complicated. It means that there were many levels of connection between the two of you, not just sex and romance. You may have loved him for the person he is. You may have treasured the companionship and stimulation he gave you. You may have come to rely on him as a person who would always be in your corner. Those qualities are important components of a good friendship, and you may loathe the thought of having to forgo that with him also. The good news is that you may not have to.

Some relationships that don't work romantically work perfectly as friendships. One reason is that expectations which couldn't be met as lovers no longer need to be. Other parts of a positive affiliation still remain, and when those expectations are removed, a friendship can develop. For example, he may not have been able to give you the kind of attention and emotional support that you require from a lover. This could have easily frustrated both of you. As a friend, you don't expect that. You can be much more relaxed with each other and get along fine.

Another possibility is that the force which keeps some people together is really friendship, but is erroneously perceived as love. In such a situation the men may like each other and each desires a partner. Unfortunately, this alone cannot create romance. The sexual excitement, the indefinable chemistry, and the numerous other components of amour are, for whatever reasons, not there between them. The men may be in denial about this and pursue a relationship nonetheless. Of course, as I have previously said, reality ultimately catches up. When the tears end and the hurt lifts, they may still find that they have a wonderful friendship in place of a failed romance.

I realize that friendship is a somewhat puzzling term. What I define as friendship may not be your definition of it. There are also good friends and best friends and great friends, so the term is a loose one at best. To complicate the picture even further, what you may want and/or be able to sustain with him may not be a friendship as you define it. Yet it may still be some kind of relationship. Perhaps it will mean calling each other once in a while. Maybe it will mean going to a movie or out to dinner every now and then. Conceivably it will be birthday cards and Christmas greetings only.

If you are thinking of resuming contact, it is helpful to think about what kind of an association you want. If you know that you would not want something as intimate as weekly contact, it's a good idea to be aware of that so you can clearly express to him what you do want. Keep in mind there will be a lot of unknown variables that will become clear only when you begin living your new relationship.

You may want one thing and he may not. He may tell you right away that he wants to "go back" and you may have no desire to do so. That could derail any resumption of contact before it even begins. And, oh yes . . . about that first phone call. (I am assuming you are contacting him first.) Before you even make it, it's imperative to be clear about why you are doing it.

You have been out of touch with your ex for a while, I am assuming. If you feel now that you want to see him again, something has triggered this desire. Perhaps you ran into a friend of his on the street and it started you thinking about the good times. Maybe you have reached a point of emotional distance and feel ready to welcome him back into your life. Perhaps a tragedy has occurred (someone close to you has died) and you don't want to be out of contact with people you care about. Or perhaps your life has been particularly difficult lately, and you remember the emotional support he used to provide.

This trigger implies an aim—there is something you *want*. You may not have thought about it in these terms, but there is a goal behind your desire to reconnect. This is where you have to start. If it is a realistic, healthy goal, it will be a good idea to pursue it. If not, you should refrain from trying to see him. At least for now.

This is not as simple as it sounds. You may think you are operating in your best interests when in fact your emotions are overriding your logic. Emotions are likely to play a major role in this kind of situation even if you are thinking with your head on straight.

A healthy motivation entails giving up the fantasies. He is not able to be your lover and you emotionally accept that. He is not able to be the guy you demanded that he be but he simply never was. You don't feel like a lover toward him any longer, and you *unmistakably desire a different kind of relationship with him now.* You want him in your life because there is still much each of you can offer the other. You know that he is a person with many good qualities. He's a good man, and it's not good to let that kind of person slip out of your life. You feel strong enough to pursue this now. You will be OK whether or not it works out.

This may be your plan on the surface. It may indeed be the whole picture, and if so, you are on safe ground. But take a close look at the list that follows. Are these motivations also operating? Are they playing a significant role in your urge to involve yourself with him once again?

- You really want to be lovers with him again. Once you get together you will both realize what a big mistake it all was, and you will get back together. You can envision that meeting; you will both look into each other's eyes and both of you will cry. It will all work out now. You know that. You don't know how or why you know that . . . you just know it.
- You have had no contact for months and you can't stand it. It feels like he died and the only way you can get rid of that feeling is by seeing him.
- You feel he's slipping further and further from your life. You had better do something fast before it's too late. Someday you may want to see him and then it will be too late. You don't really desire to see him now, but you have to think about the future.
- People you know have great relationships with their exes. What the hell is the matter with you, you think. You want to be grown up like everyone else.

- Your mother loves him and speaks with him on the phone occasionally. She's been after you to give him a call. "He's such a nice boy," she reminds you. You want to placate her.
- Everyone tells you he's such a great guy. It's time to stop being so stubborn. You don't want to look like such a hard-ass to everyone.
- He sent you a letter telling you that he wants to see you. That took so much courage. It was so sweet of him. Surely you must see him now. He deserves it. It's the least you can do.
- A close friend just died. You realize how short life is. What if he should die suddenly? You don't want to be guilty for the rest of your life because you didn't talk to him. However, you still feel very angry and uncomfortable with him, and really don't desire to see him.
- It's Christmas. It's time to forgive.
- It's his birthday. You have to be with him on his birthday.
- You have been separated one year. It's time. You don't feel any differently but it's time.
- You got a big promotion and you are swimming in the dough. You want to make sure he knows about this.
- You have a new boyfriend. You want to make sure he knows about this.
- Something bad has happened in his life. You heard it through the grapevine. You feel you have to take care of him.
- Something bad has happened to you. You need him to take care of you.
- He seems to be doing just fine without you. You feel less important. You want to find out about all the difficulties he is really having.
- You know almost nothing about his life now. You have an intense curiosity to know what is going on. Lack of information makes you feel out of control.

This list could go on. You may want to add a few. The salient point is that reinvolvement *is* a big deal. If you are doing it for the wrong reasons, it's bound to backfire.

Even if you are doing it for the right reasons, this is not to say you have a guarantee it will work either. It's one thing to feel you are ready to create a different form of relationship with him. It's another thing to live it. You also have no idea where he is with this. All you can do is try. If you go into this with the attitude that you are attempting something that may or may not work out, you will be in a better psychological position. We all know that to get anywhere in life we have to take risks. This is a risk. You must understand before you begin that it's OK if it you don't succeed.

CONTACTING HIM

Writing may be somewhat less intimidating than calling, because you will have time to craft what you want to say. Do what makes you comfortable. Acknowledge that it has been a while since the two of you have been in contact. Let him know that you would like to get together to see if you could begin to have some kind of dialogue once again. I wouldn't use the term "friends" at this point because that's precipitous. You also shouldn't go into detail about how you still think going back to being lovers is not going to work. That could create an antagonistic situation. Be friendly, direct, brief, and clear. An example of a good letter would go something like this:

> Jeff, I am writing you to see if perhaps we could get together for coffee. It's been quite a while since we broke up, and I would like to see if perhaps we could reestablish some kind of contact. I feel ready right now to try this; of course I don't know how you feel. Could you please give me a call and perhaps we could talk. I am still at the same number. . . . Hope all is well with you.

> Michael

What If He Does Not Respond?

Unless you have legitimate reason to believe he did not get your message (you know his answering machine doesn't work well, his mail gets lost often), I would end it right there and then. If you reach him on the phone and he refuses to talk with you, I would also leave it right there. His refusal to communicate is very clear communication. He's told you what he wants. For some of us rejection becomes unacceptable. It's a narcissistic wound that we have difficulty tolerating—how dare he decline our olive branch? So you may be tempted to try it again, either to get him to change his mind or to maneuver yourself into the position of rejecting him. Give it a rest. That's a waste of energy and off track from your goal. Before you contact him, prepare yourself for a lack of response. If you are not ready to take that outcome in stride, you are not ready to attempt a resumption of contact. The following is a good example of a rejecting phone conversation. José has initiated the contact:

José: Hi Tom, it's José. . . . How are you?

Tom: Fine . . . well, this is a surprise. I didn't think I'd ever hear from you again . . . Also heard you left town. . . .

José: No, just rumors from some tired queens, I suppose. I'm at the same place, same number. . . . . it's been a while. . . .

Tom: It certainly has.

José: You know . . . I needed some time apart from you. . . . I think we both did, although I certainly can't speak for you. But you have been . . . are . . . important to me. . . . I would like to still have some contact with you. So I was wondering . . . would you like to meet say for lunch so we could talk about this?

Tom: Actually, no.

José: No?

Tom: You heard me, José. I'm still very pissed off at you . . . very, very pissed off at you. The way you left . . . all that shit you said about me. No, I don't want to get together.

José: I am sorry you feel that way. . . .

Tom: Remember what you said? . . . How you didn't need me . . . that I was such a disappointment to you. That was real shitty of you.

José: I really don't want to get into a rehashing of that . . . at least not right now. I would like to get together with you but you are quite clear you don't.

Tom: Damn right!

José: I respect that. If you should change your mind at any time, please call me.

Tom: You know you have a nerve calling me after what you did. . . .

José: This is not the time and place to get into that. You don't want to get together and I accept that. Take care of yourself, Tom.

Tom: [Hangs up.]

Not a ride in the country, but José made the best of a bad situation. He was clear, he refused to be manipulated into bickering with Tom, and he respected Tom's decision. He also made his intentions unambiguous and left the door open for Tom to contact him at another time.

YOUR FIRST MEETING TOGETHER

Let's assume now that your conversation went much better than José's, and you and your ex-lover are going to get together. But where? I suggest you start on neutral ground such as a restaurant. You want to avoid powerful emotional triggers. It may be disconcerting to go back to the old apartment and be bombarded with memories. It can also hurt to see how the place has changed. You may even see evidence of someone else in his life. In time you may be able to handle that quite well. Now is not that time.

You will want some measure of privacy, but a quiet booth may suffice. Although this will be, at least initially, somewhat uncomfortable, it's not likely to create the depths of emotional stress your breakup discussion caused. Indeed, the goal of this talk is a happy one.

You may be apprehensive that he will see your life as something less than perfect. You may feel pressured to impress him with how well your life is going without him. Give that a rest also. If he knows you well enough, which he probably does, he's going to see through that baloney. Relax. Be yourself. There is no contest here, no reason to prove anything. You may have been very competitive when you were together, so it can be tempting. Keep in mind that the competitiveness was injurious then, and is not going to serve any useful purpose now. You asked for this meeting to create a different relationship with him. Begin this new creation by starting on a different path.

It's terribly important to make it clear in this meeting that your desire is *not* to be lovers again. You want to communicate that he remains very important to you, you miss him in your life, and you want to see if both of you can form a different kind of relationship than the one you had in the past. One of greatest areas of problems in all kinds of relationships is confusion and misunderstandings. We run into trouble when we expect one thing and the reality is different. To begin a new relationship that is healthy, it imperative to begin with clarity. Moreover, if your intentions are not presented unambiguously, all of your efforts to resume contact may be in vain. If he has fantasies and desires that you really want to go back, he is going to be in for an awful disappointment when that does not materialize. That can result in lot of painful feelings for both of you, and dissolution of the connection you are trying to develop.

Of course, it's true that in life the unexpected sometimes occurs, and it's not inconceivable that you could both discover you want to be lovers again. *If* that happens you can communicate your feelings at that time. Right now it's important to communicate reality as you know it.

No matter how well this encounter turns out, remember to take it slow. Don't start making plans for the next six months or conclude that you are going to be the best of friends for the rest of your lives. You really don't know what is going to happen. You could discover an hour after your meeting or the following week that you are very upset and do not want to continue seeing him. Nothing "bad" would necessarily have happened. Your ex-lover represents powerful feelings for you, and you could realize that being involved with him again, on any level, is just too uncomfortable. Be open and honest about this when you talk with him. You hope you can be in each other's lives again but it may not work out. The same, of course, goes for him. It may seem that everything went perfect when you met, and then he doesn't initiate any further contact with you, nor does he return your phone calls.

YOUR NEW ASSOCIATION

If you do begin to get together on a regular basis, however, I suggest you monitor what is going on rather closely. I'm not trying to encourage you to turn your time with him into a scientific experiment. You can have lots of fun with him and be spontaneous! You may find yourself smiling and laughing with him more than you ever did when you were together. But this new association, especially during the early weeks, is not a casual affair. You have both "been away," and each of you may even look different. You are getting to know each other again but in a very different way. Feelings will be triggered. Adjustments will have to be made. Part of you will still see him as your lover and the other part will know that it no longer exists. There may be some regrets and "what ifs." Old angers may come up. You may feel confused. There will be lots to talk about. Hopefully you will have some heart-to-heart talks, and bring about more healing and clarity and closure. But no—this will not be a lazy day in the park with an old buddy. At least not in the beginning.

Some activities with him should probably be avoided. Taking a ride to a romantic spot, going to your old favorite restaurant, or falling asleep in the same bed are not good for you because of the feelings (and confusion) it may engender. How much contact you have should also be watched. If you find yourself constantly on the phone with him, or you are seeing each other daily, I suggest you slow down. You know the expression "too little, too late"? Well, this would be too much, too soon! Although it may seem exciting and gratifying at first, this can overwhelm you. You can be over-stimulated with feelings that may make you uncomfortable (regrets, anxiety, anger, sexual stimulation, etc.). This could actually serve to push you away from him. It could even operate unconsciously. All of a sudden you may find that you are avoiding him and not even know why. It would be sad indeed, if your budding friendship unraveled because of that. Take it slow and easy. If it looks like the potential for a good friendship to develop exists, there's no need to push it.

What If He Has a Lover Now?

> . . . I thought to myself, well, it's not fair to wish unhappiness on Henry (my ex-lover) so for his sake, I'm glad he's happy. And granted, the guy was nice to me. But I hated him. And I don't care for him to this day. And I know he never did anything to me. Even Jesse, my new boyfriend, has pointed that out to me, "Why blame him? He's innocent; he didn't do anything to you." . . . Maybe because I still feel something for Henry. . . .
>
> Kevin, 35, computer consultant
> Kansas City, Missouri

Let's assume that your get-togethers continue to go well, and you feel that you are becoming good friends. You haven't approached that scary topic called "involvement with others," but since he hasn't said anything you think he's probably still single. Of course, even if he is not, that would be OK with you, you tell yourself. After all, you are no longer lovers. A lot of time has passed. It would be fine. Well, maybe . . .

Then the bomb drops: He is, in fact, involved. Since he has been feeling so comfortable with you, he feels now he can let you know. He's in a *wonderful* relationship, actually. His new lover is every-thing you were not and could not be. He doesn't put it that way, of course, but that's the fact, and you know it. He's in love with the guy and they will be moving in together very soon. They plan to share a life together. He's very happy with his life and he wants to share this wonderful news with you. Wow!

And where are you in your life? Well, things are not going all that great. You are doing well in your job, and you do make more money now. But you haven't been quite so lucky with men. You've dated but nothing serious has materialized. You would like a relation-ship—just like the kind he seems to have.

You really don't want to go back with him. You see it clearly now, as you did when you first broke up. A romantic relationship with him could never work. The two of you are very different people, and you think "all power to him" if he is able to find someone who can meet his needs. You also care about his welfare and want him to be happy. Nevertheless, *you were not about to throw a party when he told you this.* You would have liked to rejoice with him, but you felt more like crying. Actually, you felt as if a dagger had been driven through your heart! What's the matter with you? you ask yourself. Why are you feeling this way? Didn't you let go a long time ago? Aren't you over him by now? Why don't you just grow up? Are you some kind of jealous brat? you wonder.

It's quite reasonable to experience ambivalence in such a situation, especially if you learn this shortly after you resume contact. There are many reasons for this, which I will address shortly. To cope with this, you first have to give yourself permission to feel this way. The worst thing you can do is to tell yourself that you shouldn't, and endeavor to suppress your emotions.

Attempt, also, to discard "moral" dictums that say, "If you really ever loved him, you'd want what's best for him." These feelings do not mean that you don't want what's best for him. They actually have nothing to do with that. They are about your pain, not his welfare. And I do mean you will have *ambivalent* feelings. On one level you really may be very happy for him. On the other hand, you may wish his lover gets deported to Siberia.

This example assumes that you are single. But even if you are involved also, it doesn't mean that you will feel entirely comfortable. There are a variety of reasons why this is a problematic situation no matter what is going on in your life. Kevin, in the previous quote, had a boyfriend, but still was uncomfortable with the fact that his ex-lover Henry was involved.

Learning this kind of information when you first resume contact can be particularly challenging. At this point you don't have any history with him other than your relationship as lovers. (In situations where you had a friendship first, it's still likely that your connection with him will be that of a lover. It is the most recent relationship you had with him, and amour carries much more intense affect than friendship.) Thus, although you know, intellectually, that you uncoupled, your emotional reference with him is still from your relationship as lovers. You have not yet developed a history as friends, postbreakup. Thus, emotionally, it may feel as if someone has "stolen" your lover. Your emotional system needs time to catch up with your cognitive understanding.

As I have already mentioned, breaking up triggers feelings of failure and inadequacy. You may feel this even if he was single. Seeing someone "take your place" can worsen those feelings.

Again, there is likely to be conflict between emotions and logical thinking. While you may know that you were simply not right for each other (thus no one is "bad" or "inadequate") it doesn't mean that you won't entertain thoughts that "something is wrong with me" because it didn't work. At times you may think "if I wasn't such a high-maintenance guy" or "if I could have trusted more, everything could have worked out well." To see someone else accomplish that (or at least appear to) can aggravate those thoughts and trigger painful feelings of inadequacy. "He can do it and I can't. I'm a mess," you may think. Anyone can experience this kind of thinking. If you already have low self-esteem, it can be severely unsettling.

One of the best ways to cope with this is to force reality to override those distorted perceptions. Think back to what made it impossible for you to be with him. Then ask yourself if trying to be OK with that really makes sense. If he could rarely tell you where he was going and who his friends were, for example (even if he wasn't doing anything "wrong"), is that something you can or should be comfortable with? Is that what you want? Is there really something wrong with you if that is not acceptable?

Seeing your ex-lover with another lover can also stimulate thoughts about "what if." In a sense, you identify with his new lover. You see yourself in him, yet he is able to accomplish what you were not able to. (Or, as I said above, it at least seems that this is the case. If your ex is saying all is wonderful with him, and you have no other information, it may become your reality, whether or not it's true.) Psychologically, you may then try to rewrite the script so that you can actually be the lover who succeeds. Hence, the "what if" questions: What if you both didn't have so much baggage then, what if you had really been over your former lover when you met, what if your jobs were not so pressing, and so on. Of course, this will backfire rather rapidly because he is with another now, not you. This may then be followed by thoughts about "bad timing" and "losing your chance" and letting him "slip away." This is a destructive mental exercise because it will get you nowhere other than down the road of royal misery. "What if" things were different is equivalent to "what if" a person who died in airplane crash never got on the plane. It wasn't that way and you can't change the past. Thinking like this is a form of mental diarrhea. If you find yourself engaging in it, it's best to try to stop it forthwith.

Your ex-lover's involvement with new a new lover can also trigger possessive and competitive feelings. There may be a sense that a stranger is taking what rightfully belongs to you and "getting away with it." He has your ex, you don't, so the new guy "wins" and you "lose." You may also feel competitive with your ex. He was able to find love and ride off into the sunset. You, on the other hand, found nothing and are riding off into Prozac! He wins, you lose. Of course, that's not exactly how it is.

I certainly don't mean to make light of the discomfort this may engender. But humor is actually one way to help you cope with it.

Your thoughts, although not rational, come in large part from the male socialization I have previously described. Overcoming this pain means acknowledging that there is a real source of learning (although laden with false information) that has played a role in causing you to feel this way. Let yourself off the hook. There is nothing intrinsically wrong with you for feeling this way. You learned to react in this manner because you were taught to be competitive and possessive. You can also make a commitment to yourself to do battle with these thoughts. Unlike the situation if a friend of yours becomes involved with your ex, accepting a stranger is more likely to be achieved.

Once again, take aim at these thoughts with doses of reality. You really don't possess him, you never did, and there is no contest. He and his new man did not win anything, nor did you lose. There is no finite pie of happiness either. You can achieve happiness also if you want to. And is your life right now really that rock-bottom horrible? Is all gray and bleak because there is no man in your life?

If you would like to have a relationship like the one he seems to have, what can you do to bring that about? Do you really think he possesses some magic that you have no access to? Concentrate on yourself. Do you want love in your life now? If so, what can you do to make that happen? And perhaps you don't really want it right now. What else can you do in your life to give you contentment? Perchance you'd like a relationship but you're not ready yet. If so, is there anything you can do to help you become ready? You may discover that you simply need time. That's OK too. There is no deadline for love.

Good, supportive, understanding friends can also help. Tell them how you feel. Own all those embarrassing feelings. Talk about the competition and your jealousy. Come out of the closet and speak of your desire for your ex's new lover to ache with gout! You may discover that they have been there also, and that you are in good company.

It's also possible to discuss some of this with your ex, but I would advise you to be very cautious. This is emotional land mine territory, and this goes double if the two of you have recently begun to communicate. You could easily sabotage any gains you have already made. Furthermore, it will be difficult for your ex to be objective. He has been involved with you and is now involved with someone else. Not exactly a disinterested party!

Hopefully, in time, you will be able to work through these feelings and meet (and even become friendly) with your ex's lover. Give it all the time you need. It's also possible that you will never be particularly comfortable with him. If that is how you feel, respect your feelings. Hopefully, your ex will understand, and the two of you will still be able to maintain a relationship. If he is not able to accept how you feel, this will say volumes about the feasibility of the two of you continuing to have a connection. At the end of the day, you should never deny what is right for you. While it's certainly preferable, there's no law that says you must embrace the lover of your ex. If keeping a distance from him is what is right for you, then you need to do that. If that means you don't have a relationship with your ex because he won't accept that, then you aren't able to have a relationship with him. You must take care of the relationship with yourself first.

You may be the person with the new lover when you get together with your ex, and he may be single. Some of the feelings of sadness and regret previously described may also plague you. You also may feel like you are doing something "wrong" because you still have that emotional connection with him as a lover. Obviously, you have nothing to feel guilty about if you are involved and he is not. Recognize where your feelings are coming from, and then use reality to help you cope. You have broken up and you are entitled to happiness. You are entitled to a new relationship if that is what you desire. No matter how miserable, angry, etc., your ex may feel. You are not responsible for his happiness nor for his life. Be sensitive to what he may be going through, but don't abdicate your needs for him.

Sex and Your New Relationship

If you are spending time together, eventually you will be together in each other's homes. His legs may still be as good as they used to be. He may pull off his shirt and show you how much he has worked out since you broke up. You may think that he would look attractive if he never saw the inside of a gym. And so you may wonder, "Should we have sex again, maybe under certain circumstances?"

My advice? *No.*

Having sex with your ex-lover can be trouble. Lots of trouble.

For better or worse, sex does have emotional meaning for most of us. Even hasty, anonymous sex affects people emotionally. In the least complicated relationships, sex still affects feelings, and plays a role in defining what is going on between the participants. Developing a relationship with your ex will be a complicated endeavor. There are deep feelings that have to be managed, and a different way of relating has to be developed. A major task will be to create a new definition of what you mean to one another. There will be changed expectations with novel rules.

The most important tool you have to achieve these tasks is clarity of thought, supported by and developed in part from clear boundaries in your behavior. Having sex with him can confuse those boundaries. Sex is often part of a romantic connection and it was definitely part of your romantic relationship with him. To engage in sex again may fuel those old feelings. It can cause a lot of trouble because those feelings will not correlate with reality. When you leave the bedroom and you are back to friendship or even less, it may feel very strange to live by the new rules of your association. Emotionally your mind could be saying, "I just had sex and made passionate love with him like we used to. But tonight he goes out on a date (or gets together with his new lover) and I am supposed to feel OK and not think twice about it. That doesn't make sense." Psychologically it doesn't, and it may be very painful and confusing to handle.

> [I felt] more confused because the sex that we had, at least on my part, it wasn't just physical. . . . I was putting emotions into the physical. . . . [I thought] maybe there's a chance for us again. . . .
>
> Kevin, 35, computer consultant
> Kansas City, Missouri

Sometimes we use sex as a substitute for intimacy. Whatever you finally develop with your ex, your attempt to create a new connection with him is an indication that you want some level of intimacy again. You are saying, in effect, "I don't like this noninvolvement with you any more. You mean something to me. I still want something from you. I still want to give something to you." Intimacy takes work and causes discomfort because it mandates openness, self-reflection, and vulnerability. Doing this work is taking the "hard road," but ultimately the only road that can lead you anywhere worth going. It may be tempting to forgo that work and try to create the intimacy through sex. Sex is relatively easy and can give you an instant feeling of connection without the hard work of processing anything. But that may interfere with the real work you need to do to create a workable relationship with him once again. Sex, alone, creates a rather shallow connection.

If the First Meeting Turns into a "Disaster"

Suppose a very different outcome ensues during your first meeting with your ex. You do not begin to develop a new relationship. In fact, the encounter itself unravels quite rapidly. Within moments of getting together, you discover that nothing has changed. You find yourself arguing about the same old issues and feel very uncomfortable. If you're clear that the encounter is going nowhere, end it as soon as possible. You may feel very angry and disappointed that you went through the effort for "nothing." The old anger may come back with a vengeance. You could find yourself saying: "I knew I should have never seen you. You are the same jackass you were when we broke up. Thank god I am not with you any longer. I must have been out of my mind to think anything will ever be different. It will be a cold day in hell before I ever get together with you again."

Leave before you get to that point. Such statements are unnecessary, likely to be inaccurate, and potentially very damaging. Perhaps neither of you have had enough time apart. This really says nothing about the future when both of you may have resolved issues that could make a relationship viable. Why get into a fight that may accomplish nothing more than foreclose the future?

Prepare yourself, before you get together, for the possibility that it could turn into an unsuccessful experience. Plan a strategy. Plan what you would say. For example, you could state: "You know, Ted, this is really not working. We are getting into the same arguments that we used to. Maybe we're just not ready. I am going to get going now. Perhaps we can try this again another time."

This may not be as easy as it sounds because your ex may not share your conclusion. He may feel abandoned and rejected by your leaving. He could scream, "Go ahead, bitch, walk away just like you always do from everything, just like you did from our relationship." It would be unfortunate if he talks to you that way. But if you need to walk, *remember that you must honor that which you know is right for you.* Furthermore, you don't have to take the bait and retaliate verbally. You told him you needed to go, so all you have to do is leave.

WHAT IF YOU HAVE NO INTEREST IN EVER SEEING HIM AGAIN?

When we are locked up in anger and pain, it is difficult to be objective. You may be in tremendous pain over the breakup. This could result in a belief that you have no desire to see him again when that is not actually the case. The very thought of connecting may be so threatening that you remain in denial. The disturbing feeling is replaced with the absence of any feeling.

If this is what is happening, you are foreclosing potential opportunity for the sake of avoiding uneasiness. Sit yourself down in a calm place when you have no pressing needs and think about this. If he has meant a lot to you and there were parts of him you truly adored, why is there *no* feeling now? Imagine what it would be like to see him again. Would it be very painful if he is in love with another man? Are you afraid to start over? Are you at a loss as to how to go about contacting him? Are you afraid of rejection?

It may help to write out your thoughts in a journal or speak about this with a good friend. If you are in therapy, this is an important issue to address. The main question you need to answer is this: Is lack of desire really at the core of your lack of interest? Or is it anxiety or something else? If it is anxiety, I refer you to my discussion of that phenomenon. You need to control anxiety, not the other way around.

The "something else" may be that you are not ready yet. If you have not been able to sufficiently let go, the possibility that he is involved with another man, for example, may be too much for you to handle right now. That is different from having no desire. The more you are in touch with what is really operating, the better position you are in to do what is right for you. Thus, you may know you can't see him right now but you would not rule that out for the future. You may even want to work more consciously on getting ready.

Having said this, it is also possible that you simply have no interest in your ex any longer. That can happen. We connect with people because of different needs that they meet for us. Whether or not we like to admit it, if someone meets few or none of our needs, we are not going to be interested in that person. This has probably happened with you and a friend (or friends). This person was a buddy at one point in your life but you drifted away from each other. You both changed, and no longer was there a locus of mutual interest. No bad guys, no terrible fight—simply no interest.

While you would not want to foreclose a relationship that can be meaningful to you, you also don't want to force yourself to develop a relationship that you have no investment in creating.

One way to gain clarity on this is to determine, as I just mentioned, whether your lack of desire is defensive. You can also take a hard look at the type of person you are now, and the person you know him to be. (Keep in mind that he may have made some major changes that you do not know about. On the other hand, adults are not likely to undergo core personality change, and you may know him as someone who is unlikely to make many changes anyway.) Try to push away all the "judgment" coloring your thinking. Forget about whether it's good or bad to be reinvolved with an ex, or what others think. Go outside of yourself and act like an objective scientist trying to learn the *truth*. Do these two people have much in common? Can they add to each other's lives? Can they be happy with each other? Is there something worth sharing? Is there anything worth saving?

Some other questions you could ask yourself are: What will it mean if I have no contact with him again? Will I miss that? What would I lose? Do I care if I lose that? What does being involved with him *do* for me? Will it have a significant impact on my life if I never see him again?

WHEN YOU SHOULD HAVE
NOTHING TO DO WITH HIM AGAIN

Sometimes you shouldn't see him even if you want to. Certain relationships are truly pathological and severely destructive. These are the kind of unions in which any or all of the following may prevail: control by one or both partners that results in a brutal attack on freedom and an assault on legal rights, extreme codependency, pervasive dishonesty and betrayal, violence, and drug and alcohol abuse.

I don't mean for this description to be exhaustive. You know if your relationship was your private experience of hell on earth. If you consider it that, then that's what it was for you. If you survived such a relationship and had the fortitude to leave him, you need to be especially cautious before initiating any contact.

Pathological Control and Violence

There are people who lose their freedom as an American citizen in a relationship. They literally lose their power to make decisions for themselves. They can't go where they want, do what they want, or talk to and see who they want. Sometimes their partners will listen to their phone conversations, read their mail, and/or follow them in the street. Sometimes they threaten them. Sometimes they beat and kill them.

Danger

If you are considering initiating contact, you first must assess your safety. If he has been pathologically controlling and intrusive, for example, how will getting together with him affect that behavior? Better yet, how will the mere act of contacting him affect that?

Let's take a look at the following scenario: Let's say he was almost delusionally suspicious of anything you did without him. When you told him you were leaving, he could not accept it. He showed up at work, in a restaurant while you were on a date, and at your door at four in the morning. The telephone calls were incessant, and you finally changed your number. Eventually, he relented, and there has since been a long period of calm.

If you contact him now, will that somehow give him license to begin harassing you again? Certainly you intend no such message, and you are not responsible for what he does. But people who engage in that type of behavior are not likely to hear clear messages or operate logically. The bottom-line issue is your protection and peace of mind. Some people, because of their psychopathology, do not or cannot play by the rules. You must therefore craft your behavior in a manner that accounts for this. That might mean you can't have any contact with him. At all.

If he has been violent in the past, how do you know he will not be violent when you meet with him? Violence can happen in public, it can happen with one of your friends present, and it can happen during a one-time meeting. When there is potential for violence, you have no guarantee of your physical safety, perhaps even your life. Catastrophes do happen, and murder is not unthinkable when there is a history of domestic violence. Before considering anything else, consider whether there is a possibility of this. Since you may underestimate risk, check in with someone who you feel is clear-thinking and can be objective. If you are in counseling, you definitely need to address this with your counselor before you do anything. The best option would be to discuss this with an individual who works with victims of gay domestic violence. *At the end of the day, you should never put yourself in a situation to meet with an ex-lover if there is any chance that you could be physically attacked. No exceptions.*

REASONS YOU WANT TO SEE HIM

Given all that has happened, you certainly need to figure out why you would even consider seeing him again. Take a good look at the list of inappropriate reasons I provided earlier in this chapter. Do you find some of the reasons why you want to see him on that list? There may also be other reasons, equally inappropriate, such as the following.

A Desire for Closure

As I pointed out earlier, achieving closure is fundamental to letting go and psychologically moving on. If you had to leave your lover by escaping in the dead of night, there was no closure. Unfortunately, you may never be able to achieve that with him if he is incapable of having a rational discussion. If he has behaved in an out-of-control manner as I have described, the chances are quite low that he will be able to be rational. At the very minimum, he would have to have had significant psychological treatment over a significant period of time. Certainly people can change, but you need clear-cut evidence that this has happened. Absent that, you will need to accept that closure with him will be impossible. (You can still work on this on your own, although it's best if it could be accomplished with him.) This is a bitter pill to swallow, but it's the fact of the matter. Engaging with an irrational person will bring you significant risk, but no closure.

Responsibility Confusion

In an abusive relationship there is often confusion about responsibility. When there is violence, for example, the batterer often blames the victim for provoking him, and the victim frequently believes this. Suffice to say that *a victim is never responsible for his abuse; that is the sole responsibility of the batterer.* If that was your situation, do you want to reconnect because you believe the battering was your fault? Do you feel guilty for the breakup? Do you feel responsible for the unhappiness your ex is experiencing (or you believe he is experiencing) in your absence? This is misplaced responsibility and a poor reason to become reinvolved.

Drugs and Alcohol

As with the previous issues, drug and alcohol abuse in a relationship mean serious problems. If your ex is still abusing chemicals, all the serious problems you experienced while you were with him are likely to still be there. Remember the out-of-control behavior, the drama with the police, the irresponsibility, the broken promises? You may feel strong and detached now that you have had so much time away from him. But if he is behaving just like he used to, what effect will that really have on you once it begins happening again?

You should also ask yourself if you were in an "enabler" role with him. Did you make excuses for him, take care of him, and try to save him from himself? Do you remember what effect that burden had on you?' Did it really ever help him? Will you now fall back into that role?

If you abused drugs and/or alcohol, and have been clean and sober for a while, what effect will getting together with him have on your own sobriety?

Loss of Self

You may have extreme difficulty with your sense of self when you get involved with a lover. You may feel as if you don't exist when your focus becomes fixated on the life and needs of your partner. There can be an obsessive focus on what he does, who he is with, and the way he views you. Approval from him is fervently sought. Disapproval and/or rejection are agonizing. His presence may feel like a narcotic fix, the lack of his presence terrifying and tormenting.

This is a snapshot description of a host of various psychological problems in an individual that can be played out in a relationship. If this describes you in a significant way (you don't have to have all of the characteristics and may have some I have not mentioned), it's imperative that you address and resolve those issues before you will be ready to be involved with anyone. Moreover, certain people may have a tendency to "bring this out" in you more than others. Your ex is likely to be that kind of person, if you have this kind of history with him. It's important to consider whether these kinds of problems will resurface if you resume contact.

Keep in mind that time away from him may have softened your memory of what was a truly horrific experience. The kind of dependency is a form of imprisonment. It's exceedingly painful and psychologically depleting. It is also very difficult to let go of once you are back in the thick of it.

> . . . If someone has had a breakup they are in a position where tremendous growth is possible—if they can manage the pain of separation from the codependency. If they get "swept away" again, it can often take even longer to extricate oneself and move on.

Thomas J. Caldarola, MFCC
psychotherapist, private practice/CAMFT
San Francisco, California

IN SUMMARY

A bad romantic relationship does not necessarily foreclose a future for the people in that relationship. When the pressures and definitions of lovers no longer apply, a wonderful friendship may develop. There are many ex-lovers who remain close friends throughout life. An ex-lover is sometimes the one person you can count on. If you were in love with him, there is a fairly good chance that something genuinely good existed between the two of you. That good does not have to be lost because your dream to remain lovers was. That being said, it also true that some people are toxic and injurious to our well-being. Those people need to be avoided, even if we were in love with them, and even if we continue to love them.

Where denial can cloak motivations even to oneself, and when so much is at risk, it's imperative to be very careful. I will state categorically that anyone who has been violent, pathologically control-ling, and/or chemically dependent must receive professional inter-vention for significant change to occur. If you are going to see him, make sure this has occurred. Likewise, be very clear about your reasons for wanting to see him now. If you have been involved in this kind of relationship in the past, hopefully you have a support group or professional therapist with whom you could talk this over. Take your time—talk it over and over before you make any moves. I would be very suspicious if you feel you must see him right away. Make certain the persons you are discussing this with can be objec-tive and not blindly support you because it's what you want. And it doesn't hurt to have that quiet conversation with yourself in the mirror when you are away from the stresses and pressures of the world. If it helps to go to the beach or the mountains by yourself to think, then do that. Perhaps writing your feelings down in a journal will also aid you.

I have addressed in this chapter the possibility of creating a different form of relationship with your ex-lover than you had with him in the past. But what about actually going back together as lovers? Is that always a mistake? Can it never work? People do change with time. Cannot the crisis of the breakup itself jump-start the two of you?

People can and do change, and occasionally people do get back together and it works. It's important to keep in mind, however, that one's personality is fairly developed by the time one is an adult. If you're expecting a personality transformation in either yourself or him, you are in for a serious letdown. The other issue is that you probably gave your relationship a lot of chances to work, and it didn't. You stayed together even when you were in a lot of pain. You thought long and hard before you made that final decision to leave him. What is different now? Why should it work now?

In the next chapter I will examine the circumstances under which going back can be a rational decision. On the other hand, I take a close look at how psychological factors can distort reality and seduce you into making an erroneous decision. Time and distance have a way, not infrequently, of taking the sting out of a bad experience. Psychologically re-creating the past to make it seem less depressing is the antithesis to building a happy future.

Chapter 7

Remembering the Misery:
Why You Shouldn't Go Back

Leonardo and Joshua live in Tampa, Florida. They were together for a year and a half before they uncoupled. They stayed apart for two years. Their rekindled relationship lasted for eight months and ended in a huge argument. They now hold each other in deep contempt and are no longer on speaking terms. They are a good example of how circumstances and unresolved emotional issues can create cognitive distortions and make something that is really impossible seem attractive and viable.

During the two years they were apart, they remained fairly distant although friendly. Occasionally they spoke on the phone. Less often they got together for drinks and dinner.

Leonardo is an attorney in his early sixties. He is a partner in a prestigious law firm and is accustomed to being in charge of others. His aphrodisiac is power, and his second love is money. He confesses that he has a lot of trouble getting close to human beings. He openly admits that he doesn't care. Leonardo is the son and only child of a powerful and wealthy Italian family. He was born in England and spent most of his life in the States. Both of his parents are deceased. He was raised by nannies and remembers his parents as essentially distant and formal.

Joshua is fifty-two, and a supervisor for a large construction company. He never knew his father, who died when he was very young. He was raised by a mother who was alcoholic and a grandmother who was in the early stages of Alzheimer's when Joshua was eight. Joshua had two sisters. His oldest sister was a drug addict, and committed suicide five years ago. His younger sister, age forty-one, is a born-again Christian, and has disowned her brother. She feels his lifestyle is despicable and sinful, and she wants him nowhere near her two teenage sons.

Joshua has been searching for love all of his life and has always found partners who were unable to provide that. His year and a half with Leonardo was like one long feud. He wanted a monogamous home life, while Leonardo wanted the boys in passing. He wanted to move in with Leonardo, but Leonardo wouldn't dream of sharing a home with anyone. He wanted Leonardo to tell him that he loved him. Leonardo told him *repeatedly* that he did not.

After their breakup, Joshua "swore off men." He decided to create the "Three F Club" ("Find them, Fuck them, and Forget them"). He experienced one empty sexual encounter after another often with men less than half his age. He would meet them in a bar called The Howard Street Station and have sex with them in the street or in his car. He'd visit Club Tampa (a bathhouse) quite regularly and sometimes have sex with six guys in one evening. While he enjoyed the excitement and the ego boost of all the sex, he felt very empty and lonely all the while. Usually, in the middle of one of his escapades, he would think about Leonardo, and how he missed "lying in his warm bedroom with him."

That feeling was greatly intensified after he was robbed and beaten by a young man he had taken into his car for sex. The conclusion seemed inescapable and overwhelmingly poignant. He had idiotically left Leonardo for this sordid life. He could be with a man who was of real value—instead he was wasting his life on the trash in the street. How did he ever let Leonardo slip through his hands, he wondered?

At three in the morning, bleeding from the mouth after the mugging, he was on a pay phone on deserted Armenia Street in downtown Tampa, calling Leonardo. He cried into Leonardo's answering machine, begging him to forgive him.

Leonardo was with a prostitute that evening whom he had hired through a magazine ad. The prostitute was a young Mexican man who was an illegal alien. Leonardo would never bring young men such as these to his home, so he rented a room in the Hyatt, also in downtown Tampa. Leonardo loved the fact that this boy would do anything he wanted as long as he paid for it.

Leonardo was not feeling too well that evening, or for that matter, during the past year. A business venture had gone sour, and he had lost a huge amount of money. He was also being sued by a former male secretary at his firm who had accused him of sexual harassment. Leonardo knew that he was guilty in the legal sense. He had fondled the man's penis on more than one occasion when they both worked late. The man resisted and Leonardo threatened to fire him if he did not comply. But Leonardo "knew" that the man, a twenty-four-year-old black student at the University of Tampa, was gay and really wanted it anyway! He believed that the lawsuit was just a ploy to get his hard-earned money.

The telephone call from Joshua felt like redemption. Joshua never should have left him, and now he was realizing the folly of his actions, Leonardo thought. Of course he'd take him back, why not?

In the weeks that followed, he and Joshua started dating again. It seemed so good to Joshua that he was away from the emptiness of the past few years. All the problems he experienced with Leonardo in the past seemed vague and unimportant. Whatever was so bad anyway? he asked himself.

Leonardo turned on the charm and Joshua was enraptured. Fancy dinners, the theater, flowers at his doorstep . . . all of it told Joshua how important he was. All of it told Leonardo *how important he, Leonardo, was!* He may fail in business and be sued up the wazoo, but he was power to one man by the name of Joshua.

Before long, the old problems resurfaced with a vengeance. Joshua wanted a home and monogamy. Leonardo was interested in neither. It finally ended when Leonardo took one of his "high class" boys to Morocco for a vacation. When he returned, Joshua confronted him. Joshua told him that he was sick and heartbroken that he would take a whore on vacation instead of him. Leonardo responded by accusing Joshua of being a pathetic old fool who would always be a "nothing." He said that it was a blessing that his sister was dead, and that it was too bad he didn't join her the night he was mugged. Joshua told Leonardo that he never really loved him, and that he was a worthless human being hiding behind money. He informed Leonard that his "delusion" had him believing that people respected him. Joshua said he never wanted to have anything to do with him again. It is likely he never will.

For whatever Leonardo's psychopathology is, and I could make a good case that there is plenty, he was essentially complacent with his life. Terrorizing and abusing subordinates and buying the boys of the night was his life. Joshua's return certainly fed his ego at a time it needed feeding. But Joshua's presence or absence in the larger picture of his life didn't really matter to him.

It was a different story with Joshua. He was love-starved and desperately desired love. He was also capable of loving. After breaking up with Leonardo the first time, he did not examine what had happened and how he could grow from the experience. Instead, he remained "insightless" and trapped in his own rage. When his self-destructive path finally reached rock-bottom, he was able to see Leonardo *only by contrast.* Leonardo was not a delinquent and a threat to his physical life. His money and power presented the facade of security and safety and the antithesis of Joshua's life on the street. *But Leonardo was totally incapable of giving Joshua what he needed. Joshua did not remember this in his state of despair, and in a sense psychologically rewrote his own history.* Joshua not only wasted more time by going back, but grew increasingly unhappy and more desperate. Most sadly, on a very deep level, he believed, and his going back reinforced the belief, that he could not get what he wanted. Ironically, there was no evidence other than his poor decisions to support that assumption. A self-fulfilling prophecy indeed!

SELF-ESTEEM ISSUES

As I have mentioned earlier, a relationship is a voluntary creation designed to meet the needs of both partners. When you have adequate self-esteem, you tend to see it in this light. When your relationship no longer meets this criterion, it becomes clear that it is time to end it. This kind of view implies that you believe that your destiny is not to accept something which is uncomfortable. It also means that you consider as true that there are other potential relationships that can satisfy your needs. You have no doubt in your right to be happy and your ability to obtain it. This is your bottom line, even though the breaking-up process may still be very painful.

Unfortunately, we don't all have adequate self-esteem. If you remained for a very long time with a partner who was not right for you, poor self-esteem may have been a material reason. The fact that you broke up may mean that the pain was so terrible that you couldn't tolerate it any longer. If your self-esteem issues were not addressed postbreakup, however, you could be at risk for returning to your former relationship inappropriately (or for that matter to another equally destructive relationship).

This is exactly what happened with Joshua. After he left Leonardo, he continued to believe that he was not worth much as a person, and that he could not expect a great deal out of life. His conclusion that "all men are trash" was really a conclusion, although unconscious, that "the only men I can ever be involved with are trash."

Time does have a way to soften painful memories for many of us. This can be a much more serious problem, however, if you don't hold yourself in very high regard. People who suffer from low self-esteem have unacceptably high thresholds for tolerating pain. They also tend to make themselves "superresponsible"; somehow when everything is said and done, it's their fault. If you just weren't so demanding, if you just could have worked a little harder, you may think, everything could have worked out.

If you are considering going back with your ex, you should start with this question: Do you suffer from poor self-esteem? If you do, deem yourself at high risk for distorting reality. It doesn't mean that you will necessarily make a mistake. But turn your emergency flashers on—you really are more likely to misread reality, so it is especially important to carefully consider your reasoning.

REMEMBERING THE MISERY (EMOTIONALLY)

You need to revisit the reasons you left your lover. Start by going back mentally in time. Do your best to forget about, at least for the moment, what is going on in your life now. We will get to that next.

To do this, it's best to set aside some quiet time in a private, calm environment. If it helps to put on some relaxing music at a low volume, do that. You may also want to make the lights dim or burn some candles. Make certain that you avoid distractions such as the telephone. Give yourself a lot of time—do not schedule something important to take care of right after this. Other than using chemicals, do what you can to make yourself feel relaxed, unhurried, and open to examining feelings.

Begin by asking yourself a series of questions. It may also help to write out the questions and answers. Don't feel you have to come up with the answers right away. The important thing is that you are *thinking.* If you write out the questions, it may be easier to come back to them later on if you can't come up with the answers now.

What was happening at the time that you left him? What was going wrong? How long was it going wrong? What were your expectations of him? What were your expectations of a relationship? How did he fall short? *What was day-to-day life with him like? What made it so painful to be with him?* (This is very important. When we distort the past about an unviable relationship, we often think in a sort of Hollywood romantic way such as "the love that was lost." That distortion can be counteracted with the not-so-romantic memories of day-to-day life together such as incessant arguing.) What did you want out of breaking up? What were your hopes for the future then? What were you missing by being with him? What frustrated you so badly? What were your feelings? Were you sad, rageful, frightened, disappointed, stressed out, confused, jealous, insecure, sexually frustrated, all the above? What factors finally convinced you that there was no hope? How did you first try to avoid breaking up? Did you have long talks? Did you go for counseling? Did you try new things that didn't work out?

You are not going to be able to do this in one session. Do as much as feels comfortable. You will come back later. The important thing *is* to come back. It may help to make an appointment with yourself so you stay with this.

Since you are doing this to get in touch with feelings, it's important to avoid turning this into an intellectual exercise. Keep focusing on your gut—how you *feel* as you are asking yourself these questions. Try to visualize the past. See yourself waiting in your house when he did not show up, or your face when you found out he was cheating, or the discomfort you felt when you had that loud argument in a restaurant. You can help your visualization by trying to remember details of the scene. What does the room look like in the old apartment? Where were you standing when he admitted to you he was having that affair? What is the layout of that restaurant? What was the look on that waiter's face when you started to yell at each other?

This exercise is skewed to have you clearly experience the "bad" in a very real way. My reason: if you are considering going back, you have to give this part its full due in relation to your different, positive feelings now. Perhaps there has been massive change and the right thing is to go back. This is a method to help ascertain if that is happening, or if you if are just fooling yourself.

HOW DO YOU RATE YOUR CURRENT LIFE?

In conjunction with this exercise, it's important to look at what is happening with your life right now. Are you unhappy and somehow the "good old days" seem better? Did you have expectations that life would be wonderful after you left him, only to discover that you are more unhappy than you were when you were with him?

You may be employing "contrast thinking" just as Joshua did. The current pain makes the old pain feel like "nothing" in contrast. *But of course it was not and is not "nothing."* Thinking like this is a clear-cut form of cognitive distortion, and it can get you into trouble. Your life may not be going well now, but that doesn't mean that life with him was fulfilling. As with Joshua, the answer lies in an alternative focus—get to the bottom of why you are not achieving happiness and move in the direction to achieve it.

By getting in touch with the old feelings via the previous exercise, you may be able to clearly see this.

Real and False Insight

Another issue to explore, which is related to the above issue, is what you have learned about yourself since you broke up. You could come to a correct discovery about yourself, and a mistaken conclusion about your relationship.

Maybe you assigned blame to your ex for everything from your low self-esteem to the death of your dog! You realize now that you have to take responsibility for your own life. You realize you have unresolved emotional conflicts that have nothing to do with your ex. *That still doesn't mean, however, that your relationship was healthy. It doesn't mean that breaking up was a mistake.* It may seem that conclusion number one (he really wasn't the cause of my general discontent) creates conclusion number two (it was a mistake to break up). *Not necessarily so.* On the contrary, a poor relationship is often an external manifestation of internal conflicts.

Why Do You Want to Go Back Now?

Another area of inquiry is the question, "Why now?" What makes now the time to go back to him? In Chapter 6, I listed a number of inappropriate reasons that can stimulate a desire to attempt a friendship. Most of those reasons also apply to stimulating feelings of wanting to go back. The reason they are inappropriate is because they are deceptive; they have little or nothing to do with the foundation of a viable relationship. Take a close look at them. Are these kinds of pressures playing a substantial role in your thoughts about returning to him?

The Hazards of Going Back

You may ask yourself, "Why am I making such a big deal out of this?" So what if you go back and then learn it was a mistake? So you'll find out and leave him again. It won't be an intractable mistake.

It certainly doesn't have to be *intractable.* But there are distinct disadvantages to returning to a relationship that is likely to fail again, especially if you are using poor judgment. Among them are:

- Returning can be a form of conceding to the difficulties of remaining uncoupled. This can have psychological and behavioral implications. Your "observing ego" may record this as "unable to do it, having failed." This can make it significantly more difficult to deal with letting go at another time (which is likely to be necessary if your relationship is in fact unviable). In essence you will be telling yourself, "I wasn't able to do it then—how can I believe I will be able to do it now?"

- Lowering self-esteem. You may tell yourself that you weren't strong enough, that you just didn't have what it takes, that you are "weak" for going back. If you already suffer from low self-esteem, this will be like pouring acid on an open wound.
- Profound disappointment.
- Profound anger.
- Reactivation of old painful feelings that had been put to bed. The old jealousy, feelings of rage, abandonment, mistrust, etc. will come back to life like Frankenstein in the castle on that dark and stormy night.
- Taking you from a relatively calm, stable place in your life back to a state of crisis and high drama.
- Intense confusion.
- Distrust of your own judgment.
- Significant interference with your self-development. Instead of concentrating on ways to improve your life, understand yourself, and grow, your energy is focused on the relationship again, how it's not working, and how unhappy you are.
- Wasting precious time. If you are quite young this may not feel that important, but it is. *Time is finite. Wasting time is a major loss. It is one of the few things in life that can never be recovered.*
- Preventing you from being open to and pursuing relationships that can meet your needs.
- Intensifying feelings of dependency, particularly if that is one of the issues that you were struggling with in your relationship. You convince yourself that you need him to be OK.
- Having to go through all of the pain of a breakup again.
- Economic disruption. You move back in, give up your apartment, and then have to move out again.
- Social humiliation. You feel that you don't know what you are doing in the eyes of others. (While I can certainly make a case that it's no one else's business what you do, people are judgmental and you may still feel very sensitive to their opinions.)
- Increased feelings of hopelessness about gay relationships. This puts the nail in the coffin of your "jadedness." Once you are out of this, you tell yourself, you never want to think about having a lover again.

- Remaining together. The whole breakup thing all over again seems just too hard. You pay for this dearly—you remain chronically dissatisfied and trash the best years of your life!

The Case for Going Back

Now, I am not trying to make you crazy! But having said all of the above, resuming a romantic form of relationship with an ex-lover is *not always* a mistake. Indeed, there are reasons why a separation can play a role in making a relationship viable once again. Among them are:

- Anger can significantly decrease. You get space to cool off and be more objective about what is really going on.
- You get an opportunity to process your experience and develop insight. Example: You realize you did demand too much of his time and were not developing your own life.
- Related to the above, you grow emotionally. You *desire* to develop more of your own life and do not *need* to demand so much of his attention. A major problem that you had has now been solved.
- While you were together, one of the most intense pressures you felt was your hunger to be "back in the scene." You realize now that it's not as wonderful as you thought it was, and that interest will no longer aggravate your relationship with him.
- You are now able to value in a heartfelt manner what he was able to give you. You did take it all for granted because he was always there. The problems overshadowed the benefits because of the little weight you gave to the "good." Now that he is not around, you are able to appreciate on a visceral level his immense worth in your life. The relationship will feel more balanced now.
- You recognize, undeniably, that you are in love with him. That was a question that plagued you while you were together. The space of the separation has made that unquestionably clear in your mind, and it will no longer pose a problem in the relationship.
- You are motivated to work on problems. The reality of losing him has impelled you to do the difficult work of making a rela-

tionship function. Your problems were never really intractable. It was just "too easy" to do nothing and assume the problems would take care of themselves. You've grown up now and you are ready to "roll up your sleeves."

The above scenarios, among others, can be sane reasons to try again. There is never an absolute formula and in the final analysis you have to use your judgment. Your judgment can be enhanced by being able to clearly answer the following questions: What has changed in both of us, and what is my evidence that this has changed? And, at the end of the day, am I going *from* something, or *to* something?

"From" means trying to escape the pain of loneliness, emotional problems, guilt, and so on and thinking that reconnecting will solve those problems. "To" means you don't need the relationship to fix your life. There is something to go to, something that will be better for your life. The former implies regression, the latter suggests growth.

Emotions will play a strong part in this. There is nothing wrong with that. They have to. The problem is when emotions override logic and convince you of something that is not really there.

For going back with your ex to be successful, I strongly recommend that you have evaluated all the criteria mentioned above. To summarize, the following should prevail if you are seriously considering being lovers again:

- Your self-esteem is adequate. If you struggle with self-esteem issues, you know your "buttons" and are able to avoid acting upon them. Going back is not satisfying one of those buttons.
- You have a fulfilled life irrespective of him. You want him to enhance your life; *you don't need him to give you a life.*
- You have revisited "the misery," and have a clear *emotional* memory of that. It is outweighed by other factors that make it unlikely for that to happen again.
- Related to the previous point, you are certain that there has been major change with both of you and *you have clear-cut evidence to support this.*
- There is an appropriate reason as opposed to an inappropriate reason why you want to go back with him *at this time.*
- Your insight is sound; you are not coming to faulty conclusions based on otherwise judicious mindfulness.

A UNILATERAL DECISION AGAIN

As with breaking up, your decision, in the same sense as I described it in Chapter 3, has to be unilateral. Of course you will discuss it with him, but it's you and you alone who has to decide whether going back is right for *you*. No one else is going to be living your life and your experiences.

Obviously, the same has to go for him. Thus, you may want to and he may not. You may desire to make a strong case for your position to him, and there is nothing wrong with doing that. But if he doesn't want to be lovers with you again, it is truly the end of the story. When you are going through the process of self-reflection, it is imperative to be prepared for this. His refusal can be powerfully disappointing to you, especially if it is clear to you that it can work.

Couples Counseling

Assuming that he wants to try again, it's not a good idea for the two of you to "go it alone." Going back is going to be scary, uncharted territory. Short-term couples counseling can help both you in a variety of ways. A therapist can assist you with anxiety. He or she can help both of you articulate expectations, and facilitate communication. A therapist can also help you distinguish between the inevitable disquietude you will experience at times, and signs that indicate your new relationship is *not* going to work.

Your Relationship Is Not Set in Stone—You Are Simply Trying

Even if you do everything "right," there is still no 100 percent guarantee that going back will work. Breaking up meant you had very serious problems, and you may discover that those problems weren't resolved after all. If you used good judgment in your decision to return to him, in a sense you did not make a mistake. You used the data you had available and made a reasonable judgment with it. Failure, in this scenario, will be easier to accept than having gone back because you denied reality.

IF THE FUTURE IS WITHOUT HIM

As it turns out, it really is over for you and him. For many of you who are reading this book, it was never even a question. Once it ended, it was done with.

But where does that leave you? You have been alone for some time now and you don't like it. You don't even like the word "alone"; it seems so *lonely*. Being alone is simply not your nature; not your style . . . you are the relationship type.

You do want to get involved again, but you know you're not ready right now. You have gone out on some dates but nothing serious has materialized. So how long does this go on? Are you going to be alone for the rest of your life? Remember what Uncle Sidney told you about homosexuals? *They all end up old and alone.*

Being Alone

It's easy to be frightened of being alone, and go on a desperate search to find another partner. Unfortunately, if you are not ready and have not worked through what happened in your former relationship, that is not likely to work. Being alone is necessary for growth. Being alone helps you discover who you are, what your strengths are, and that you are able to stand on your own. This makes you a healthier and happier individual, and more likely to develop a solid relationship when the time is right.

Some people never seem to have had a period in their adult lives without a partner. Aside from the rebounding problems this reveals, these people rob themselves of an important growing experience. Even the people who have had one partner from the time they were young adults are, in my opinion, missing out on an important learning experience.

It's thus better to slow down and take a frank look at what being alone is all about. You may not want to do this because it will tend to make you focus on it. It will fuel some unpleasant feelings. That is true, but it will also help you cope, and therefore enable you to pursue a partner when you are truly ready. It will also help you see that being alone has distinct advantages. I am not asking you to view being without a partner as preferable. I personally don't view it that way. But there are some characteristics that you might as well take advantage of! To understand this state, we still need to look at why it is so painful. Why do many of us settle for unhappy relationships rather than risk being without a partner?

I touched upon some of this in the beginning of the book. Society does frown upon and pity people who are single. Homophobia and our collective history of developmental isolation make this phenomenon particularly unwelcome. There is also another truth: a relationship meets profoundly vital needs for most human beings. It is no accident of the cosmos that humans often bond as couples. Without a meaningful relationship, we can suffer.

Does that mean, however, that we have to be miserable without a lover? Must we experience a period of being alone as always potentially permanent? Can we see some advantages to being without a partner? Can we accept it without a fight, even embrace it?

Obviously, I am presenting you with loaded questions. Being alone has taken on demonic characteristics in our culture. This view can be powerfully injurious to your well-being. You can get yourself into deep psychological peril if you believe that being without a man in your life is intolerable. It need not be something you avoid at the cost of staying with the wrong man. It can also be a highly productive period of your life. It really can be an era of unmatched opportunity, an exciting and developing and very *happy* time of your life!

If you are single and feeling lonely and sad right now, what I am saying may be very difficult to believe. You know by now that I like evidence to back beliefs! So let's take a look at the evidence. . . .

Chapter 8

Alone Again: Facing the Difficulties, Appreciating the Benefits

GROWING UP

How you experience this status is affected not only by the "external reality" of not having a lover. What being alone means to you will be greatly influenced by your developmental history.

One part of that history is your experience of simply being by yourself. How did you feel as a child? Were you able to entertain yourself and soothe yourself if no one else was present? Did you feel strong and confident when you were by yourself? Was being alone a welcome relief from being around too many people? Or did it frighten you? Did you feel abandoned? What happened when your best buddy went off to camp, or when you moved to a new neighborhood and had no friends? Did you have good coping skills or did you feel lost? Did you view being alone as a form of punishment? Was it used as a punishment against you?

Another component is the messages you received as a child about adults with and without partners. What do you remember about your parents, the "old maid" next door, your divorced aunt and uncle? Were you raised in a one-parent family where the parent was chronically depressed? Were you raised by two parents? Were they happy? Did marriage seem like the royal road to achieving happiness in life?

The various combinations of developmental factors are multitudinous and beyond the scope of this book to investigate. Suffice to say that they will affect your experience of being single today. Revisiting those memories will help you to fully understand your current experience. If you are having a particularly difficult time, it is likely that you have absorbed many pejorative messages. Being alone can be painful but it shouldn't feel catastrophic. It's consequential to bring those memories into consciousness. That can help you see the distortion in the childhood perceptions, and decrease your suffering. The process is likely to require the assistance of a professional therapist.

Growing Up and Homophobia

Homophobia is likely to have played a major role in your developmental history. Most of us lived some of our lives, especially during our formative years, in secrecy. What is particularly destructive is that we were in the closet not only from the world at large, but from our family and other loved ones. That is, quite frankly, a bizarre experience; guarding a "terrible secret" from those you would otherwise be intimate with. It's why so many gay and lesbian people grew up (and grow up) feeling "I am the only one." Such an isolating experience can create significant psychological wounds. It can cause you to associate being alone with those awful memories. It can therefore transform the normative discomfort of being without a partner into a nightmarish psychological experience of feeling "cut off" and "floating in outer space."

Interestingly though, I have also encountered the opposite to be true. Some gay men I have spoken to have said that the isolation of childhood actually helped them. Since they were already used to being alone, it actually facilitated coping when they uncoupled. My personal belief is that the former scenario is more likely to occur.

Homophobia and Adulthood

If you survived the loneliness of your gay secret as a child, there was still more to encounter. Homophobia "teaches" you that in the end you are still screwed. You will "end up old and alone."

I have seen twenty-five-year-old single men terrified by this. So what if you are fifty-seven and just left your lover? The gay-positive changes in society and the ability of your adult mind to challenge prejudicial dogmatism will certainly help you. But as I have said earlier in this book, messages told to us repeatedly, especially during our early years, have a way of remaining with us on some level. Homophobia may thus make the experience of being single more frightening. You may feel pressured to end this state as soon as possible, or end up "old and alone."

Homophobia is best dealt with by acknowledging the "politically incorrect" fact that you feel this way. A supportive gay group, supportive gay friends, or a gay-positive therapist can help you weather the storm. They can help remind you on an emotional level that the homophobic "scripture" is, as we'd say in Brooklyn where I grew up, "a crock."

THE REAL LOUSY PARTS
OF BEING WITHOUT A LOVER

The above all being true, having no one in your life is painful and challenging. None of us moves forward in life by denying the obstacles to our happiness. To overcome a barrier, we have to first acknowledge that it's there. A basic tenet of psychotherapy, for example, is that we must acknowledge the reality of what hurts in order to manage and overcome it.

So goes it with being single. There are certainly many benefits, and assuredly many exaggerations as to how awful it is. But we must also acknowledge that when all is said and done, *it actually does hurt, and you can miss a great deal when you are alone.*

To deal successfully with this period of your life, you need to take a close look at what a relationship does offer, so you can *emotionally acknowledge what you do not have.* From there you can move to effectively coping without it. This will serve another purpose: by accepting loss, you become more peaceful and unencumbered. You are then in a position to experience this time as an extraordinary opportunity for personal growth and joy.

For those of you who truly prefer to be without a partner, I don't take issue with the fact that it can be a preference. I do not think you must be psychologically disturbed to prefer being alone. I do believe, however, that many who may think they prefer being alone actually prefer avoiding the serious problems that can come with a relationship. These people often have had a series of unhappy relationships, and have simply given up.

Whether it's an actual preference, a false preference, or simply where you find yourself now, there is a material difference in the way you experience life when you are single. Having a lover is an occasion to experience deeply gratifying feelings that are simply unavailable in other forms of relationships.

There exist, of course, ardently satisfying relationships between friends, and between parents and children and siblings. Those relationships may even meet needs that a lover cannot. But they do not replace a lover.

THE NEED TO CONNECT

What we need from an intimate loving relationship with a partner can be traced to the deeply human need to connect. I define connection in this context and in its most basic form as a psychological link between two human beings which makes the fact of one's existence significant to the other (connection may be in only one direction and therefore the fact of both people's existence is not necessarily significant to each other).

We enter and leave this world completely alone, but in the interval we have a powerful need to bond with other human beings. During our primary formative years, connection, particularly with a parent or parental figure, is the principal means of developing our own identity. The parent mirrors back to us the kind of person we are. *It is our connection with the parent that allows that view of us to have significance.*

Connection is the mode by which we are socialized. When we connect with other human beings, we learn from them. If someone is psychologically irrelevant to you, his impact on you is far less. In psychotherapy, for example, the relationship between client and therapist is the most significant factor in facilitating change in the client.

Connection with others, therefore, vitally affects the way in which we perceive the world, perceive ourselves, shape our roles, and navigate through life. Connection gives psychological coloring and depth to being alive. Without connections to others, life would be a barren existence analogous to floating in the blackness of outer space. Connection provides the means for us to encounter external psychological reward (when someone gives us approval). It enables us to identify with others and to view life from alternative perspectives. It makes it possible for us to share with and care for others. It's a vital component of the capacity to love.

Bonding with a lover is, in my view, one of the highest forms of connection. When this kind of relationship is working, you occupy a very privileged place in the world. He is permitted entree into the deepest levels of your being. No one else but he is allowed there. He knows how you think and feel. He is privy to your shame and shortcomings and strengths. He appreciates your deepest fears and greatest joys. He knows the history of your life before him, and why you are who you are today. While he may not like or agree with everything about you, you know that he accepts you for who you are. You feel comfortable, safe, secure, and joyous with him. You are in love with each other, and you are permitted access to the deepest recesses of his soul. You accept him for the man he is. The value of this for both of you is boundless.

The needs this kind of relationship meets could be described in volumes without being exhaustive. A short list, however, is in order here to underscore what you are struggling with when you don't have it.

• The world is a complex, stressful, and at times frightening place to live in. A lover gives you solace. He provides deep human contact in a world where quality contact appears increasingly scarce. He provides momentous emotional support when the world is doing the very opposite.

• The sense of being "all alone" in life is greatly diminished. Friends and family can certainly provide companionship but they are unable to be there for you in the same way a partner is. One of the major roles of a lover is consistent, deep companionship. You and your lover "belong" to one another. You are profoundly meaningful to this person. You are part of each other's day-to-day lives, and what happens to one of you significantly affects the other. You are sharing a journey, and your dreams and plans are interwoven. This creates a powerful feeling of security in an uncertain, indifferent world in which your welfare and mere existence is irrelevant to most of the inhabitants.

• Being loved as someone's partner in life is intensely ego boosting. No matter how good one's self-esteem is, outside validation is still necessary for all of us. While it's dangerous as an adult to require outside approval to feel acceptable as a human being, outside validation to some degree is still necessary. Could you imagine how you'd feel if no one ever let you know they felt good about you? Being loved by your partner is a supreme form of validation. It means you occupy a place in his life that no one else does. Since you are in love with him, his granting of that access is very meaningful to your view of yourself.

• Some events meaningless to others become unique and magnificent to lovers who share the experiences. Two lovers I knew would go to a special doughnut store in Staten Island, New York on some Sunday nights. They would take the ferry across from Manhattan. The ferry ride and eating the doughnuts was a terribly meaningful event to them even though the reality of what they were doing hardly seemed special. It was "their private little joy "shared only between the two of them that made it so wonderful. Years later, after one of the men died from AIDS, the memory of those trips was bittersweet indeed to the surviving partner.

• Events in general take on added color and intensity because they are being shared with a special person. A friend of mine described a city he was visiting with the man he loved as "all electric."

• Shared events create a shared history. A shared history gives one a sense of belonging.

• Feeling love for your partner is profoundly rewarding. Although it is very difficult to describe why, the experience of being in love delivers indescribable pleasure to the self. Many characterize this as the most intensely pleasurable feeling a human being is able to attain.

So you are missing out on a lot when you are single. Now that I have made you completely depressed, what are you supposed to do about it?

BEING IN LOVE AGAIN

Start with recognizing that your present state is temporary if you want it to be. You can have a lover again. You can be in a viable relationship. If you are in the midst of grieving, it will be very difficult to believe this. Don't worry about that. Tell it to yourself even if you don't believe it right now! In time your painful feelings will let up, and telling yourself repeatedly may actually help convince you.

Obviously, I cannot guarantee that you will find another lover, and being in the right place at the right time is necessary. But you have *tremendous,* repeat *tremendous power* over making it happen! Suffice to say that we often believe "there is no one out there anymore" when the real issue is that we are not ready for what is out there. We are not ready to do what it takes to make a relationship work. Once we are ready and therefore open to it, it is much more likely to occur.

One way of thinking that may help you right now is to view your chances of finding a another lover on a purely mathematical basis. Even if you don't live in a city such as San Francisco or New York, there is a good likelihood (unless you live in a small town in a remote area) that there are literally *thousands* of gay men in your area. You need only one of them to become your partner. You are not the only one who is single. You are not the only one who wants a relationship. You are not the only one who would be willing (when you are ready) to do the work necessary to make it happen. Of course, the chemistry has to be there. Nevertheless, *the odds are overwhelmingly in your favor!*

For our purposes of coping with being alone, it's important to view it this way (or at least work on viewing it this way if you are feeling very sad). Pain is much more bearable when an end is in sight. It can also take the desperate feeling out of being alone. Fear of being and remaining single can spawn another unworkable relationship. That is the last thing that you need now.

So sit back and relax. Throw the schedule out the window. You will get back into a relationship when you are ready and *if you want to.* And when you are ready, all of those good things I mentioned above will be yours for the taking.

Now that you are relaxed, I have more good news for you. Being partnerless has some great benefits. As I said, you may not always be single. Now is the time to take advantage of what you have before you lose it by falling in love again!

Let's take a closer look.

You're absolutely in control of your life. . . . When you're alone, it's all about you.

Juan, 44, research psychologist
New York City

THE BENEFITS OF BEING ALONE

Freedom

Yes, you are really more free now. You can stay out all night. You can paint the house any colors you want. You go visit your friend in LA without asking anyone or giving explanations. You can flirt with whoever you damn well please. You don't have to think about monogamy versus "tricking" at all. If you want to go wild (practicing safer sex) in your local sex club, you can go ahead and do it! Yes, there are illusions that freedom is all wonderful and the truth is that it can feel lonely. You can be daunted by the lack of structure. But freedom is not worthless. Indeed, it's a precious gift. Freedom is, of course, imperative in a relationship. Nonetheless, the level of autonomy you have without a partner can never be matched. A relationship mandates compromise that *compromises,* to some degree, your freedom. Now you need not compromise with anyone. Perhaps this sounds selfish. It is. As a general mode of relating to the world, being selfish does not work. Indeed, having this level of independence is not necessarily what you want all of your life. And this is not, I would be the first to admit, a great argument to stay single forever. But it's something you possess right now that you won't when you are in a relationship. Recognize it and go ahead and enjoy!

Power

Related to this freedom is a new sense of power. Being single puts you in total control. Decisions are totally yours; there is no need to check in with anyone about what you want to do. You are the supreme commander. And while you must also take full responsibility for your decisions, there is no one to criticize or blame you for your mistakes. You don't have to be embarrassed (except to yourself) or have to justify what you did. You also don't have to get angry with someone who makes decisions you never fully endorsed.

Having this kind of power after a breakup can make you feel competent and strong, and back in command of your life. People in unhappy relationships often feel that their lives are out of control. Having a sense that your world is spinning unchecked is terribly disconcerting. Reclaiming your life is priceless.

Exercising this kind of puissance after a breakup is not the same as "needing total power" as a personality description. Such people are often thought of as "control freaks" and "high maintenance." They have tremendous difficulty being in any situation where they don't have total control. Indeed, being able to share power with others is prosocial and ultimately in your best interest. The authority I am referring to is related to primary decisions about your life. It doesn't mean that all of your friends now go only to the movies you like!

Having such control serves another function. Perchance you have spent years with your lover compromising your needs down to the bone. You may have been doing this for so long that you are not even sure what those needs are anymore. This power will now serve to meet needs long denied, in addition to making you feel you are back in the driver's seat.

A word of caution. It may feel strange to consider that you can actually get what you want in life. Indeed, if you were in a relationship where your needs chronically took a back seat to your lover's, this may say more about you than him. Perhaps you suffer from serious low self-esteem. You may therefore continue to have a problem getting your needs met. You may believe, consciously or unconsciously, that you are not deserving.

If you have been in the kind of relationship described above, and continue to feel that your needs somehow can never be met, that is a signal to get help. Since you are in major transition in your life right now by having ended your relationship, capitalize on the change momentum by making another one. Go for psychological help.

Getting to Know You

Being alone is a superb time for self-discovery. Obviously, we learn about ourselves in the context of relating to others. An intimate relationship affords us great opportunities to learn about ourselves. Often our lover will let us know loud and clear about parts of our personality that we'd perhaps rather not know! That might be painful, but it also helps us grow. However, a relationship is an entity with a life all its own. The "relationship entity" absorbs power. That need for energy can impinge upon your ability to learn about yourself.

Often, in the thick of intimacy, we lose some focus on ourselves because so much energy goes, understandably, to making the relationship work. Your focus can become somewhat external: You may think, "How will doing this affect him, our relationship, and our future?" not "What do I want to do, what are my needs in this situation?" Of course it doesn't mean that thoughts about yourself are nonexistent when you are part of a couple. It's just that you have a job called "managing a relationship" at that time, and therefore have less energy and less impetus to focus on yourself.

Being alone gives you more time and space and serenity. It's like getting out of the city and going to the mountains. You can slow down. You can perceive and appreciate and remember parts of yourself that you may not be able to in the "rush" of a relationship. When you are by yourself, you are not reacting to someone else's demands. You are not dancing to the tune of your lover's approval. You are not reacting to his negative sanctions. You can be more open and honest with yourself. There is no need for defensiveness. There is less pressure, less distraction, less "noise." There is no chance to confuse his needs with yours.

Timing and Personal Dreams

Your dreams also have no relation to someone else's time frame. "Oh honey, that's nice that you want to change careers now. But I am in the middle of medical school. We really can't afford that. You have a high-paying job. You can't quit now."

If you want to change careers, or chase any other dreams, the only clock you have is your own. Indeed, major life changes are very dependent on one's own time frame. A principal change that succeeds often does so in great part *because it was at the right moment, meaning it was the right time for you.* At that time you were open and ready to do what you needed to do. If you have to wait around for the time when it's right for your lover also, a window of opportunity may be lost forever.

REEVALUATING YOUR LIFE: A TIME FOR MAJOR LIFE CHANGE

Let's take a closer look at this. Perhaps you want to pursue a new career. Maybe you should try for a promotion that will require new responsibilities. Perchance you want to relocate to another part of the country. Since you have been able to be more focused on your own needs, you may now have answers to questions you didn't even know. Asking questions is good. It helps you grow. Don't be frightened if at first you have lots of questions with few or no answers.

Having More Energy and Time for Change

In terms of actually creating major change in your life, the early aftermath of your separation is *not* a good time. The breakup, itself, is enough major change for the moment. At that juncture you are likely to be in crisis and you will need all of your energy to deal with emotional upset. Furthermore, your judgment may be impaired. You may fervently desire to make a change just to dispel acute discomfort. That could interfere with your ability to think through the long-term ramifications of your decision.

However, after the smoke clears and you are in a more stable position, it may be the perfect time to consider change. A relationship demands significant energy, and you may now have more stamina to take on new tasks. A lover also takes a considerable amount of your time, and since there is only a limited number of hours in each day, you had fewer of those hours for other parts of your life. It doesn't mean that you can't pursue change when you are in a relationship. It just may be easier now. This is an advantage!

You can grow in many ways. You can take on new projects, pursue a hobby, go back to school. You can develop friendships that you may not have had time for when you were together.

> After breaking up, along with having the energy that I didn't have to spend on the relationship, I had energy to spend on making some changes. . . . It allowed me to focus again on thinking about going back to school for another degree. . . . It was after we broke up that I started teaching. . . .
>
> Milton, 62, physician (HIV specialist)
> New York City

> I would have never, ever, ever been able to move to Asia . . . had I had a lover. . . . I would have never been able to go back to college had I had a lover.
>
> Edward, 44, clerk
> New Orleans, Louisiana

You may even be able to improve your health. Perhaps you spent so much time arguing with him that you never got to bed at a decent hour. Maybe you were so stressed that you couldn't sleep once you did get to bed. Now that can change. You can take better care of yourself in general. Maybe it's time to get that medical checkup that you have been putting off for years. Perhaps it's time to lose some weight and get into the habit of eating healthier foods. Maybe you want to get into an exercise program and join a gym. The choices are endless. Think creatively! There is a big space in your life, and you don't have to fill it with depression. You can replenish yourself with gratifying endeavors.

A Mental Health Vacation

While intimacy is wonderful, it takes a great deal of psychic work. Letting someone inside is not an easy venture, and involves considerable emotional risk taking. It involves stripping the layers of your being before an outsider and trusting he will accept you. Indeed, trust is the operative word, and it means trusting him in multitudinous aspects of your world. You did that.

The coming apart process also took a tremendous amount of your psychic energy. From the very beginning, when you sensed something wasn't right, you began the difficult work of disengagement. It may have been unconscious, but it was happening and it was work. Then there were the thousands of discussions, the endless attempts, the hurt and sadness, and the making up and being disappointed again. Finally the actual breakup occurred, with all the attending emotional upheaval. You have been through a lot indeed!

You now have a break from that. You don't have to take risks and feel anxious. You don't have to be emotionally vulnerable. You don't have to experience the difficult process of letting someone in and trusting. You don't have to worry about being rejected, or that your trust will be abused. You don't have to worry about breaking up; *it has happened and it is over.* You can turn all that off and enjoy a hiatus from this kind of work.

> I felt calmer, I got control of my life and felt like it wasn't going to go off into a tizzy at any moment. I wasn't on edge anymore. It was just more peaceful.
>
> Jack, 56, pet store owner
> Miami Beach, Florida

You may find yourself saying, "But intimacy is wonderful and I accept the 'work' that goes with it." That is fine and I am not encouraging you to forgo intimacy. But it's also delightful to have a break from that kind of pressure. That, in itself, has value.

But there are other benefits. Repose from mental stress is efficacious—it gives you a chance to collect yourself and recoup. It can improve your mental health and may even improve your physical health. It can assist you with confronting other challenges in your life. It may enable you to better tolerate intimacy in the future.

No One to Worry About

Jack was devastated when his lover Caesar's mother passed away. It was extremely difficult for Jack to bear witness to Caesar's pain. Caesar was depressed for months afterward. He went on disability and sat home most of the day staring into space. Jack tried everything to cheer him up. He took on most of the responsibilities of the house—paying the bills, doing the shopping and cleaning, and so on. He suggested to Caesar that they go away for a few weeks. Caesar was not interested. Jack kept in constant contact with Caesar's doctor, and became very upset when Caesar skipped a dose of his medication. They'd get into loud arguments when that happened, and Jack usually wound up with a severe headache afterward.

Jack's friends became worried about Jack. They told him he always looked bad and tired, and implored him to take better care of himself. His boss told him that his work was not up to par and that he was putting his job in jeopardy. Jack's best friend, Ted, confronted him about this, and told him he had do something. "Do what?" he asked. "He's my lover, I care about him . . . what is there I can do?"

We take the bad with the good when we are in love. It's hard to dispute that and most of us accept it as part of the bargain. The magnificence of being in love is also being able to experience, to some degree, that which happens to our lover as if it is happening to us.

But this has high costs that we sometimes don't acknowledge in our rush to accept "the bad with the good." As cold as this may sound, if your lover is diagnosed with metastatic cancer, it does not mean *you* have been diagnosed with metastatic cancer. But you may experience it in almost the same way. There may be serious psychological and even physical consequences to you. Yes, it's part of love. But it's also your body and your life.

When you are single, you are released from the connection and therefore the pain of what can befall a person you love. I don't mean that if something terrible happened to your ex, you wouldn't be greatly affected. But in general, his pain is no longer yours. On a day-to-day basis, you don't have to be concerned about how he is feeling or what he is going through. You don't have to wait for his telephone call, or worry where he is or if he is safe. You don't have to be concerned about how others are treating him. His poor mood no longer can bring you and your whole day down. You are liberated from this weight.

Getting to Know Your Strengths

Relationships create roles with divisions of labor, so to speak. You are good with cooking, he takes care of the plumbing problems. He pays the bills, you are the social maven who arranges parties and Sunday brunches.

This arrangement can become a very comfortable state of affairs. You may never have liked to balance a checkbook, so it's wonderful that he is willing to do it. The problem with this is that after a while, especially in a relationship of many years, you may have come to depend on him for this. You may believe you do not have the ability to perform certain tasks. Let's take a look at John and Marc and how this played out with them.

Marc is a clinical psychologist and grew up in Philadelphia. He met John a number of years ago at an American Psychological Association convention in Washington, DC. John is also from Philadelphia.

After four years together, they bought a beautiful three-bedroom home in Rockville, Maryland. While Marc always wanted to own a home, he was terrified of having anything to do with caring for and/or improving it. Plumbing, cutting the grass, electrical work, and so on, were all John's department. Marc's distaste for it went beyond the actual physical work. He "had no idea" how to call an electrician or a contractor, and desired much less to learn how. "You know that's just not me," he would tell John. This from a man with two master's and a PhD!

When they decided to break some walls down and add extra rooms for a Jacuzzi and sauna, Marc did not want to deal with the contractors. He contributed his ideas about what would be done, but then it was John's responsibility to carry it out. "Just tell me where to sign," he joked. John actually didn't mind this. He loved their home and he felt building it was a labor of love. He had no problem talking to contractors and handling all the business aspects.

Four years later when they uncoupled, Marc bought out John's interest and was left with the house. Within a month, everything seemed to go haywire. First, the sliding door leading to the backyard wouldn't close properly. Then the ceiling in the hallway began leaking. A foul smell started emanating from the basement and he couldn't figure out what was causing it. Then the washing machine went crazy, going into perpetual spin cycle. Marc grew increasingly anxious because of all this. Then one evening, without thinking very clearly, he stood on top of his bathroom sink to change a light bulb. The sink was not built to hold up 190 pounds, and came tearing out of the wall. Marc went crashing to the floor, luckily onto his butt. The pipe connected to the wall split in two, causing water to pour onto the floor and into Marc's face. Marc had a meltdown. He didn't move and just sat there and cried as the bathroom and living room flooded. He sat there for about ten minutes. Then he sprang into action. He discovered a dusty Yellow Pages and within minutes learned how to call an emergency plumber! Two hours later the pipe was fixed and the flood was cleaned up.

If you depended on someone else to perform duties you have convinced yourself you are incapable of handling, you can become extremely frightened and dismayed when you break up. But you can also discover just how incompetent you are *not*.

Your fear can actually be turned into emotional muscle that can have far-reaching positive psychological effects.

There's a song that contains the lyric, "Got along without ya before I met ya, gonna get along without ya now."[1] When you feel overwhelmed with anxiety after he is no longer with you, this is where you have to start.

The fact is *you did get along without him before you met him.* Some of the tasks you have to do now may not be your favorites, and you may be rusty from all the years of letting him do it. But that does not mean you can't. It doesn't mean you won't survive. Also, when you take on responsibilities and activities you believed you were incapable of, another process unfolds. You are able to realize you have strengths that you forgot you had, or believed were non-existent. This will bolster your confidence and self-esteem. You will feel very strong and liberated.

This will be uncomfortable at first, but in the long run it will benefit you. The fact of being single now is an advantage because you are forced to grow. You don't have a choice. Your bills have to be paid. You need a working toilet!

One of the pitfalls of a relationship is that we can become so comfortable with an arrangement that we can also stagnate. Most of us are familiar with the physical manifestation of this: "Oh, she's as big as a house now, but you know, she's married!"

This is not as funny and innocuous as it sounds. It is very dangerous to lose sight of your strengths and take the easy way out. There is something very sad about this also. It's one thing to not be able to do something. It's another thing to have the potential but not know it. *It's unfortunate to forgo opportunities in life because you believe you can't do something.*

It may seem as if I am inappropriately expanding this concept: if you have to call a plumber or learn how to balance a checkbook, will you not have to "forgo opportunities in life"? Actually, yes. There is *great power* in realizing that you can do "simple" things which you believed you were unable to do. This can have profound effects on your willingness to face bigger challenges that will materially affect your life.

I am certainly not making the case that all people in relationships are stagnant and the royal road to growth is being single. But challenging situations such as being thrust into a world without the security of a lover can help you reap unforeseen benefits.

DATING: FUN WITH A PURPOSE

It is important to spend a significant period of time alone after you uncouple. That includes no dating. Being without any form of "amorous distraction" is important for many of the benefits that I have described. Among them are the opportunity to grieve and let go, and to give yourself an opportunity to gain clarity about who you are and where you want to be going.

But there comes a point when it's apropos to get back into the scene, so to speak. At this juncture you will want to begin dating again. Dating can and should be gratifying in its own right. It can also been seen as rehearsal in preparation for another commitment later on. It's a first step in a process, which means your first date doesn't become your lover. Natural circumstances are likely to create this—one doesn't usually fall in love with the first person or first few people he dates (obviously there are exceptions). But it's also important to go into this phase with the aim of *not* finding a lover initially. The reasons are numerous. First and foremost, you are not ready. The pressure and responsibilities of a lover are not what you need now. You need time now to explore, and to try out, blunder, and learn. Learn is the operative word. Learn about relating to men again in a romantic sense. Learn again about the fun and joy of having a partner. Learn about what you want and what you don't want, what you will put up with and where you will draw the line.

Dating can be a lot of fun with little displeasure. There is little pressure. As I am defining it here, it is romance "light." You don't have to plan years ahead, worry what your mother will think, or be concerned about how he takes care of his bathroom. There is no agreement on monogamy or exclusivity about your or his affections—he is free to do what he wants and see who he wants, as you are. You can experience companionship and sexuality and romance and excitement without the obligations of being with a lover. You, as a single man, now have this to look forward to. You did not have and could not have this opportunity when you were in a relationship.

Some men consider themselves lovers but, by mutual agreement, are free to pursue dating arrangements with others. I believe this is more the exception than the rule. In situations where there is a mutual agreement, it does not come without complications. Being in a committed relationship is quite complex, and dating others concurrently can create a myriad of problems. Since you have no lover right now, none of this applies to you. You have the opportunity to try out dating without any barriers or hesitancy.

You may never have had this opportunity. Perhaps you were young and became involved with a lover before you had a chance to play the field. Men in such relationships often feel cheated and that they have missed an important life experience. In a sense that is true, and if this is the case, you now have the opportunity to make up for lost time.

There is another advantage to your current single status. Even if you had dated before, you may not have had the mindfulness that you have now. You might have just done it automatically—dated some guys, not particularly paying attention to the process, until the "right one" came along. Given your experience with your ex, you can now date with a different awareness. You can notice what is good and bad about each guy—what qualities you find pro and con for a relationship. You can monitor your feelings. You can monitor how you distort or assume qualities in a person that may not really exist. This an excellent learning opportunity that can ultimately prepare you for a healthier relationship in the future.

It should be mentioned that this will not be easy for everyone. Indeed, dating can certainly create some disquieting feelings. You may like him more than he likes you. You may not fancy the idea that he is seeing others. You may feel uncomfortable seeing more than one man at a time. You can certainly opt not to do that. But if you are dating as I am depicting it here, you can't require him to do the same.

Perhaps it is effortless for you to develop strong deep feelings early on, and "fall in love." While it is certainly possible for that to happen, it's likely that this is not love. The propensity to fall so quickly may cause you to ignore vital information. That data may tell you that the object of your affections is not an appropriate choice for a committed long-term relationship.

It may be uncomfortable to manage this impulse at first, but the endeavor can become a superb learning and growing experience. With the awareness you now have from your breakup, you can observe your feelings without acting upon them. By pulling back and closely observing, you can figure out what this is all about, and why you do it. In the process, you will be developing a keen awareness of how you can distort reality when you become excited about a guy. You may then be able to distinguish this feeling from the feeling of actually falling in love. That can go a long way in helping you find, in time, the *right* Mr. Right!

The period following your breakup is complicated and challenging. It's a time of pain and joy, a period of sadness and rebirth, and a juncture filled with uncertainty and possibilities. You can make this time work for you when you recognize and seize the opportunities it has to offer.

Despite this, being alone is difficult. Acknowledging this difficulty is requisite for overcoming it. Furthermore, when you deny and therefore are not fully aware of what is bothering you, you are in the greatest danger. The pain can take over and cause you to make choices that ultimately will cause you more pain.

Pain is absolutely unavoidable after breaking up. Some people are terribly intolerant of emotional pain, and will go to great lengths to obliterate it. It cannot be achieved. This is sometimes the reason, or I should rather say the seductiveness, of rebounding. There are others. Whatever the draw, rebounding creates many problems and solves little. One of its most serious flaws is that it operates as an avoidance strategy to bypass the difficulties of being alone. It's an avoidance strategy, not a coping behavior, and as such, does not work. Being alone after uncoupling is absolutely necessary. In the early aftermath of a breakup, you should not even be dating.

In the next chapter, we will visit rebounding up close. We will examine what it is, why it doesn't work, and the myriad of ways it is destructive. We will address how to avoid it, and what to do if you are already in the midst of living it.

Chapter 9

How to Say No to the Rebound Trap: Taking a Relationship Vacation

... it allows you to sort of skip over processing certain emotions about the whole relationship, and move forward without really dealing . . . that's what I think it really does, I think that's the main attraction to it.

Jason, 24, fitness instructor
Atlanta, Georgia

... like any loss . . . there has to be a recovery time. . . . Without that process, I think you are going to find yourself in some of the situations you may have been in the first relationship.

Milton, 62, physician (HIV specialist)
New York City

Michael, a thirty-four-year-old New York University graduate student, was feeling energetic and vivacious only days after he left Troy, his partner of two years. One of their many problems was their poor sex life, and Michael often fantasized about sleeping with other men. They had an agreement to be monogamous. Michael felt, however, that it was more like a covenant for mutual celibacy. So on the first weekend after they broke up, Michael headed toward a bar on Sixth Avenue in Manhattan. On the top floor of the bar was a back room, where guys would masturbate with one another. Michael had an erection in the cab, and dashed up the steps to the back room immediately after entering the bar. He happily paid the entrance fee and rushed into the dimly lit room.

Michael had sex with three men and finally had an orgasm. He was about to go to a lower level in the bar and get a beer when he was approached by a young man in the dark. Though this was normally not the place to carry on a conversation, he nevertheless found himself engrossed in a discussion with this very attractive guy. Jorge was a twenty-eight-year-old Latino man who worked as a clerk in a bookstore. He had also recently separated from his boyfriend. Michael decided he wanted to see Jorge again, even though he told himself that he was thinking like a crazy man. They were both new divorcees, and a back room just didn't seem like the place to begin a romance. But Jorge was very interesting and sexually attractive to Michael, and he felt he could not let this pass him by. They exchanged phone numbers.

They dated for a month, and went to a few very upscale restaurants for dinner that neither could really afford. But Michael was enjoying himself immensely. What the heck, credit cards existed for a reason, he joked to himself. He thought about how Troy would never do anything like this with him, which further convinced him of the wisdom of his decision to break up.

On Sunday, four weeks after they had met, Michael invited Jorge to his apartment. They made love for hours, and as Jorge ejaculated for the third time, some of his semen inadvertently got into Michael's left eye. It burned for about five minutes, even though Michael immersed his eye in cool water as fast as he could. Michael was HIV negative, and so was his ex, Troy. Jorge told him that he was HIV negative also, and that he shouldn't worry. But of course, he didn't really know Jorge, so how could he not worry? He silently panicked for about an hour, but then calmed down when he convinced himself that semen in the eye was an unlikely mode of HIV transmission.

Later in the afternoon, they went window shopping at Macy's, and Michael began thinking of all the times he went to Macy's with Troy. During those excursions they would fantasize about how they would decorate the apartment they would someday have. The afternoon with Jorge grew ice-cold and empty rather quickly, and by six p.m. Michael was having an emotional meltdown. He couldn't stand the living sight of Jorge and vowed never to see him again. He felt dirty and guilty and stupid, and was convinced again that he would contract AIDS. He now viewed it as just punishment for leaving the only man who ever loved him. He told Jorge he was feeling ill and rushed home. He dove into his bed and stayed there for hours. He could still smell Jorge on his sheets and it made him nauseous. He wondered how on earth he ever got to this place in his life. All those reasons for breaking up now seemed far away and small. He had an intense impulse to call Troy and beg him to take him back. But he resisted making the call. As much pain as he was in, he also knew that he really didn't want to go back.

In the aftermath of a significant life change, emotions can be quite intense, confusing, and labile. This is easily observed in the bereaved. A grieving person can be laughing and crying and feeling numb all in a short span of time. One day he feels he's over it and ready to move on with life. The next morning all the anguish has returned and he feels he won't make it through the day.

You may experience similar feelings after uncoupling, particularly right after you break up. It's important to recognize that this is to be expected, and to be easy on yourself. You're not going crazy; you're grieving. It's equally significant to control self-destructive behavior engendered by distressing emotions.

When Michael began to date Jorge, he was experiencing some of the excitement of his newfound freedom. But he was also denying the profound loss that was equally real. The ejaculate in his eye was a rude reminder that his new life also meant new dangers and less security. Thus, it put him in touch, rather abruptly, with a feeling of profound loss—the loss of refuge from the world he experienced with Troy (the health fear, thus, was only the tip of the iceberg of numerous other feelings about safety). It further worked as a trigger to get him in touch with diverse feelings of loss that were now more poignant than they would have been if he had not met Jorge. Being with Jorge underscored Troy's absence—they were going into the store just like he and Troy did, but this was not in fact Troy. The love, the bond, the meaning that he shared with Troy were nonexistent with Jorge. This realization of who Jorge actually was also created a jarring feeling of disappointment—he had been experiencing a connection in fantasy, when in fact there was little connection in reality. He was alone after all. It made him feel very foolish for being so silly, which only made him feel worse about himself. This then played into his guilt—he was ambivalent about leaving Troy, and guilty about being involved with another man so soon. What better way to self-punish than to become fixated on fearing he had contracted HIV during the act of being "disloyal"?

YOU NEED A VACATION

Taking a vacation from relationships with men after you uncouple is not only good for you. It will not only bring you all of the advantages of being alone I have described. It will not only help you avoid the kind of experience Michael had. Being without a man in your life is requisite for your best interests. Let me put it very simply and directly. *You must go on vacation. This a required leave of absence.* And I have some other strong news for you. In the very early aftermath of a breakup, *no dating*. That's right, *no dating*. As we used to say in Brooklyn, *no nothin'*.

WHAT IS REBOUNDING?

I define rebounding as the act of getting involved in a new relationship *due to* the severe deterioration and termination (or immanent ending) of a previous one. As such, some people rebound before they actually end their former relationship. I do not delineate a specific time period after the previous relationship to qualify the new one as a rebound. Most likely, it is very soon after the breakup. The salient point is that the new relationship comes about primarily *in reaction to* the failure of the old one.

There are many reasons why people rebound. Chief among them is an unwillingness to experience the severe emotional pain that comes with a breakup. But there are other reasons. Fear of being alone and anger at one's former partner are also high on the list.

Rebounding really never removes pain. Indeed, it causes a great deal more of it. Everyone comes out a loser, and bad feelings abound. Emotional growth is delayed or stunted. People become jaded and more angry. Self-esteem is trashed. Disappointment and shock reign supreme. Therapists get new patients!

At the heart of rebounding is the act of fooling oneself. One may actually be thoroughly unconscious of the need for a break between lovers and believe that he is "just moving on." Another knows "something isn't right" but somehow feels it won't blow up in his face. Not *his* face. "Somehow I just know it will work out." "It just feels so good to be with Jim; I'm not going to let that pass me by. Life is short." "I am really in love with Cedric. Really."

Nah, not really.

It's Not Real

You may truly believe that you have fallen in love with your new man and that you can create a wonderful relationship with him. Sorry to disappoint you (and/or piss you off), but neither situation is very likely.

Being "on the rebound" means reactivity—you are doing something *as a reaction to* something else. In this case, it's your ex-lover. Because of this, your new relationship is compromised from the start.

Why we get interested in others as potential mates is complicated. But there is something very clear and simple about a rebound. A significant part, if not all, of the interest in the new person is because of feelings about another. Thus, a large part of the attraction, the driving force, has nothing to do with the person who is the object of that force.

When the excitement of this new person dissipates, and you have to get down to dealing with the person who is really this man, you may be in for big-time trouble. Since your interest in him had little really to do with *him*, you may find that you have no interest at all in creating a real relationship. You are as likely to be deeply disappointed as he is likely to feel angry and used.

GRIEVING AND REBOUNDING

Breaking up is a process that does not end when you walk out. It ends when you successfully grieve the loss. That is the point at which you truly say good-bye to the old period of your life with him and are able to welcome a new life with someone else. The grieving requires time and there is simply no getting around that fact. Only when you have grieved and therefore let go will you be emotionally ready for another man in your life.

> ... it would be difficult to develop a new "us," a new relationship with somebody, if you haven't let the other one go.

> Milton, 62, physician (HIV specialist)
> New York City

Being able to develop a mature, committed relationship requires emotional capability. With your ex-lover still at the center of your psychological vista, you will not be able to do this. He will get in the way whether you like it or not.

Grieving is what enables you to move your ex-lover away from the center. He will always be there, but in a very different psychological form. Successful grieving enables you to experience powerful emotions in a substantially altered and less chaotic feeling state. This, then, gives you room and hence ability to be involved with another lover.

It is relatively easy to see this with the actual death of a person. And loss by breakup is similar, psychologically, to loss by death. If someone very significant to you died, there would be a big difference in how you feel and behave before and after you successfully grieve his or her death.

I will assume that you have had the unfortunate experience of losing someone close to you. Take a moment and think about how you felt the day he died. Undoubtedly, you were quite upset, anxious, and sad. You probably didn't go to work that day, or left early when you found out. In the days that followed, you may have had no appetite. You spent many hours on the phone and in person talking with others about him. You probably cried a great deal. Now think about how you experience that death today (I am assuming "today" is at least a year later). You are not thinking about him as much as you did when it happened. You are sad when he comes to mind, but you experience that emotion in a significantly dissimilar manner. You are not crying as much, if at all. You are back in balance. You don't feel overwhelmed. You go to work. You can concentrate, you can sleep. You have accepted it and *you are getting on with your life.*

More on Grieving

Sometimes after a rebound fails, a person repeats the act—he gets involved once again, and once again the relationship goes up in smoke. The cycle can indeed become vicious. Ironically, only when you stop running and accept the pain do you begin to rid yourself of it.

This is extremely important because you can be stuck forever. Not just a failed rebound relationship. Not just the one after that. *Stuck forever,* imprisoned by the past and unable to live in the present. Have you ever met someone who was still angry with a partner who left him *twenty years previously?* Did it sound as if they had split up a week ago? If you have, you were staring down the barrel of ungrieved loss. This is tragic.

Failure to grieve may not appear to be the problem when indeed it is. For example, a man may spend years going through multitudinous affairs that are unfulfilling. The man attributes his discontent to the belief that "there is just no one out there any more," or worse, that "all men are pigs." What's really causing the problem is a torch that obfuscates real opportunities and attracts unviable partners.

If the right man appears before his eyes, it's likely he won't see him. He won't be attracted, or he will forget to call him, or something else will happen that will just not let that relationship happen. The wrong man, on the other hand, will get his attention. In time there will be high drama and a breakup and "confirmation" of his belief that there is "no one out there." All this can come from failure to grieve, which can be a result of rebounding.

Rebounding robs you of the grieving process. You stay falsely and temporarily protected from pain as you focus on your new love. This is a nonreality scenario that will hurt you. You may find a plethora of rationalizations as to why this will not be the case in your case. It will be.

If that wasn't enough, rebounding causes a lot more trouble. Such as . . .

Compromising the Learning Process

We have much to learn from a former relationship, as we will examine in the next chapter. An unsuccessful relationship can teach us volumes about ourselves. Not only can we learn how to do it better the next time around, but our insight can give us valuable tools to negotiate other aspects of our lives.

Developing insight often requires refraining from certain kinds of behavior. For example, someone who is sexually addicted is unable to process much about why he is behaving in that manner until he refrains from the sexually addictive behavior. When he abstains from going to a sex club, for example (over a period of time), he is more likely to get in touch with the feelings underneath the behavior (such as loneliness, emptiness, and depression). Since these feelings propel his behavior, avoiding the behavior causes the feelings to rise to the surface of his consciousness. While he is "behaving," these mental processes remain concealed because the behavior is "addressing" (dysfunctionally) the issues. Sometimes mental health professionals refer to this as "acting out."

Without understanding his feelings, he is likely to engage in the same destructive behavior repeatedly. He remains chronically unsatisfied and frustrated, and doesn't have a clue as to what is really wrong.

The behavior of being in a relationship soon after a breakup can obscure from consciousness some of the problematic issues you may have experienced in your previous union. For example, if you experience feelings of abandonment when you are not the center of attention, your rebounding boyfriend's fascination with you may obscure that issue. Since the behavior continues—you seek and receive inordinate amounts of attention—you don't have to experience the abandonment feeling. You may therefore never learn that (a) you have this problem, (b) what role it played in your breakup, and (c) that you will continue to have this problem in any relationship unless you address it. Only when you are without a partner for a period do you have the opportunity to experience this feeling in a psychologically meaningful way. This produces insight and gives you a chance to do something about your real problem. But rebounding interferes with more than that. It compromises the entire learning process. One often needs psychological distance from an experience in order to fully comprehend it. Rebounding prevents you from viewing your ex-relationship from the outside looking in.

As you probably know, it's much easier to be objective about something when you are not knee-deep in it. Think of all the truly wonderful advice you have been able to give friends about their boyfriends, and compare that with the advice you are able to give yourself! I know this as someone who has worked as a psychotherapist for many years. I can dispense sound advice as a therapist, but ask some of my closest friends how well I do that when it comes to me!

In a rebounding situation you are, of course, involved with a different person. But you are still in a relationship. You are at another ground zero, in a manner of speaking. You are still relating on a daily basis to another guy instead of being able to gain some distance from the phenomenon. This will compromise your ability to be objective about relationships, and interfere with your understanding of what transpired between you and your ex-lover. For example, all relationships have covert "relationship rules" (I will address this in detail in Chapter 10). One rule you may have lived by in your previous relationship is that "painful issues are dangerous to address, so never openly confront." This rule may have played a major role in transforming small problems into insurmountable ones.

In your rebounded relationship, you will become involved (as we all do in relationships) in covert relationship rules with this man. By having no space between relationships, you forfeit the opportunity to look back and realize, first of all, that covert rules existed. Furthermore, you won't discover that some of them (such as your "don't address painful issues openly" rule) didn't work for you. As you charge forward into the new relationship without taking a breath, you may set up the same dysfunctional rule, never realizing that it was, and still is, there (and that it is destructive). Once again, you lose out on very significant learning.

Processing an experience and gaining insight also require an environment in which you can think. Introspection requires a dearth of external distraction. You need solitude and mental energy and the comfort of no other pressing needs in order to accomplish this. Think of it in this extreme example: Could you imagine an airline pilot trying to figure out what went wrong between him and his ex-lover as he lands a DC-10? Not helpful to our pilot. Not helpful to the other people in the plane (and on the ground)!

If you rebound, you deny yourself that environment. You will get caught up in the distraction of your new affair. That will take energy and focus away from learning.

Disappointment and Cognitive Distortion

Although you are not likely to be thinking about this consciously, one of the reasons you rebound is to replace some of the positive aspects of the relationship you are losing. Perhaps you loved the way your ex held you in the middle of the night. Maybe he made you laugh when you were sad. Perchance he reassured you when you were frightened.

Your rebound man is not your ex, and sooner or later you will realize he cannot replace what you lost. In the very beginning when you are needy and he holds you tight, all may feel well to you. The hell with your ex, you think, you now have him and he's willing to do anything to make you happy. But on another night when you really need him but he needs to be with his friends or, worse, another love interest, you may experience penetrating disappointment.

And then something even worse can happen. Your ex may stop looking so bad all of a sudden. You may think, "Yeah, it was wonderful when he held me. He didn't run off with friends on a night like this. He was real, this isn't. Maybe I should call him."

This thinking is likely to be as logical as thinking the rebound could work. However, your overwhelming disappointment could create a memory distortion about your ex-relationship and tempt you to resume contact prematurely. It could even entice you into wanting to go back to it. This is playing with fire.

Anger, Guilt, and Regret

Often, when you uncouple, there is ambivalence. The relationship wasn't working and you had to end it. But it's not as simple as that. Many parts of what you and he had together were also very good. You were in love with him at one time and may still be. He, like you, is likely to be experiencing a lot of sadness. If you initiated the ending, as sound as you know your decision was, there may still be a part of you that feels bad for the pain you "caused" him. Not logical, not real. But feelings often don't correlate with reality.

You may have also been sick of, fed up, and angry with him for all the misery he "caused" you, all the time you wasted, all the nonsense you had to endure. Then, two weeks after your breakup, along came your rebound. When you made love with him like you hadn't done in years, you felt even more justified in your decision to leave your lover. When he gave you the attention that you sorely missed for longer than you can remember, you felt even further justified in what you had done. "Damn, the hell with Anton. He is nothing like Chen," you thought. You compared the two and mentally came out attacking your ex for his lack of what your rebound appeared to provide.

Of course, whatever a rebound can give will pale next to what your ex gave you. Your rebound provides you short-term excitement and gratification, which is fine and dandy in and of itself. But at the end of the day, you are comparing diamonds and golf balls when you compare your ex and him. When the rebound situation falls apart, or even before that, you will know that one was deep and real, and the other is cotton candy. This can intensify your guilt about leaving. Seeing the shallowness of the new relationship, which only a week previously looked superior, can make you feel guilty about having "trashed" your ex. Although this was only done in your mind, we often (though not logically) feel guilty over what we think and feel. Since you're probably harboring many other guilty feelings about having uncoupled, this could set off a chain reaction of spiraling guilt.

Diminishing Self-Esteem

Our minds watch our behavior and draw conclusions as to who we are based on that behavior. When we engage in something destructive, we don't only suffer from the overt impact of our behavior. Our self-esteem also suffers. For example, if you got very drunk and brought someone home who robbed you, you would not only have to endure the horror of being robbed; you are likely to attack yourself for your poor judgment that led up to it—"I should have never drunk all that beer and then to top it off bring someone home like that. I remember he was kind of strange and elusive. What kind of an asshole am I?"

After a rebound does not work out, you are left with pain and disappointment and more loss. On top of that, you may be able to see that the endeavor made no sense in the first place. While you are in a better position than someone who is in denial, it may still be very hard for your ego to accept how "foolish" you have been.

Early postbreakup time is not when one has the highest amount of self-regard anyway. No matter how appropriate your breakup was, you are still feeling a sense of failure. It didn't work out after all that energy you put into it, after all of that trying. Your ego is further bruised due to the fact that there is no one in your life right now, no one to give you (at least occasionally) the strokes you used to get (as bad as he was otherwise!). What you don't need is further diminishing of self-regard by having engaged in something that is destructive, and something you know you could have prevented. Thus, the failure of your rebound is adding vinegar to an open wound.

You "Need" Your Rebound More Than He Needs You

Although the man you rebound with may feel victimized after his relationship with you does not succeed ("you just used me to get over your ex"), he is likely to be in a much more powerful position in that relationship. Your connection with him comes out of desperation on your part—you "need" him to get you through your breakup. You obligate him to deliver you from pain you want to escape from. Perhaps this is not conscious, but it is still very much what is happening. While we do not know what his issues are, unless he is in a comparable frantic place, he is likely to be in want of you a lot less. Maybe not the first week. But soon. This is a setup for creating an unbalanced power differential and an unhealthy dependency on him. Aside from being another factor that makes your involvement with him unlikely to succeed, you will experience a lot of pain. As you need to obliterate the memory of your ex while he needs slow courting, the two of you will be doing a very awkward dance. Your magnified dependency on him is likely to make you frustrated and angry when you see he does not feel the same way. Intense dependency on another can also seriously impair self-image. Such feelings, and behavior that manifests as a result of those feelings (continuous calling, excessive requests to be with him almost all of the time, jealousy and anger if he wants to spend time with others, etc.) tell you that you are weak, out of control, and pathetic. Again, this is a particularly poor time to experience additional assault on your sense of self.

This is a perfect example of how rebounding displays a false face. At first glance it looks nurturing. In time (and not that much time) it transforms into emotional bleeding.

BAD FEELINGS ABOUT GAY RELATIONSHIPS

Why we gay men have negative feelings (and sometimes many negative feelings) about relationships with other gay men is a topic for another book. Suffice to say our community is ambivalent, at best, about relationships. Certainly we want them. We pursue them. We have them. But oftentimes we harbor animosity toward fellow gay men. For example, can you find a gay male community where pejorative joking about men is rare? You know, where people hardly ever talk about how men are pigs! Where it is uncommon to hear, "He just wanted to fuck me," or "Never heard from the son of a bitch again," or "Had a lover and didn't tell me." And so on. And so on.

OK, so find one . . . I'm waiting!

But you say it's just joking. Sure! Sure, sometimes a cigar is really only a cigar. But joking frequently communicates the unacceptable acceptably.

It's to be expected that one's faith in men and relationships will be challenged somewhat after a breakup between lovers. If we had no preconceived negative feelings about our fellow gay men, this would probably still prevail. In light of the fact that we do, it's a particularly problematic state of affairs. If you add on top of that a short-term, ill-conceived rebound relationship that causes pain to everyone involved, you are aggravating an already serious problem. You are likely to feel significantly more sour about gay men and having a relationship with one.

This can also play into creating a self-fulfilling prophecy, which can develop into a nasty, long-term, vicious cycle. You feel hopeless about men and relationships, and you repeatedly do your best (unconsciously) to prove this point. Augmented by the dynamic of unresolved grief as described previously, you may find yourself imprisoned in multitudinous failed relationships, and haunted with the question of why all men are no goddamn good.

BAD FEELINGS ENGENDERED IN YOUR EX

Certainly you may be able to live a very fulfilling life without having anything to do with your ex-lover ever again. Maybe that's what would be best. But what if it's not? Perhaps, in time, a friendship will make a lot of sense, and you will want it then. *Will want it then* is the operative phrase. Right now you may feel that a friendship with him is a very unfunny joke. At present you may want to do everything you can to stick it to him real good. A new relationship in his face could meet this desire.

Aside from this also intensifying your guilt later on, as described above, what effect will this have on him? How will he feel about the fact that you were able to get so easily involved with someone else so quickly after him? Never mind you know the new guy meant nothing to you. He doesn't necessarily know that.

I certainly am *not* saying that you are responsible for his thoughts and feelings. But what you do can have an effect on what you may be able to expect from him later on. When *your* anger clears, his feelings about this may not. It can even bring him to question the value of what the two of you had.

> He quickly got into a new relationship. . . . If it was that easy for him to just put me out of his mind and fall in love with someone else, what did he really think of our relationship and me? That really sucked.
>
> Jason, 24, fitness instructor
> Atlanta, Georgia

This may then have implications for developing any kind of a relationship with him later on. Sometimes we can't take back or make up for something we did. Watching one's ex-lover get immediately reinvolved can be very difficult to bear witness to, and may never be forgiven.

BUT NOT EVEN DATING?
COME ON, GIVE ME A BREAK

OK, you agree you won't rebound. You recognize it can hurt you. But of course you want to date. You uncoupled, you didn't join a monastery. So why do I think dating is not OK?

First, let me define "dating" as I see it here. This would be a conscious attempt on your part not to fall in love or become seriously involved, but to have companionship in *a quasi-romantic way.* Thus, a form of "playing lovers" would exist that would (likely) include a sexual relationship. I see this quite differently from developing friendships in which you would have the aim of obtaining companionship but where it is clear there is no sexual and/or romantic interest. I recognize that these definitions are arbitrary and our relationships may not be so clearly defined. But in your early post-breakup period, it is very important for you that your relationships with other gay men are clearly defined. Clarity means you will be less likely to wind up in situations that are destructive to you. Remember, this is a difficult and vulnerable time for you. You need to do extra leg work to make certain you are taking good care of yourself.

Now let's get back to that sticky area of dating. What do I mean, "no dating"? Didn't I say that was one of the advantages of being single?

I did say that. But I meant that it is an advantage later on. Right after you break up you should refrain; that is, until you have become used to your new status and gained emotional homeostasis. I can't come up with an absolute amount of time you shouldn't date, but the neighborhood of about six months is probably a good ballpark figure.

OK, but why no dating? Why until "I have become used to my new status and gained emotional homeostasis"? And why, my god, *six months?*

Because . . .

Maybe It's Really Rebounding

What you think may be "light dating" may really be an attempt to do full-blown rebounding. Not intentionally, but the line between dating and rebounding can be very blurry.

If you experience respite from pain when you're with him, you will be inclined to keep that going. All of a sudden you may be seeing him every day. You may begin to have feelings. You may begin to feel you need him in order to be OK.

You can be up to your neck in no time with emotional overload. It's best to stay away from that temptation.

Denial

Right after you break up, you need to face the fact that you are now partnerless. That familiar guy by your side is not part of your life now, and it makes no sense to pretend he still is. It's important to experience a clear sense of being single.

You need to go through your days and nights without any form of relationship as a frame of reference. You will therefore be experiencing, without confusion, what truly is your present status—you are single. When you are clear with this status, you are in the best position to meet the challenges of your situation, and to grow.

Dating can be a form of denial because it's a way of denying that there really is no guy at your side. Dating at this time can be a form of playing house in order to avoid facing the fact that there is no house.

Necessary Down Time

Dating may look as if it can give you an emotional boost that you sorely need. You are used to being with someone, and being alone appears very difficult. But your "aloneness" is also the way you will be able to rest and process what has happened.

Early postbreakup is a very stormy time when you need all of your emotional resources to take care of and give to yourself. Dating, or "love light," still requires focusing, to some degree, on another person. It's likely you won't be able to do an adequate job, which is not fair to him. But more important, you need your strength to deal with all of the changes and to appropriately navigate in this time of crisis. You will be robbing time and energy from yourself to give to another. While dating may appear to be nurturing, it's more likely nurturance will come from within you if you are undistracted by dating.

Emotional Vulnerability

This is not an easy time for you. You are depressed. You hurt. You feel scared. You are very needy. Thus, it's going to be very difficult for you to date in a relaxed, carefree way. While it may appear that dating could help you get through some of the pain (you will feel more secure with a man around), on balance, it's more likely to produce the opposite. *You still have to give something to him emotionally if you date*, and right now you might not have it to give.

Dating Can Cause Emotional Conflict

Relationship issues are hot issues for you right now. There is a lot of emotional fire surrounding them. They are your buttons, so to speak. If you had been in an airplane crash recently, flying would be a hot emotional area for you now. Dating, even without the emotional heaviness of a committed relationship, still hits on many of these issues such as togetherness, trust, connection, and sexuality. You may find it very troublesome to deal with this. Dating can increase your level of stress at a time when you are quite stressed out. You don't need any more!

HOW DO YOU AVOID REBOUNDING?

The first step is truly believing that it will not be in your best interests to get involved. If I have not convinced you, speak to a friend who can be objective. Or talk to someone who has had a rebound experience. As I indicated at the beginning of this chapter, the heart of the problem with rebounding is the ability to fool oneself. One believes that the relationship with the rebound can be viable. Until you believe that that is very, very unlikely, it will be hard for you to resist what may feel like a huge gift.

If you are convinced, it's important to create some structure for yourself. Decide that for a specific period that you will *absolutely not get involved with anyone*. Such a structure can function as protection against your emotions. If you make a serious commitment not to get involved, you will be better able to do this should you meet someone.

I suggested a time period of six months for no dating, but it's imperative that you use a period that is comfortable for you. If you try using my formula, it may feel very uncomfortable and increase your chances of giving up. However, be realistic. If you decide to not get involved with anyone for only three weeks after you uncouple, you will not be accomplishing much.

When you set up a structure like this, make it very public and ask a friend to act as a sponsor with you. You are making a commitment to both yourself and him that you will not get involved. If you find yourself tempted to break the commitment, you will talk with him about it first. The act of committing to others and making it public increase support to abstain.

Unlike deciding not to drink or not to go to a sex club (sorry for the addiction examples—I am *not* implying that rebounding is any form of addiction), "getting involved" can be insidious. You can be talking to some guy in a cafe, next week you go with him to a movie, and before you know it you are involved. Think beforehand about the indicators that show you are interested in someone beyond a friendship or casual acquaintance. Be honest with yourself. If you meet a guy at school whom you are seriously turned on by sexually and emotionally, it's probably not a good idea to arrange a "casual dinner just between friends." All of this is much easier to do if you think this through thoroughly before you encounter anyone.

Now this may sound like I want you to wrap yourself in plastic. "What if I meet someone really nice? Am I supposed to just let that pass me by? How often do I meet really good people?" you ask.

Of course, you don't stop good people from coming into your life. But if you meet someone whom you feel you could get seriously interested in, why not just tell him what is going on? Why not say, "You know, Justin, I would love to go out with you. But I just broke up with my lover and am not ready now to get involved. In a few months it may be a different story. I would like to contact you then."

Obviously, he has no obligation to wait for you, and he could meet someone in the interim. But if you are not ready, you are not ready. By doing this you are letting him be aware of your interest, and he may just be available when you are also.

What If You Are Already Rebounding?

If you are already in the midst of a rebound, it's going to be harder to do something about it. Nevertheless, you need to do something, and need to do it *quickly.* That means going cold turkey *and ending it forthwith.* Of course, explain to this man what you are doing and again, just be frank. "Peter, I really can't continue this with you. I need to first let go of Reginald, and that is going to take some time. This was a mistake, and I have to stop it before it becomes an even bigger mistake. I am truly sorry for any grief of yours that I have contributed to."

If you believe that there is a chance a relationship with this man may succeed at another time, let him know that also. Of course, he may be very angry and disappointed, and not want to consider that. If such is the case, so be it.

What About Sex?

It's not necessary to abstain from sexual experiences per se, although you may want to take a rest from that also. However, if you do not want to, sexual experience devoid of emotional involvement is not a form of rebounding and should be OK. "Devoid of emotional involvement" includes, in my view, fuck buddies in addition to anonymous sex and the numerous forms of "tricking." By definition, you are not romantically attached to a fuck buddy.

I do think you have to be clear whether or not this is really OK for you, however. That is, is sex with no emotional attachment acceptable? While for many gay men this is fine, for others it is not. If it isn't, this is certainly not the time to pressure yourself into doing something that you are uncomfortable with. Keep in mind that you are emotionally vulnerable now. Something that normally upsets you is likely to be significantly more unpleasant. Thus, you may have to forgo sex until you are ready to begin dating. Yes, you read correctly! I know that is not fun, but the higher good of healing from your breakup needs to be the focus. I promise that you won't go blind and/or insane!

WHEN YOU ARE READY TO DATE

When it is time to begin dating again, it is still not the time to make a serious commitment. I described the reasons for this in detail in Chapter 8. Essentially, you are probably still not ready to be involved with another lover (especially if you were with your ex for a considerable amount of time), and you can learn a great deal via the process of dating different men. This is not to say that it is impossible for the "right man" to come along. If you feel that is happening, I wouldn't recommend telling him to come back later. *But I would take it very slowly. Make certain this is not just a disguised form of rebounding.* The same goes for someone you met earlier whom you told you would contact later on (as I described previously). I would be especially suspicious if you fall in love with the first guy who comes along. A serious commitment is a serious commitment—it may mean spending many years with this man. You therefore need to take your time in deciding if he is right for you. One of the most essential questions you will have to ask yourself at that time is this—have you been able to let go of your ex-lover? Not *not love* him anymore. Not *forget* him. Not *not care* about him. *Let go.* Very different.

Rebounding is a false treat and a fruitless endeavor. While it may appear to comfort you when you are at your neediest, it really has nothing to do with meeting your needs. It will actually take away from you. Stay away from it just like you would stay away from anything that was not good for you.

One point I made about rebounding is that it will interfere with the learning that can come from a breakup. In the next chapter we will examine that learning. A relationship is, in a sense, a school of higher education for life. Why and how you love, and how you manage the relationship born of that love, speaks volumes about who you are as a person. One of the great benefits of a breakup, if you will, is the insight that it can provide to the individuals. We certainly learn while we are in a relationship, but distance and time from it are likely to provide even more wisdom. Wisdom of self is deeply empowering.

Chapter 10

Learning the Lessons
of Your Ex-Relationship

... there were warning signs right out of the barrel that I ignored. . . . If somebody makes your flesh crawl . . . in the first five minutes, odds are you probably don't want to spend a lot of time with that person.

Edward, 44, clerk
New Orleans, Louisiana

Earlier in this book I explored the difficulty we sometimes have with accepting what we did not plan on. Many of us have colossal problems with a breakup because in our minds it was not supposed to happen. If we can let go of the presumed "supposed to," we would certainly be in considerably less pain.

A related notion is that there is great merit in the ability to perceive value in all life experience. I don't mean to discount the obstacles and valleys of life. But we forfeit a great deal when all we can see is the pain. You probably can remember a horrific experience that turned out to be one of your life's most important lessons. I know I have.

This certainly applies to uncoupling. There is a plethora of lessons in a failed relationship. If you are sensitive to those messages, you will be vastly more knowledgeable about who you are, the story of where you have been, and where you want to go. You will see your mistakes in bright bold relief, and as such, it will be hard to repeat them. You will master alternative, healthier ways to connect with and fall in love with a man. You will also discover what went right, what you did well, and the gifts he gave you that are yours to keep forever. This will aid closure to this period of your life, with a heightened sense of gratification and peace.

IT'S ALL ABOUT YOU

Lots of the time we want it to be all about us. But when it comes to lessons about an ex-relationship, we are quick to make it all about *him*. "Yeah, I learned something . . . my ex-boyfriend is a class A scumbag."

You guessed it. Ventilating your spleen about the sins of your ex is not what I mean by learning the lessons of your ex-relationship. Actually, your lessons have nothing to do with him. If you really want to benefit, if you really want to learn about yourself and how to make you achieve more during this journey called Your Life, you have to restrain yourself from concentrating on his faults. Turn the spotlight squarely on you and keep it there.

It's Not All Bad News

Whatever happened between the two of you, no matter how bad it got, there was a time when you had very good feelings for him. He was also very happy and excited about you. Most likely, you guys were in love. You spent times together sharing the stories of your lives. You made passionate love in the middle of the afternoon. You experienced wonderful feelings of intimacy and caring. You were happy to see each other; you couldn't stand it when you had to be apart. You surprised each other with "silly" gifts, and cards, and flowers. You left messages on each other's answering machines for no reason other than to say, "I'm thinking of you, baby." You laughed together. You cried together. You have a history that only you and he will ever have on this planet till the end of time. *All of this is precious. All of this is wonderful. Not everybody in the world gets to have these kinds of experiences. You had them.* So no matter how much pain came later on, it never cancels out what you had. This is an important lesson. If you can see it in this balanced light, a sense of profound gratification, rather than failure, is more likely to be what you take with you.

Were You Ready When You Met Him?

It has to be the right time and place for you to meet the man of your dreams. The chemistry also has to be right. These are somewhat uncontrollable and unidentifiable variables.

We can do a lot to maximize our chances of meeting a man, but some level of fate or luck also has to be operating. Only that can put you and him in the exact spot at the exact time for both of you to come together.

"Chemistry" is an elusive "something" that makes it right for both of you. You can predict with fair accuracy that a man who is diametrically opposite to all of what you stand for is not going to create chemistry with you. But many with similar personality characteristics and worldviews, good men with good lives and good things to offer one another, are unable to create that chemistry. We simply don't know why this is so. But we do know this: no chemistry, no relationship, pure and simple.

That being said, much of what goes into creating a successful relationship does not come from the stars, but from a much more worldly source—namely you! A material component of that "success potential" has to do with one's readiness to commit to a serious union with another man. Many cry out to have a lover. But not all are really ready to do what they have to do to live their desire.

There are multitudinous reasons why one may not be ready to get involved. Some of it I covered already. If you have not let go, psychologically, of a previous relationship, you are not ready. But you may not be mature enough, either chronologically or psychologically. You may prefer to play the field. You may not be able to handle the emotional vulnerability.

An important question to ask yourself is this: were you ready when you met your ex? If you were not, why was that so? This is vital data, because if those same factors are still operative, you will be wasting your time going through the motions of bonding with another man. That's like constructing a building without a foundation.

YOUR NEEDS

We enter relationships with different needs that we want met in the relationship. It's imperative that we own this. Putting it rather candidly, we become involved with others because of what they can do for us. I know how blunt this sounds, but human beings do behave this way. Think of that wonderful boat ride down the Hudson River or the cabin you rented in the woods with your ex-lover. Something about who he is made that experience special for you. It would not have been the same alone or with your best friend, Joseph. Your ex did this for you. He met a need of yours.

Sometimes we have been so damaged early in life that our needs are insatiable. For example, if you wanted your lover, psychologically, to be the mother or father you never had, that will not occur. He would always fall short and you would always be disappointed.

Often, however, your needs are quite reasonable, it's just that your lover is not the right man to meet them. For example, you may be the worrying type and need someone to give you that extra reassurance when you go to the doctor or when you have problems at work. Your ex may have been the type of guy who thinks reassurance is "babying" you, and he refused to do it.

This kind of scenario becomes particularly destructive if that need becomes pathologized. He can't meet it and calls it sick and crazy. You buy it.

Again, we have to stick with you and your needs, not what a bad guy he was for not meeting them. What were the needs you had that your ex could not meet? Were they reasonable? Did you wind up believing there was something wrong with you for having them?

Think about all the legitimate needs you had (and still have) that he was not able to meet. Some of these may be: You needed to be held when you cried; he was not the "touchy-feely" type. You wanted the world to know about your love; he was too much in the closet to hold your hand in public. Mountains and lakes turned you on, and your picture of romance was making love with him in such an environment. Mountains and lakes and starlit skies put him to sleep.

My list is but a fraction of the potential needs that may not have been met. So make a list of those needs right now. Title it: "My reasonable needs that have to be met with a guy I get involved with." Put it away for the time when you begin to consider another man in your life.

Unreasonable Needs

Perhaps you do have some needs that cannot be met by any partner. One hint that this may be operating is if you have had the same kind of frustration over and over again. That is not always the case, however. The problem may be that you have continually chosen partners who could not meet your needs. It's best to take some time out to think about what you are looking for and how realistic it is. A good friend, a group, and/or a therapist can help you with this.

Many kinds of needs simply cannot be met in a relationship between two adults. Perhaps you want your lover to keep you "safe" from life, or you have a deep sense of loneliness and want him to be around almost all of the time. Perhaps you suffer from significant problems with trust, and anyone close to you immediately becomes suspect.

The first thing you have to do is *not* place a pejorative value judgment on yourself. Because you have some problems does not make you "fucked up" and "unlovable." The fact that you are realizing that you have some problems will go a long way toward helping you change. Deep-seated problems obviously need the help of a trained professional.

"Your Type" May Not Be Your Type

This is an area where a lot of us can run into trouble. "I am only into Asians." "I just like guys under thirty-two." "I like the rough type." "Only beefy guys for me."

A type often refers to a combination of physical and psychological attributes that one finds especially attractive. There is nothing wrong with looking for and being excited by what turns you on. The problem comes when you are inflexible and will pursue only the men that fit into such a range of characteristics. Not only will this limit your options, but *your type may not be the type who can develop a workable, satisfying relationship with you.* Ask yourself the following questions:

- Would I consider my ex my type?
- Was he my physical dreamboat but unable to hold an intelligent conversation?
- Was he young and cute but about as emotionally ready for a relationship as a twelve-year-old?

- Did he meet a certain income and educational level require-
  ment of mine, but there were no sparks because I was not emotionally attracted to him?

A type may also mean particular psychological characteristics
primarily. Some questions (in relation to your ex) that may reveal
whether this was operating are the following:

- Did he have a boyfriend that he was just about to leave when you
  met? Did it make you feel very special that he was giving him up
  for you? Do you often get involved with "married guys"?
- Was he essentially emotionally unavailable, but it turned you
  on when, at times, you could "penetrate the hard exterior"? Do
  you enjoy that kind of challenge?
- Was he someone in a socioeconomically lower class that you
  were going to help? Did it make you feel good that someone
  like you could be interested in someone who had so much
  "less" in life? Do you tend to be threatened by people who are
  more like peers?
- Was your ex very significantly younger or older than you? Do
  you like to be the "daddy"? Do you like to be the "young boy"?
- Did your ex have difficulty understanding the word "truth"?
  Were you aware, at least on some level, that he was dishonest
  with you? If so, why did you tolerate it?
- Did "commitment" mean to him "time spent in a mental institution"? Did you want a commitment? If so, why did you tolerate his inability to commit? Do you often become involved
  with men who have this difficulty?

Again, the focus is on you. Why did you (or do you often) find a
partner like this? What can you do not to get involved, exclusively,
with men like this in the future? At all? How can you expand the
range of men you would be willing to try?

You may know very well that you have a type and what he is. Or
you may be only dimly aware of it. Without a doubt, if all of your
ex-lovers feel like the same guy with different names, it is likely
you are pursuing a type!

It's important to take a frank look at what you are getting out of
this and what you are missing. If you are really turned on by guys

with muscles, obviously you get something out of it if your lover is big and beefy. It's important to own this. Your type does give you something. The question is how much, and what are you not getting by being exclusively or primarily into this type. What is the cost? This may motivate you to work on being more flexible in your approach to men. Sometimes what gets in the way of being more flexible is the erroneous belief that "I'm just not interested in other kinds of guys, it just won't feel natural." You may need to force yourself to go out with someone you are sure you could never get serious with. You may then discover that you were wrong. *But you have to start by not ruling out someone who is not your type on sight!*

Furthermore, interest in types that are self-destructive is often linked to emotional problems. The type is an external manifestation of the internal, emotional problem. Thus, getting involved with people who can't commit may reveal your own ambivalence about commitment. As one resolves the psychological conflicts, one's old type may no longer appear attractive, and formerly boring men may be terribly exciting. It's important to ask yourself if this is operating with you (or did operate with your ex-lover), and formulate a plan to address those emotional issues if it is.

IGNORING RED FLAGS

In the beginning of this book, I discussed at length various signs or "red flags" that indicate a relationship in serious trouble. That was information you needed to consider in your uncoupling decision. Another area to explore now is this: Were there many red flags? How aware were you of them? Did you consciously choose to ignore them? Did you tell yourself untruths in an effort to minimize the seriousness of what was taking place? Are you clear about what those red flags were?

Answers to these questions will give you valuable information about yourself. If it took numerous red flags before you were ready to do anything, you may have a terribly high tolerance for accepting the unacceptable in a relationship. If you weren't even aware that they were there, that is another problem of equally grave degree. Perhaps worse. This is analogous to someone who has lost his ability to experience physical pain. Obviously, physical pain is a major defense for the body because it lets you know something is wrong. If you are not able to feel pain, your foot could literally be on fire and you might not even know it. If you are in deep denial you may not be aware that your relationship is on fire. You may not look for the exit until it's too late. Perhaps you will never look, and will be consumed by it. Thus, if nonawareness is relatively descriptive of your experience with your ex, you know you have your work cut out. You have to make certain your danger receptors are operating, so that it never happens again.

Look back closely. Take your time. Go slowly. Talk to others about it. Seek professional help if you cannot gain clarity. What exactly was going on? What were those red flags? Did you perceive a red flag as a slight annoyance? Were you "kind of" aware that he was cheating, for example, but thought "What I don't know won't hurt me?" Was he beating you? Did you consider that part of what you had to accept?

Understanding the red flags of your ex-relationship, and asking the right questions both of yourself and a potential new partner, may prevent you from getting involved with the wrong person in the first place. The red flags of this past relationship may never appear again because you will screen out an inappropriate individual. To achieve this, you could explore inquiries such as the following.

For a red flag about violence:

> How did you happen to get involved with a violent man in your past relationship? (I am not implying that it was your fault, or that you were responsible for his battering.) What clues did you ignore with him? What signs should you look for now, and what questions should you ask? Do you have a counselor or a group who can help you make sure you are not repeating an old pattern when you meet a new guy?

For a merging versus separation/individuation red flag:

> How do you prevent merging that paralyzes? What boundaries did you cross and permit your ex to cross that impeded each other's individual growth? Have you worked on your own separation issues so that you don't become attracted to someone

who cannot tolerate individuation? What questions can you ask a prospective boyfriend (very early, maybe the first time you have coffee) to get a sense of how he tolerates separateness?

For an "in love with a fantasy" red flag:

How do you distinguish between the real personality of a man, and what you want him to be? What did you demand your ex to be? What was he really like? What data about him did you ignore? How did you ignore it—that is, by what process did you screen that information from your perception threshold? How can you avoid that the next time? What questions can you ask a guy very early in your association with him that will give you a sense of his values and interests, and the person he really is?

If you are very aware of the red flags that came up with your ex, and you begin to see some of them appear in a new relationship (despite your attempts at screening), you will be in a position to address them forthwith. You may be able to avert the rise of a serious problem, or derail the development of an unhappy union at its inception.

YOUR COMMUNICATION STYLE

We often hear this dictum: "Relationships are all about communication." I would only add that they are also about the lack thereof. We form a relationship in order to connect—the way we communicate is the vehicle by which a connection or a nonconnection is fostered.

Styles of communication are related to the way communication was modeled in your family. If your family dealt with painful issues by becoming silent, for example, you are likely to do the same.

Communication plays a major role in the viability of a relationship. If you can't get across to your lover what you want, or he is receiving a communication you are *not* giving, or do not intend to give, fertile ground for serious misunderstandings has been created. Communication problems can turn a potentially viable relationship into one that becomes unworkable. You may be right for each other in many ways, but are simply unable to let each other know that. If this is the case, it is indeed sad. It's one thing if you have actually outgrown each other. It's another thing to mistakenly believe that.

Once again, peer back into the past with you and your ex. Address the following questions:

- How did you let him know what you wanted? Were you able to tell him directly, or did you just assume he should know your needs? Did you let him know indirectly? Did you get angry, for example, and inform him of this by "forgetting" to call, or staying out all night?
- How did you handle his feelings? If he was upset about something, were you able to express support? Were you able to do it verbally and physically? Did your verbal and nonverbal communication seem to be at odds? For example, would you tell him how much you cared that he had a rough day while you continued to watch television? If so, how did he react?
- What are your listening skills like? If your lover was conflicted about something, were you right in there telling him what he should do? How did he respond? Did he appreciate it? Did he stop talking abruptly, and tell you everything is OK, forget it? Or were you able to just listen? If so, how did he react in that scenario?
- Were you the "strong, silent type," avoiding discussion about complicated and uncomfortable issues?" Did you joke about serious problems because it was too scary to directly address them? Did that interfere with resolution of those issues?
- Were you a "talkaholic," discussing and processing everything (and usually late at night or at other inopportune times) until both of you were exhausted? Did it get you anywhere? Was it a way you actually avoided real issues by talking around them? Does leaving a discussion for another time give you a lot of anxiety? Do you feel disagreements must be resolved immediately?

Keep in mind that looking back will not only help you see what you did wrong and how you can do it better the next time around; you may also learn about your strengths. You may find that you communicated well in certain ways or under certain circumstances, and want to continue to do that. The aim here is education; find out what works, and discard that which gets in your way. The aim is not confession and/or self-attack.

Conflict Resolution (or the Lack Thereof)

I have touched on this in the previous section, but let's take a closer look. First of all, did you guys express conflict? I shudder when I hear people say, "We've been together for years and have never had an argument." If that applies to you, it doesn't mean there was no conflict. It means that it was either too threatening for you (and/or him) to express feelings, or you (and/or he) were not in touch with anger. A relationship cannot be healthy without open expression of dissension. If that never happened, this is an area for you to work on. Even if it was mostly his problem, you still went along with it. You participated in the system. Yeah, it's still all about you!

Assuming there was open disagreement, let's investigate the following areas:

- How did you disagree? Did you talk fast and scream in an effort to drown out your partner? Did you have a substantial investment in winning? Did you use personality assassination? Did you dredge up everything that you didn't like about him since the Eisenhower administration?
- Were you able to listen? I didn't say hear. I said *listen.*
- Were you able to develop and stick to "fair fight" rules? What do you consider "fair fight" rules?
- Were you able to see his point of view, even if you did not agree?
- Were you ever able to admit you were wrong? If so, did you take *real responsibility* for your mistake, or did you somehow toss it back in his lap? Example: "Yeah, I am sorry, Ben, that I embarrassed you in the restaurant. I should never have yelled at you. I should know by now how crazy you get when you have a bad day at work and I should avoid *letting you get me that pissed. Next time I see you are in a mood like that I'm not going out to dinner with you.*" (Not just fake taking of responsibly, but punishment also, all in one breath. Cute!)

- Were you able to say you were sorry? Did you ever say you were sorry when you did not mean it? If so, why? What could you have done differently?
- How did you decrease pressure when the going got too rough? Were you able to walk out of the house to cool off? Did you walk out almost every time you became uncomfortable?
- Did you ever become violent? If so, have you received help for that?

THAT GAY PROBLEM

Those of us who are very out, or who live in very openly gay communities such as San Francisco, may think that internalized homophobia is a thing of the past. It is not and it can negatively affect a relationship.

To learn from this, you first have to acknowledge that it is there. Despite what you may feel on a conscious level, it's important to probe under the surface. Try as much as you can to get the internal critic off your back. Keep in mind that negative feelings about being gay have nothing to do with moral weakness or betrayal of your community. They have to do with an intolerant homophobic society that imparted hundreds of thousands of prejudicial lies upon your head from the day you were born. If you need to blame anyone, it's the homophobic outer society that owns that distinction!

Thus, do you believe you may have some uncomfortable feelings about being gay that affected your relationship? Answer the following questions. Feel free to add your own.

- Does being gay make you feel like you are less than a "real" man?
- Did you have a fatalistic belief about the longevity of gay relationships? If so, what role did this play in your breakup?
- Was it difficult to integrate your lover into your work life? Your family? If so, do you want to do something different now? How can you?
- Do you need support for your conflicts? Are you willing to open up to others about this? What kind of resources are available in your community to help you with this?

Since this is difficult material to look at, it may be problematic to gain easy access to your feelings. As I have advised various times in this book, when you need to be contemplative, take your time, and be in a comfortable, safe space. You need to be free of distractions and other pressures. You may want to have a number of these "quiet sessions" to help you access your internalized homophobic feelings.

That Male Gay Problem

As gay men we do have some clear disadvantages in our relationships because of male socialization. As men, we were not taught some of the most basic skills requisite for intimacy. Awareness and validation of feelings, accepting passivity and emotional vulnerability, and so on, are areas where women and men are differently socialized in our culture. Unfortunately, this means that many men are somewhat deficient in their ability to successfully negotiate a relationship. Heterosexual relationships also have their share of difficulties because of this. We, as gay men, have it worse because both partners are men. Furthermore, because our masculinity is, by definition, questioned, we may have more of an investment in attitudes and behavior that are incompatible with a healthy relationship. Explore the following questions:

- How have these issues affected you as an individual? Do you find yourself struggling with our culture's definition of masculinity? Do you often feel you have to "prove yourself" in this area? What role did this play between you and your ex?
- What are some of the powerful "male messages" you received during childhood (e.g., boys don't cry, you're a "sissy" if you show fear, a "real" boy likes sports, etc.)? How much of this is running your life today?
- Was it difficult for you to address feelings with your ex?
- Was it difficult to know what your feelings were?
- Did you become upset or anxious if he was sad, if he cried?
- Were you frightened of letting him get too close?
- Were you fearful of getting too close to him?
- Were you very competitive with him?
- Were you afraid to appear vulnerable? Did that mean you were weak?

- Were you able to overcome some of this male socialization? What aspects? How?
- What do you think you need to modify in order to successfully relate to another man? Why? How does it get in the way? How could you go about doing this?
- What "male characteristics" are you *not* willing to let go of? Why? Can that work in a relationship? How?

HONESTY AND DISHONESTY

Honesty is a very hot topic among gay men. Many men I have spoken to are fearful of being lied to, and can describe a past relationship where they were deceived. Many gay men have problems with intimacy, in my experience, because they are fearful of trusting.

A relationship cannot work without honesty. If you were dishonest with your ex, you have some work to do. But before we get into that, I want to describe what dishonesty is *not*.

All of us keep some secrets from our lovers. When we do share information and feelings, it also requires diplomacy. Raw truth should not permeate every discussion. You may then ask: Am I saying that all relationships have some level of acceptable dishonesty?

No, that is not what I am saying.

Honesty never means you cannot retain private aspects of your life. Although you may share some of the most cloistered parts of your world, you do not fully merge with your lover. It's imperative to maintain your individuality in order to remain free and psychologically healthy. *Not* sharing every thought and every aspect of your life is one way that is achieved. You need boundaries to keep your separateness. This is good for you as an individual and ultimately good for the both of you. This is not dishonesty. Honesty never implies unqualified access to one's brain.

Raw truth also must be managed. A relationship in which you are brutally honest all of the time can become brutally destructive in no time. This is not to say that occasionally you won't have to communicate in that manner. If you are no longer in love with your partner, for example, you eventually will have to say, "I am no longer in love with you." But that style of conversation need not come to describe how you impart information. You can be perfectly honest in a manner that minimizes the infliction of pain. Again, this is not a form of deceit.

On the other hand, there are many kinds of outright dishonesty that are called by other names. For example, some gay men have an explicit agreement that they are monogamous, but have sexual liaisons with other men. They may rationalize this in the following manner: "Well, we both know we are doing this. We have an unwritten don't ask, don't tell understanding." "Unwritten" usually means "has not been discussed." To believe you are being honest in such a situation is, frankly, absurd.

A man who has such liaisons is violating what he has explicitly agreed to do. That is being dishonest. To assume that an unwritten rule can replace a rule you agreed upon is illogical. Furthermore, the man's lover may not really subscribe to this unwritten accord. If it is not discussed and is in opposition to what has been decided, how can he know for sure that his lover is doing the same thing? Even if he were accurate, there would still be a serious problem. They would then be lying to each other.

I define dishonesty rather simply: any form of purposeful interaction that overtly or implicitly communicates a falsehood. Assumptions, "good" reasons, "everyone does it," and so on changes nothing. Communicating falsehoods to your lover is dishonest.

Obviously, there are different levels and forms of dishonesty. You may say that you walked the dog when you didn't. That's different from telling him you went to the movies when you were really having sex with the cleaning boy. You may lie on rare occasions, or you may live a lie. None of these behaviors are constructive, and none are good for your relationship. But there are differences that may have different effects on your relationship. I am saying this because all lies are not created equal. But I am not implying that any form of lying is ever OK.

Omissions can also be a form of dishonesty if they create an implication that is not true. For example, let's say you normally go to work on Monday but you take the day off to see your ex-lover. You don't tell your current lover this. He then asks you how the day went (and you know he's referring to your job) and you say "fine, nothing particularly exciting happened." You may really have had a "nothing particularly exciting happened" day with your ex. Your involvement with him may pose absolutely no threat to your current relationship. You may rightfully feel it's not necessary to tell your lover that you were seeing your ex. That is all beside the point. If you responded in this manner, you were presenting a false impression. You were being dishonest.

People very often justify lying. When you do this, you are in effect saying, "Yeah, I know it's wrong, but there was a higher purpose." Then you are lying to yourself! Perhaps lying made it easier in the short run, and it saved you from confronting an uncomfortable situation. Perhaps it prevented your lover from experiencing discomfort. As a society we have a propensity for pain avoidance, but that isn't a "higher good." Indeed, pain is often necessary for growth.

There are many reasons why dishonesty is literally *relationship poison*, including the following:

- It's a way to avoid taking responsibility for one's behavior. Avoidance of responsibility is a generally destructive form of interaction in any form of relationship.
- By avoiding responsibility, you are engaging in immature behavior. Immaturity is counter to developing a committed adult relationship with another man.
- Lying is the antithesis of intimacy. Intimacy means stripping away the masks and exposing the core. Dishonesty means creating walls. Lack of intimacy is the antithesis of a nurturing relationship.
- Dishonesty interferes with problem solving. If you are not telling the truth about what is going on, there is no chance to address problems. Lying takes the place of dealing with issues. Enough lying over enough time will create insurmountable dilemmas because problems will be left to fester. If you decided on a monogamous relationship but you really want to open it up, you need to talk about it. If your lover is threatened by an ex, you need to deal with that.
- Dishonesty creates a false view of what is transpiring. This can be very destructive when reality catches up. Let us say, for example, that you were seriously questioning a future with your ex, but spoke as if there was no question in your mind that you

planned to grow old together. When you finally had to tell him that you were leaving, it's more likely that this would create shock and dismay for him. It's probable that the uncoupling process would be much more difficult for both of you.

- Dishonesty is deeply disrespectful. When you lie to your lover, you are devaluing him. While you may not be consciously thinking this, you are, in effect, saying to him, "You don't matter that much to me. I don't have to tell you what is real if I so desire. I don't owe you that much." Since you are also compromising your integrity, you are devaluing yourself in your own eyes.
- Dishonesty destroys trust. When your lover discovers you are lying, which he is likely to do, he may have difficulty believing you when you are being honest.
- Dishonesty in one partner can trigger dishonesty in the other. Although you are not responsible for your lover's actions, if you lie to him he may feel justified in lying to you. This can create a very destructive, vicious cycle.
- Dishonesty falsely weakens you and your partner. You are telling yourself that neither of you can handle the truth.
- Lies often beget other lies in order for one to stay consistent. Like a boat taking on water, before long both of you could be drowning in deceit.
- The idea that we'll benefit by lying is the ultimate lie. We lie to "give" ourselves something, but it actually "takes." Sometimes it "takes" a relationship.

Perhaps the best lesson you can learn from looking back on how you conducted yourself is that compromising the truth has high costs. If you had difficulty with honesty, you need to commit yourself to telling the truth in the future. Before you can do that, however, you have to be sold on the idea that being honest works better. Look at the points that I just made about the destructiveness of dishonesty. How do they apply to your former relationship?

Keep in mind that it doesn't make sense to castigate yourself. Of course you need to take responsibility for what you did. But don't put yourself on an endless guilt trip. Not only will you make yourself miserable, but you won't gain anything by it. Instead, why don't you try to understand what you were trying to accomplish? For example, you could ask yourself:

- Did it seem like the easy, less complicated way out?
- Did you believe that "what he didn't know wouldn't hurt him"?
- Were you too frightened or unsure of yourself to be more assertive and deal with the discomfort of confrontation?

These and other questions can provide you with a road map as to what work you have to do.

YOUR SEX LIFE

Review your sex life with your ex-lover and address the questions I am about to pose. When you do this, also ask yourself how these issues interfered with the viability of your relationship. What will you do differently now?

- How comfortable are you with having sex? How comfortable are you with gay sexuality?
- How frightened of sex has HIV made you? Be careful here, it may not be "politically correct" to admit you may be frightened of "ridiculous" ways to contract HIV. Forget about political correctness and be honest with yourself. Some gay men do have irrational fears (I once had a sane, intelligent client express his fear to me that he could give himself HIV) and the only way you can begin to address them is by first admitting that they were/are there. Irrational or not, if you have them, they will get in the way of your sex life.
- How satisfied were you with him? Were you compatible?
- Were you able to talk about your sexuality? Were you able to discuss what you liked and did not like?
- Was your risk tolerance respected, or did you feel pressured to engage in behaviors you were not comfortable with? Did you pressure him to do what he was not comfortable with?

And Your "Arrangement"

Unfettered by heterosexual norms, we gay men are free to create our own rules about fidelity and openness in the sexual arena. Gay men have numerous forms of agreements that are limited only by the creativeness and willingness of the participants. For example, some men will permit openness on particular days, or only when they or their partners are a certain distance from home (the hundred-mile rule!). Others will agree on "tricking" as long as there is no emotional connection. Then there are details within such an understanding such as: "no emotional connection" means (a) you cannot exchange numbers, and/or (b) you can't see him more than once, and/or (c) sex only in a sex club. While in theory this may sound wonderful, some gay men find that living the agreement is more complicated than making it. Kelsey and Fred learned this.

These men live in San Francisco. They agreed that Monday would be "freedom night." Their rule went as follows: "Do whatever you want with whomever, no questions and no discussion afterward." This was fine for a while. Each man didn't really know what (if anything) the other was doing on Monday nights, so it didn't seem to bother either of them. That is, until one Monday evening when Kelsey was walking into a bar called The Stud and Fred was leaving at the same time (with a man). As fate would have it, Fred was kissing this guy as he bumped into Kelsey. Agreement or no agreement, Kelsey became very upset. He screamed, "You goddamn bitch!" and ran off. Fred, completely taken by surprise, said, "Holy shit, that's my boyfriend." The man Fred was with became irritated and looked at him with incredulity. "I thought you had an agreement with your boyfriend." he said. But before Fred could respond, he added, "You know, you're a pig." He then walked away. Not a good night for anyone!

Agreements may seem to work in theory but not when it's actually "in your face." Agreements may work for a time but then cease to as you and your partner change. Still another problem is that pressures within the gay community may cause you to agree with something you really never endorsed. Sometimes, you may not even be consciously aware of that. I believe the greatest potential for this is in the domain of accepting an open relationship. Nonmonogamy is fine for many, but not for everyone.

In my view, monogamy, at least on a long-term basis, is not positively received in the gay male community. It's thought of as unrealistic, restrictive, and destructive to the relationship in the long run. But what if monogamy is what you truly want?

It is important to be honest with yourself about this (as with any other sexual arrangement you make). Look back. If you agreed to an open relationship, is that what you really wanted? Did you want to change the agreement after a time but felt you couldn't because you already had agreed to it? Did you feel monogamy was too much to ask for? Did you feel you would not be "with it" if you asked for monogamy?

Looking at the present and your future, pose some questions to yourself: Do you want monogamy now? If you do, do you feel that no one in your community could accept it? Are you willing to be different from many who believe in open relationships? Do you have friends or can you make friends with people who could support you (even if it's not what they want for themselves personally)? Are you willing to wait for the man who also wants monogamy on a long-term basis?

THE GENERAL RULES OF YOUR RELATIONSHIP

In the realm of sexuality, the concept of rules is relatively explicit. Many gay men (of course not all, which is a mistake) sit down and create specific dictums about how they will conduct their sexuality. What a lot of us are not aware of is that most other parts of our relationships also run according to very specific precepts.

A relationship, like any social system, creates do's and don'ts, values, and boundaries in order to function. These notions are often implicit. No one may talk about them or even be particularly aware of them as rules. (Not that you are totally unconscious of them. They are just not at the forefront of your awareness.) For example, Sunday may be "the day for you and your boyfriend." The implied rule may go as follows: "This is our day together. We use this day to spend relaxed quality time with each other. We don't make plans with others on this day, and do everything we can to avoid having to be apart."

Some of the problems you had with your ex may be because you have agreed to implicit rules that you really did not want to. One problem may have been that you were not aware that they were rules. It just seemed to be "the thing you did," and yet you knew you were uncomfortable with it. One superb way that you can learn from your ex-relationship is to expose what those rules were. Make the implicit explicit! You can then decide which rules worked for you, and which ones did not. You can enter a new relationship with a clear understanding that rules will be developed, and what rules will be viable for you.

Get out a piece of paper and a pen and examine different ways your relationship "ran." Then describe that observation in the form of a rule. A few examples follow:

> **Observation:** Most of the time when we just hung out, it was in Robby's apartment.

> **Rule:** Free time with no planned activities is done most of the time in Robby's apartment.

> **Observation:** Robby's friends often came with us to the movies. Robby never asked me whether this was OK with me.

> **Rule:** Robby's friends accompany us to the movies. My explicit consent is not required.

> **Observation:** When either Robby or I were out of town, we'd call each other every day.

> **Rule:** We call each other on a daily basis when we are out of town.

Keep in mind that as with other lessons of your ex-relationship, you may discover some rules that you liked. The knowledge of this helps you understand yourself and puts you in an advantageous position when you develop your next committed relationship. You know what works and does not work for you.

AGE DIFFERENCES

Some of us prefer partners significantly older or younger than ourselves. While these relationships can certainly work, they present special challenges because of developmental differences. If you are in your forties and your ex-lover is in his twenties, there is simply no getting around the fact that the age difference affected your relationship. Your "youthful maturity" and his "mature youthfulness" could not change that.

Take a look at just how it was affected. Did you feel like a father or mentor to him? How did you like that role? Was he unable to be emotionally available to you at times because he could not understand something he had not yet experienced? Did your interests collide with his because of age differences? Did you feel in competition with him because of his more prevalent physical attractiveness to others? Did you worry that you'd lose him to some younger man? Did the future scare you when you thought that the age differences then would seem more pronounced?

These are but a tiny fraction of the questions you can ask yourself. You can learn from this first and foremost *if you are able to acknowledge that it did matter.* Again, it doesn't mean that such a relationship is necessarily unviable. By acknowledging the challenges, you can discover how successful or unsuccessful you were in meeting those challenges. You then have a blueprint for what you can do in the future. You can devise strategies to help you cope with the difficulties. Or you could decide that the challenges are not what you desire and decide to seek a lover closer to your own age the next time around.

I have covered a number of areas where you can learn about yourself when you look back. Certainly the subject matter covered was not meant to be exhaustive. There are other issues you may wish to explore. If you were in a relationship with a man from another race and/or another socioeconomic class, how did that affect you? How did your respective levels of being out of the closet affect your union? What role did the in-laws play? What effect did illness have on both of you? Develop the questions that are meaningful to you. In your search, remember to leave out your ex-lover. He is not going to be living your life or be in your next relationship. You are, and therefore "you" is all that counts.

It may be painful to view your mistakes in bold relief. There may be a strong tendency to attack yourself for being so "stupid." *Do what you can to give that a rest.* Not only will that not aid you, but it may interfere with the learning process. If you give yourself enough discomfort via self-attack, you may become de-motivated to explore further. It may even stifle your ability to process your memories and gain insight. It can derail your motivation to develop a plan to create a different type of relationship in the future.

And now what about that new relationship in the future? We have spent considerable effort exploring what *doesn't* work in a relationship, and how to leave. We have viewed numerous social and psychological ramifications of a breakup. We have addressed holding off from reconnecting (with an ex) or rebounding, and giving yourself time to be alone. We have visited the myriad of ways you can learn from your relationship that wasn't meant to be.

Perhaps a good deal of time has passed since you broke up. You have grieved the loss and let go. You have become more mature and psychologically healthy. You have a good idea of what worked and did not work, and you have a superb plan to do it differently this time around. You are ready to go once again.

What you want this time is a healthy relationship. One in which you laugh more than you cry. One where there is more pleasure than pain. One that helps you grow, not regress. You want to feel trust and security and joy. You want the feeling of intimacy and happiness. You want to see color where there was once only black and white. You want to be in love. Having a relationship with the man of your dreams is deeply gratifying when it works. So what makes it work?

Chapter 11

Starting Over: Loving a Man

I mean everyone has their baggage, but the trick is to not bring too much of it to the relationship.

Antonio, 29, management consultant
Boston, Massachusetts

. . . what makes it (a relationship) work?

Neil Kaminsky

. . . communication and trust, surrounded by love.

Kevin, 35, computer consultant
Kansas City, Missouri

Intimate relationships between gay men have never been without challenges. As we approach the beginning of the twenty-first century, we continue to be faced with a formidable task.

That these relationships are difficult is quite an understatement. They take work and enormous emotional risk taking. They endure within an outer society that literally condemns them. They exist within a gay community that, at best, is ambivalent in its support. Many gay men have been, and continue to be, denied the normal courting experimentation of adolescence. There are terribly few positive role models. Gay men struggle with internalized homophobia. Male socialization issues interfere with the development of the tools necessary for intimacy. And I could go on. Yes, we have a lot on our plate. Nevertheless, we still pursue these unions, and despite all of the above, numerous relationships do succeed. Many gay men know the magnificence of being in love.

The question, of course, is, how does a relationship succeed? How, despite all the pressures and problems, do two gay men achieve deep contentment in a union? It's beyond the scope of this book to provide a guide to a successful gay marriage. A guide would necessitate detailed advice which in itself could fill the pages of a book. Indeed, books have and will continue to be written on this subject.

For the purpose of this book, I want to outline some goals you can set for yourself. We have actually addressed many of the components of a viable relationship by looking at what doesn't work. But to aid in your learning, it's also important to address them in the affirmative—what *does* work, what *is* healthy, and why. This chapter, in conjunction with all you have already learned, can help further clarify what happened between you and your ex, and where you want to be the next time around. If you are already in "the next time around," it can still help you view how both of you are doing, and what areas could use improvement.

SOME FACTORS OF RELATIONSHIP SUCCESS

What makes a relationship successful is a combination of many factors. I define "successful" in rather simple terms—it's when two men are truly happy with each other, and their lives are greatly enhanced because they are together. Let's take a look at how this happens.

Compatibility

In a sense, this is quite simple. You have to like your lover, and he must like you. You have to be friends. You have to be in sync. You need to have fairly similar values and perspectives. This doesn't mean you are clones! It doesn't mean you won't have some arguments and disagreements. Furthermore, no relationship operates automatically, and all require some amount of work. But time together, generally, should not feel like work. A relationship exists for mutual emotional gratification, not mutual toil and despair. Most of the time together should be pleasurable.

Compatibility to a large degree has to exist before you come together as a couple. Believing you or your potential partner can undergo a personality transformation to *become* compatible is very unlikely to succeed. Choosing someone who is compatible rests on having a good understanding of who *you* are, and being able to choose a person who can realistically meet what you need from a lover. Being confused about what your needs are, or getting lost in fantasy or sexual attraction, often compromises the selection process for a compatible mate.

Respect

Your lover is someone you should *want* to take home to Mom and Dad. He is someone you want to show to your friends and co-workers. You should be proud of him. Since your attachment to him is profound, he is in a sense part of you. Respect for him materially affects respect for yourself. If you are deeply involved with someone you don't respect, what does that say about you?

Taken from the other angle, what does it say about you if you spend time with someone who doesn't respect you? Your relationship, a voluntary creation, exists to meet the needs of both you and your lover. Disrespect by either of you for the other makes the purpose of the relationship meaningless.

Respect doesn't mean blind allegiance or an inability to see what is wrong. It doesn't mean either of you must like or agree with everything the other one does. But it does signify that you have a fundamental admiration for each other, and a basic acceptance of the person each of you are.

This creates a healthy environment for two people to relate and grow. The atmosphere is positive because there is mutual validation. Respect means you honor your partner's feelings. You know what bothers him and you do your best not to hurt him. You know what he enjoys and you do your best to facilitate his happiness. You are sensitive to his needs and you take them into serious consideration in relation to your own. A healthy relationship means you don't abdicate your own needs and you don't deny that his exist. Rather, you strive for a mutually satisfying balance. You expect and get from him the same in return.

Respect means you can be free and comfortable to make mistakes because you know your lover has positive regard for you. You are not fearful of being rejected because you make an error. Basic acceptance helps one to take risks and to grow. Self-esteem flourishes in this atmosphere, because each of you can encourage and support the other. And because you respect your lover, what he does has weight and power. If you are frightened, for example, and he tells you it will be OK, you are more likely to be comforted by him if you respect him. His ability to calm you makes him feel effectual, and motivates him to help you the next time you need it.

Mutual respect can become a spiral of increasing gains for both men.

Boundaries

Being in love means connecting on one of the deepest levels you will ever experience. Perhaps the most intense level of all. Intimacy of this degree creates a form of psychological merger that can be intensely gratifying. But there is a reality we must contend with: two people simply do not become one. We therefore need to retain a sense of psychological separateness. This means perceiving oneself and one's lover as separate people with distinct paths. It means recognizing that your needs and his are not identical. It signifies an awareness that your lover does not exist to create a life for you.

Since some degree (indeed a high degree) of merging operates concurrently in a relationship (his pain affects you, you care deeply for each other), both of these realities must coexist, and coexist in peace. This is a difficult balancing act for anyone. Those who have a clear sense of self will fare better. Those who enter relationships seeking completion of self with another are bound for troubled waters.

Clear boundaries provide the best of both worlds. You keep yourself and you have him. You reap the rewards of intimacy and remain separate and free. You grow as a couple and as an individual.

Boundaries enable both of you to have separate viable lives. You can have different interests and different opinions. No one has to be bad or wrong or "less than." You can have separate friends and enjoy activities with friends apart from each other. You can tolerate time and distance apart. You may want to travel without him, or he may want to go to a party or club without you. If he is tired, it doesn't mean both of you have to stay home for the evening. When you are in social situations together, you are not attached at the hip (or any other place!). You can walk around. You can talk to others. You can make new friends.

None of this takes away from your relationship (obviously trust has to exist, and you have to negotiate how you handle your separateness). Indeed, clear boundaries will enhance your relationship. By retaining the domain of freedom, you will experience your relationship as the enrichment to your life that it should be, not as a substitute for it.

Sexual Attraction to Others

> ... we don't have on and off switches ... even when you are on a diet, you can look at the menu.
>
> Milton, 62, physician (HIV specialist)
> New York City

Some gay men feel that once you are attached, sexual interest for the rest of mankind abruptly disappears. Only the lover is supposed to be the object of one's sexual desire. Where that sexual interest goes beats me! Some men even feel guilty if they find themselves looking at others, or having fantasies.

I say this with tongue in cheek. I don't think that most gay men really believe that these feelings are supposed to disappear. But there is a sense among some that it is wrong to have them.

I want to emphasize that I am talking about *feelings, not behavior.* There is a world of difference between feeling attracted, and acting upon the feeling.

Sexual feelings for others is simply part of being human. Having a lover doesn't change that. Sexual feelings are also very powerful, and suppression of them, sprinkled with guilt, has a way of making a nice guy grumpy. Such a state of affairs can poison a relationship.

Openly accepting these feelings within yourself and your partner creates a sense of freedom and reality within the relationship. It means you don't have to fight a losing battle within yourself, nor do you have to try to control the ungovernable in your lover. It means each of you can continue to be yourselves. Men in healthy relationships openly acknowledge this, and some may find the open sharing of these feelings quite pleasurable.

Trust

Trust is a pivotal component of intimacy. It is the element that enables closeness to develop. Trust between lovers is influenced by a number of factors.

Developmental history is vital. How you learned to trust or not to trust early in life provides a blueprint of sorts as to how you will trust later on. If you were seriously wounded as a child (physical or sexual abuse, abandonment, etc.), you are likely to have considerable difficulty trusting a lover. But violation of your trust doesn't have to be this extreme to create problems.

Perhaps you were very close to a parent who suddenly died. Perhaps a parent had to go away for an extended period, and no one explained to you what was going on. Maybe your dad made promises but was inconsistent in keeping them. For a young child, these kinds of experiences can be traumatic. They may make the child feel very unsafe, confused, and deeply disappointed. He may then build a defense against the pain. His thinking may go something like this: "If I don't trust (depend on someone else), I will not be caught off guard. I will not be vulnerable. I will not be without protection. If I don't trust, I never have to suffer the pain of disappointment. If I don't trust, I am in more control."

Other factors are also important. If you have been deceived by a former lover, you may have been traumatized. You may build a "protective" shell. It may protect you from ever getting hurt, but you will forgo your opportunity for intimacy. *You cannot have intimacy without trust.*

Issues of internalized homophobia are also significant. Among the numerous "laws" of homophobia is the dictum that gay men are shallow and untrustworthy. This feeling, on some level, is more prevalent in the gay male community than we'd like to believe. When we have "tricks," dates, and relationships that turn into fiascoes, we are ready to joke that "all men are pigs." Jokes often belie feelings that are difficult to express in more direct ways. Awareness of these kinds of feelings, and working them through, is requisite for developing trust with another gay man.

Trust is also related to your own trustworthiness. If you behave in an honest manner, you are likely to view others as virtuous. If you are dishonest, you are apt to view your lover and others as potentially or presumably mendacious.

Of course, trustworthy behavior must be demonstrated by your partner. A mistake can be forgiven and it's important to work on transcending a mistake. If your lover demonstrates a pattern of lying, however, I cannot see how you could develop trust with him.

Trust is requisite for intimacy in another way. It's not just that you have to be able to trust your lover to feel close to him. *You have to be able to trust the process of developing emotional closeness.* Getting very close to someone is a double-edged sword. While it may feel wonderful, it can also feel like *engulfment*. Engulfment means, psychologically, losing a sense of who you are. You are "engulfed" by the other person. Without getting caught up in psychological discourse, a person who has difficulty with boundaries between himself and others may fear engulfment. When he gets close to someone, he may be confused about whose feelings he is feeling. For example, his lover may blame him for something he is not responsible for. He may, nevertheless, feel very guilty *because his lover is angry!* It's as if there is no skin membrane between them—his emotions are automatically determined by his lover's emotions. Such a man can become so focused on his lover that he is almost unable to think about or validate his own needs. He may not even have a clue as to what they are. He may also feel very dependent upon his lover and fear that he cannot survive without him. Such a person (for good reasons) may have significant difficulty trusting intimacy. However, if you are clear about where you end and someone else begins, intimacy is far less threatening (not devoid of danger—intimacy is still an emotional risk). No matter how close you get to him, and no matter how much you are part of him, you are still able to feel a strong sense of who *you* are. You still remember you, and take care of you. You still know your feelings and how they are distinct from his. And you do not feel your life depends on him. You feel perfectly able to negotiate the world with or without him. Thus, it is easier to trust the intimacy process and hence develop emotional closeness.

When lovers trust, they are able to expose to each other the deepest aspects of who they are. This creates powerful and profoundly gratifying feelings. He knows the real you and he loves that person. No masks, no role playing, no need to prove anything. With him you can be comfortable being just who you are. What a wonderful feeling of respite from the world! What a powerful support to your self-esteem.

Trust means you know your secrets are safe with him. He will respect and protect your privacy. He will not use what he knows about you to hurt you.

You know that he's there for you, that he is on your side, that you can count on him in the good and bad times. This can create a deep sense of security in a world of maddening insecurity.

You know that what he says is true. There is no hidden agenda. There is no reason to be suspicious, no reason to question. No reason to fear or wonder. What he tells you is *what is*. If you agree on monogamy, for example, it matters not whether he is in another room or another country. He will not sleep with someone else and you do not have to worry about it.

This is not to say he can't make a mistake under unforeseen circumstances. Human beings are fallible. But there is a difference between a mistake and betrayal. Should he sleep with another guy, he will come clean about it. You will both deal with it. You will not be living with an unreality.

Some will argue that if cheating is an isolated event, it's best to say nothing. They argue that it will cause more damage to the relationship than if you kept it quiet. I could not disagree more. Being truthful about difficult problems is the essence of honesty. That's what it's all about. Honesty doesn't just mean that you admit you forgot to change the cat litter! It means you are going to tell the truth no matter what. *Knowing that he will be honest under the most difficult circumstances is a major reason why you trust him in the first place.*

Trust creates a joyful, comfortable, safe, deeply nurturing climate for a couple. Honesty, which sustains trust, makes a relationship real. Trust helps a couple resonate. It helps them surmount obstacles, sometimes very difficult problems. It's the basis for true intimacy, which is the cornerstone of a loving union between two men.

Accepting Emotional Vulnerability

That all being said, you do take a big chance when you love. Even if you have the best of everything, you never have a guarantee about anything.

The finest relationship may cease to work one day. You or your lover may have to separate because of a career choice, or because one of you wants to relocate. Your lover could die (and sadly, this has not been particularly uncommon in our community).

You can also trust and find out you "played the fool." He can lie. He can deceive you. You *knew* that he would not betray you, but you never had a *guarantee.* Guarantees in human relationships do not exist.

For these and many other reasons, some men fight closeness. They keep their lovers at arm's length almost like an insurance policy. If they don't get too close, somehow, they believe, they can protect themselves from pain if the roof falls in. Trying to be in a relationship in this manner is like swimming while endeavoring to remain dry. *It simply cannot work. The two realities are mutually exclusive.*

A healthy relationship mandates emotional vulnerability. It means you accept the fact that you risk deep pain by getting involved. But it's also important not to confuse this with physical and emotional survival. The pain of a breakup can hurt like hell. But it won't kill you. It won't foreclose your ability to continue to have happiness in your life. You are not risking your survival or your ability to derive joy from life; you are risking pain.

When you accept emotional vulnerability you are operating in reality. You are not in a fruitless pursuit to make the impossible possible. Furthermore, your acceptance gives you tremendous freedom and release from pressure. You are free to get very close and fall deeply in love with the man of your dreams. You are able to rejoice in today and not obsess about controlling tomorrow. You don't have to try to protect yourself, and in the process destroy your chance for love.

Competition and Remembering Whose Side You Are On

We live in a very competitive society, and it's not aberrant to find competitive behavior in a couple. Men especially are socialized to compete. Openly accepting these feelings makes a relationship healthy. You don't have to hide or feel guilty about what you feel. Furthermore, the issue can be openly addressed, which can help resolve it.

Perhaps your lover was promoted for the third time in a year, and you have not been moving ahead in your career. You may experience a sense of inferiority, jealousy, and even anger. If you are open about this, you are less likely to engage in destructive passive-aggressive behavior. Passive-aggressive behavior could manifest something like this: He arranges with you to go out to celebrate, and you "forget" to meet him at the restaurant.

Being open means telling your lover that although you are happy for him (on one level), you are also upset. It's best if you can really describe your feelings in a more specific way. For example, you could say something like, "You know, Jesse, I just feel sort of bad that you seem to be going everywhere and I am going nowhere. Frankly, I feel inferior to you and jealous." If he is accepting of these feelings, he won't see this as a betrayal of your love, but an under-standable feeling. He can even provide emotional support (remind you of some other strengths you have), which may then decrease your discomfort.

That being said, it is also true that a healthy relationship signifies a limited amount of competitiveness. In truth, you are there for each other and you are on the same side. The benefit for one will also mean the benefit for both. Furthermore, your positive attachment and love for each other will make each of you want the other to succeed. The atmosphere is then set for support and nurturing of success and other good things.

Telling yourself to feel this way may help somewhat, but it's really where you have to be coming from in the first place. If you are having serious problems with jealousy and competitiveness, these are probably deep-seated problems that require some form of professional intervention.

When competitiveness is at a minimum, and each of you views yourself as part of a team, the relationship will be in sync with your individual lives. It becomes a "place" that supports, encourages, and rewards the strengths and accomplishments of each man. There is also another fruit. Your lover's good fortune truly makes you feel good. You view it as something good "for the family" and thus beneficial to you. And there is yet another gain. Part of the wonderment of love is knowing that you care so deeply for another individual that his welfare is emotionally meaningful to you. Just the *awareness* that you can care so much about what happens to him will be ardently gratifying to you.

Healthy Dependency

Yes, individuation and the ability to have a separate life independent of your lover are imperative for a healthy relationship. I have probably said it a thousand times by this point! But that is only half of the story. Interdependence is equally important. Why have the relationship if all you desire is total separateness?

One of the beauties of a relationship is needing another, being able to sit back and comfortably depend on him to be there for you. Whether it's for emotional support or being picked up late at night from work, it's a good feeling to know that he is there and that he will do that for you. This is not only gratifying for you—it makes him feel needed and important in your life.

This is another area where you have to be on guard for that "male stuff." Men are not socialized into being receptive and dependent. Yet all of us need to be that way at times, and a lover can be there for us in that manner if we only let him.

Sharing

Sharing often means getting less than. When you were a child and your mom told you that you had to share your piece of pie with your brother, you were probably not amused.

Things, like experiences, need, *to some degree,* to be separate with lovers. It's fine, indeed good for you know that you have a book and a camera that is yours and yours alone. If your house is big enough, you may have separate rooms even though you share a bedroom. It's good to be able to go there when you need to be alone.

But sharing with a lover can also give you more. There is something wonderful about knowing that this is "our house," "our pictures," "our furniture." This emphasizes the connection and belonging and structure to your life. Being able to share in this manner gives you more, not less.

Communication

A key way a relationship works is by having good communication. When you communicate well, you connect. And connection is paramount in a romantic union. That is what makes being in love so wonderful. Communication is how you get there. It's how you demonstrate that you know and understand and love him. It's how you let him know he is safe with you.

Insight

Good communication means essentially being able to get your message across and being able to understand his message. One way you can achieve this is by having good insight about yourself. When you are not in touch with parts of you, you may communicate those parts without even knowing it. He may pick up on those messages and then confusion reigns.

Let's say, for example, that you feel threatened when he spends time with others. But you are not aware of this. You think on a "logical level" that he has a right to spend time with whomever he pleases. However, your gut tells you something else. When he's going to go out with his friends, you say "have a great time," but your face and body posture communicate sadness and discomfort. When he comes back from an outing with his friends, you inevitably find something about him (not the fact that he was out without you) that annoys you, and you wind up in an argument with him. He tells you that you are really angry because he was out without you, and you tell him that that is not what it's about (and you believe this).

By having insight, you are less likely to get into a false argument. You will know what is really bothering you. This affords both of you the opportunity to address the real problem.

Multiple Levels of Communication

A related issue is appreciating that communication exists on nonverbal levels as well as verbal ones. If your lover says, "You are telling me it's OK to go out with my friends but your tone and facial expression say something else," you don't respond with, "But I *said* it's fine, what the hell else do you want?" You are open to examining those other forms of communication because you recognize that they are just as valid, if not more so, than what you are saying.

Avoid Bringing Up Every Problem
Since the Lincoln Administration

Good communication means you remain focused on the issue at hand. There is nothing more destructive than having a disagreement about one issue, and bringing up everything you have been angry about for years. For one thing, that tends to harden defenses and make any kind of working together impossible. Furthermore, you can't solve a multitude of problems, especially events that happened a long time ago, in one discussion. By remaining focused on the problem at hand, you are again in the business of finding a solution to what is problematic.

Problem Solving, Not Winning

When you are in conflict with your lover, don't enter a discussion with the intention to win and prove how wrong he is. Enter with an intention to problem solve. *See the goal as solving the problem. You want both of you to be winners.* State honestly what is going on and what you want. Do not attack the person but the problem. Also, take responsibility for your feelings.

Let's take a look at Jeremy and Robert. I will give you a good and a bad example of how Robert communicates a concern he has to Jeremy. First, the good way:

> Jeremy, I really feel uncomfortable when we go to a party and I hardly spend two minutes with you. I know I am a big boy and you don't have to baby-sit for me, but I would feel better if we just checked in with each other now and then. You know I get anxious in those situations. You know my stuff with abandonment. So could you please be sensitive to these issues the next time we go to a party? It would really mean a lot to me.

The bad way:

> Jeremy, you are such an insensitive prick. You left me all alone for the entire evening at that party while you were talking to that asshole Jim. How many times do I have to complain about this? You left me alone at Kevin and Brad's commitment

ceremony, you took a walk when we visited my mom on her birthday. Last year, damn, you practically abandoned me in Rome. . . . Shit, you have to have your "free time" all the time. What kind of goddamn lover are you anyway? Lovers don't behave like this to each other!

When one expresses honest feelings appropriately, as in the first example, the feelings need to be respected. Only then can there be openness. This doesn't mean, necessarily, that there has to be agreement or that behavior must be changed. But respect means you do not attack or get attacked for *feeling* something. Let's take a look again at Robert and Jeremy. After Robert appropriately expressed his discomfort with Jeremy's lack of attention at the party (the first scenario), Jeremy suitably responds in the following manner:

I'm really sorry, hon, that you feel that way. It really must be awful to feel so out of it and abandoned. But you know I don't really think there's much I can do about this. I don't feel comfortable checking in with you unless it feels natural with me. And this doesn't. I feel this is something you have to deal with on your own. If I check in with you, I am sort of telling you that you can't be OK without me. I don't think that's a great idea.

Obviously, there is no resolution to the dilemma between Jeremy and Robert at this point. Nevertheless, these lovers are being open and honest and respectful with one other. This creates a calm, nondefensive win/win atmosphere. It increases the likelihood that they will continue to work on this until some meeting of the minds is reached. Just because Jeremy doesn't believe he has any part in Robert's feelings of abandonment at this point doesn't mean he won't be open to a counter-argument by Robert. But even if they don't solve this problem, they have created a psychological milieu where it is safe to disagree.

Time Is Important

Problems should be addressed as soon as possible. As with any kind of issue, if you neglect it, it's likely to grow and become unmanageable. Problems, also, do not go away by themselves. If you are having a serious disagreement, you may need to stop the discussion and withdraw for a while because you are getting nowhere. *But that should be temporary, and you need to come back to it.* Not infrequently, when a problem is very threatening (for example, a disagreement over whether the relationship should be monogamous or open), it may feel very tempting to act like nothing happened when peace has been finally restored. But something has happened, and unless you find a resolution to your conflict, it will eat away at you. In the case of monogamy versus an open relationship, the man who wants to pursue other sexual liaisons may choose to do it anyway. The potential for destroying the relationship in such a scenario is very high.

Problem solving needs to take place at appropriate times. Generally this means in private when you have ample time, you are otherwise relaxed and alert, and you are not pressed by other responsibilities. In such an environment, you do not become involved with other issues and therefore can devote your full energy to the issues at hand. If, for example, you get into a big discussion right before you go to sleep (and you need to work the following day) you may get increasingly tense with each other as the hour gets later and you are not reaching a resolution. You may not be able to sleep and may be increasingly angry at your lover for keeping you up. And then if you have a miserable day at work, "dragging your ass" through it because you are so tired, you may find yourself even more perturbed at your lover. I don't know where that idea that we should never go to sleep angry comes from. Sometimes you have to go to sleep angry or you won't go to sleep at all! As long as you have good tools to problem solve, that will not matter. Expectations to solve a problem before you go to sleep puts pressure on lovers that can cause unnecessary problems.

Mind Reading

As far as we know, human beings are not able to read minds. So why do lovers sometimes believe that their partners have this ability? "He knows exactly what I want—if not, he should." That kind of attitude can cause innumerable problems.

Having a healthy relationship means you do not assume your lover knows what your needs are, or what you are thinking or desiring at a particular time. It means you directly and openly state what you want. This gives him the best opportunity to be there for you in the way you want him to be.

It's true that when people are very close, each can occasionally sense what the other is about to say or is thinking. Some guys proudly express this when they declare, "I didn't have to say anything—I just took one look at John and we both burst out laughing. He knew just what I was thinking." This can also exist between good friends.

That is fine when it happens, and it can give one a feeling of being deeply connected with another. But to *expect* that to happen when you need something from your lover is not realistic. Sensing needs at a particular moment is *not* the hallmark of intimacy. Clear, direct, honest communication is. To get angry when he doesn't respond to your thoughts is unfair and a way to get into a destructive altercation.

There is another fringe benefit to clearly expressing needs. It means each person is taking responsibility for himself—it signifies that neither man is expecting the other to do his work for him. In general this is a healthy, mature attitude that supports the relationship. Taking responsibility for oneself is adult behavior. There is a world of difference between relating to an adult as opposed to taking care of a "child-adult." The former can be deeply gratifying. The latter is emotionally draining and destructive to relationship growth.

Being open and direct doesn't only mean that you express needs and conflict. It also means you tell your lover what you love and respect about him.

Stroking

In our society there is a dearth of stroking. Many of us are quick to judge and criticize. If you are treated unfairly by a company, you may be quick to write a complaint letter. There is certainly nothing wrong with that. But are you as quick to write a letter of commendation when you are treated well?

We all respond to stroking and support. We all want others to appreciate and acknowledge what we offer. In a relationship, it is very important to communicate this to your lover. The companionship and love and care that he gives to you is something that you should never take for granted. It is a wonderful, priceless gift, and you are one lucky man to be the recipient of that gift. Obviously, what you give to him is equally magnificent. Then why not tell each other this? Exactly what will it cost either of you? Obviously, nothing. On the contrary, it will make both of you feel valued. It will deepen your intimacy. It may add to the self-esteem of both of you, which can only be good for your union. It will help you ride out the difficult times when you are not so enamored with each other. It will increase the likelihood that each of you will continue to treat the other well. It's a total win/win situation.

Unfortunately, many people are raised in homes where stroking for positive behavior is scarce. The rationale is that this is "coddling" behavior, that the child should *know* what is appropriate, and shouldn't be "babied." That, of course, is ridiculous. If this describes your family background, recognize that you have been given a false message and don't continue to live it.

Positive Physical Communication

I am not talking about sexual behavior, but rather touch that communicates other good feelings. Touch can proclaim love, caring, support, safety, and intimacy. These are some of the major components of a loving relationship. Verbal expression of this is really not enough— touch is a whole other level of communication that is needed.

Both of You Being in Love

This is one of the most powerful but equally mysterious human emotions. Many refuse to define "being in love" and say you will simply know it when it happens. The best I can do is describe how I perceive it.

Being in love, for me, is the deepest connection you can have with another human being. It involves profound caring and penetrating symbiotic experience. What happens to him in a very large sense is happening to you. It also creates deep meaning and enormous fulfillment that is unparalleled by any other experience. It imbues life with color and intensity that is unrivaled and mysterious. It's what makes starless, icy nights warm, bleak days electrifying, hot chocolates and fireplaces romantic. Pleasurable experiences take on heightened significance and depth when you are in love. Gazing at a mountain and the stars may be very enjoyable for you, but sharing that moment with someone you are in love with is a whole other story. It can bring you to a level of joyousness that is literally impossible to describe within the confines of human language.

As I see it, being in love is the best life has to offer. When a relationship provides this, you are getting the best you can. *Loving* your partner is not the same as *being in love*. I define love as having a deep fondness and concern for someone. You can love your friends and others in your life but you are not necessarily *in love* with them. Without being in love with your lover, you are being seriously shortchanged.

Being in love does change over time. There may be fewer walks on the beach, less lovemaking in the dead of the night. *But less than does not mean none.* In fact, in time you should be more deeply in love because you have a history together. Perhaps fewer romantic liaisons, but deeper feelings. You are more part of each other, more of a family.

Unfortunately, couples do fall out of love. They may still care about each other, but the passion is gone. Sometimes working on the relationship rekindles it. Some couples neglect their relationship and become obsessed with the demands of day-to-day living (getting ahead in one's career, worrying about the mortgage, etc.). Couples therapy may get them back on track as they learn to place more of a focus on themselves (getting away for a vacation, making quality time together a priority, etc.). Sometimes, however, it simply cannot come back. Not infrequently, people accept falling out of love as normal and anticipated. The thinking goes something like, "Well, you know we've been together for so many years, so you can't expect that to continue." I think that is a grave mistake. Being in love is one of the ways we are deeply gratified in a union with another. We should always expect it to be there, do what we can to nurture it, and work to bring it back if we feel it is slipping away.

POINTING TOWARD TOMORROW

If you are in the process of a breakup, or if both of you have already gone your separate ways, you are probably experiencing one of the most painful epochs of your life. Letting go of a man who was once the man of your dreams cuts to the core of your being. Once he was wonderful. All that you ever wanted, all that you ever hoped for. Sure, you know the reasons why it didn't work. For heaven's sake, you just read this book. You have looked at all the red flags, and understand all the mistakes. But when the emotional pain hits you very badly, it may seem as if you don't understand anything. When all is said and done, you don't really want this to have happened. You never planned it this way. You never imagined this would occur. How could it have turned out this way? Why did the story have to end this way? you ask yourself.

I have been through my own breakups. They have never been easy or simple. All the men in my life gave something to me, and losing them has hurt every time. Indeed, it has been difficult at times for me to write this book because of the pain it has caused me to revisit.

When a lover comes into your life, everything is wonderfully transformed. Daytime, nightfall, on the job, on the subway—he is always with you. Your boss can be angry, your car can die—nothing seems terrible. You are enraptured with his presence, and all of your troubles are a distant, benign blur.

The memories of those days can be terribly sad as you now sit alone. Remember how easy it was, you whisper to yourself. Easy to talk. Easy to listen. Easy to share dreams and plans. Easy to spend lazy Sunday afternoons. Easy to make love. Easy to fall in love. So what happened? Why did the story have to end this way? you ask yourself once again.

Of course, you *do* know why the story had to end this way. It ended this way because you fought more than you made love. Because there were more tears than laughter. Because there was more pain than pleasure.

It ended this way because your life was no longer your life. Because you were not satisfied. Because you forgot about you. Because he was not who you wanted or needed any longer. Because he was not who he said he was. Because you both changed. Because you fell out of love. Because you couldn't stand the confusion and the drama and the misery. Because you were destroying each other. *Because the relationship no longer worked.*

I never throw away birthday and friendship and Christmas cards sent to me. A few moments ago, just after I completed the previous paragraphs, I took a break from writing. I went searching through my collection of cards to find one sent to me by a friend many years ago. I remembered a note he wrote to me that I thought would provide a good quote for this book. Well, I didn't find his card, but I found a few cards from an ex-boyfriend. What he said was terribly sweet and beautiful. In one card he said he missed me when I had been away. He wished me a happy birthday in another card—he said he looked forward to spending many more birthdays with me. In still another one (boy, he sent lots of cards) he said he was just getting to know me but already I had become someone special to him. Another card had printed on it, "You are the best decision I ever made." And still another card said: "together forever." I have to admit that I felt quite sad when I saw this. Very sad. I wondered to myself, "Why did we have to break up?"

Our relationship had been doomed from the start. He was not ready for a relationship with me at the time we met—I knew that but chose to remain in denial. He didn't seem to know what he wanted from me; I wanted what he plainly could not deliver. Contrary to my best efforts, I could not trust him. He knew it and resented it. Our uncoupling was good for both of us. Yet even though I knew that, even though I knew that five minutes before when I was reading those cards, I still found myself asking, Why? Why did the story have to end that way? Inadvertently, I had proved to myself why uncoupling can be so difficult and maddening.

The men whom we fall in love with create magic for us. No one else can do that. They bestow upon us a precious, glorious gift. It's agonizing when we realize we must return that gift.

For all the knowledge I accumulated to write this book, for all the therapy I have dispensed to gay men in problematic relationships, for all the therapy I have been the recipient of, I still had a temporary lapse of memory and, some would say, sanity. Why did we have to break up? I pondered. Oh yeah, that's why, I remembered!

Guys, this is powerful stuff. We don't want to let go. We don't want to return the gift. We don't want to relinquish without kicking and screaming and doing anything we can to convince ourselves that it ain't so. We want the story to end another way.

If this can happen to me from just looking at a few cards when I am in the process of writing a book about breaking up, how are you feeling right now if your lover moved out last night? If you are about to tell him it's over this evening? If you are trying to make a decision? What about all the cards he sent you? All the love and treasured moments he brought to you? Can you really leave him? Does the story really have to end this way?

As a matter of fact, it does.

If your relationship is no longer viable, you know it. We humans are adept at denial, but there is a part of us that is aware of what is going on. We have to have the courage to listen to that part. No matter how goddamn scary it is. No matter how terribly sad it is.

We have to acknowledge the pain and our temporary lapses of memory and sanity *and get down to the business of taking care of ourselves.* If a relationship is not viable we can no longer remain in it. We are destroying ourselves by not letting go. We cannot permit that to continue. We will have to take our hits and wounds and tears but we must keep on moving.

We need to acknowledge the sweetness of yesterday and the dreams that never will be. We have to concede what we are losing and grieve the loss. We must accept that we have no guarantees about tomorrow. About anything.

We will no longer have him and life as we have known it. Perhaps we were together for a only few months. Perchance twenty years. However long, everything will be different. We will lose a lot. But we have ourselves, and we can never, *must never,* lose that.

If you have let go of a bad relationship, you have taken an important step toward improving your life. Whether you realize it or not, you have decided that you matter more than your fears.

Your dreams with him have indeed died, but your hope need not. There can be new dreams and better tomorrows and much, much more in the days, weeks, and years to come. *The days, weeks, and years to come.* What a hopeful concept. What a beautiful phrase. Those are very bittersweet words for me. It was something my late ex-lover of eleven years, Calvin, once said to me. His words were a gift. I now pass them along to you.

Appendix

Gay Community Resources

The following is a limited list of resources in various cities throughout the United States where you may be able to obtain psychological services and/or help with domestic violence. I am unable to describe the kind of assistance that is available in each listing; please contact the resource you are interested in to obtain that information. The names, phone numbers, and addresses that appear are what was available to me at the time of this writing. Since they may change, some information could become outdated. Please check with local directories if you find any information to be inaccurate. Good luck.

National

National Domestic Violence Hotline
PO Box 161810, Austin, Texas, 78716
1-800-799-7233
Hard of Hearing: 1-800-787-3224

The Gay and Lesbian National Hotline (GLNH)
1-888-THEGLNH, or 1-888-843-4564
Web site: www.glnh.org
E-mail: glnh@glnh.org

Boston, Massachusetts

Fenway Community Health Center
Victim Recovery Program
7 Haviland Street
Boston, Massachusetts 02115
(617) 267-0900

Chicago, Illinois

Horizons Community Services
961 West Montana
Chicago, Illinois 60614
(773) 472-6469
Anti-Violence Crisis Line (24 hours): (773) 871-2273

Cleveland, Ohio

The Lesbian/Gay Community Service Center
1418 West 29th Street
Cleveland, Ohio 44113
(216) 522-1999
Hotline: (216) 781-6736

Dallas, Texas

Gay and Lesbian Community Center
PO Box 190869
Dallas, Texas 75219-0869
(214) 528-9254
Gay and Lesbian Switchboard, Dallas, Texas: (214) 528-0022

Denver, Colorado

Equality Colorado—Anti-Violence Program
PO Box 300476
Denver, Colorado 80203
(303) 839-5540

Los Angeles, California

The Los Angeles Gay and Lesbian Community Services Center
1625 North Schrader Boulevard
Los Angeles, California 90028
(323) 993-7400

Minneapolis, Minnesota

Outfront Minnesota
310 East 38th Street, Suite 204
Minneapolis, Minnesota 55409-1337
(612) 822-0127

New York, New York

New York City Gay and Lesbian Anti-Violence Project
240 West 35th Street, Suite 200
New York, New York 10001-2506
(212) 714-1184
24-hour Bilingual Hotline: (212) 714-1141

San Diego, California

The San Diego Lesbian and Gay Men's Community Center
PO Box 3357
San Diego, California 92163
(619) 692-2077

San Francisco, California

New Leaf
1853 Market Street
San Francisco, California 94103
(415) 626-7000

Community United Against Violence
973 Market Street, Suite 500
San Francisco, California 94103
(415) 777-5500

San Jose, California

Billy DeFrank Lesbian and Gay Community Center
175 Stockton Avenue
San Jose, California 95126
(408) 293-2429, 293-4525

St. Louis, Missouri

St. Louis Lesbian and Gay Anti-Violence Project
University of Missouri, Dept. of Psychology
St. Louis, Missouri 63121
(314) 516-5467
Hotline: (314) 826-7067 (2-10 p.m. daily)

Washington, DC

Whitman Walker
1407 S Street, NW
Washington, DC 20009
(202) 797-3500

Notes

Introduction

1. From the song "You Can't Hurry Love," words and music by Eddie Holland, Lamont Dozier, and Brian Holland, Stone Agate Music Corporation, 1965. Best-selling record in 1966 by The Supremes (Motown). Source: *Popular Music 1920-1979, Volume 3,* Nat Shapiro and Bruce Pollock, editors. Gale Research Company, Detroit, Michigan, 1985.

2. Berzon, Betty. *Permanent Partners: Building Gay and Lesbian Relationships That Last,* New York: Plume, 1988, p. 15.

Chapter 1

1. From the song "Touch Me in the Morning," words and music by Michael Masser and Ronald Miller, Jobete Music Company, Inc., 1972/Stone Diamond Music Corporation, 1972. Best-selling record by Diana Ross (Motown, 1973). Source: *Popular Music 1920-1979, Volume 2,* Nat Shapiro and Bruce Pollock, editors. Gale Research Company, Detroit, Michigan, 1985.

Chapter 2

1. Isensee, Rik, *Growing Up Gay in a Dysfunctional Family,* New York: Simon and Schuster, 1991, pp. 9-17.

2. Ibid., p. 17.

3. Gibson, P., Gay Male and Lesbian Youth Suicide, *Report of the Secretary's Task Force on Youth Suicide, Volume 3: Preventions and Interventions in Youth Suicide.* Rockville Maryland, U.S. Dept. of Health and Human Services, 1989. Reference provided by Advocates for Youth.

4. From the song, "Touch Me in the Morning," words and music by Michael Masser and Ronald Miller, Jobete Music Company, Inc., 1972/Stone Diamond Music Corporation, 1972. Best-selling record by Diana Ross (Motown, 1973). Source: *Popular Music 1920-1979, Volume 2,* Nat Shapiro and Bruce Pollock, editors. Gale Research Company, Detroit, Michigan, 1985.

5. Beattie, Melody, *Beyond Codependency and Getting Better All the Time.* San Francisco: Harper/Hazelden, 1989.

Chapter 8

1. From the song, "Gonna Get Along Without You Now," words and music by Milton Kellem. T. B. Harms Company 1951/Milton Kellem Music Company, Inc. 1951. Introduced by Teresa Brewer. Best-selling records in 1956 by Patience and Prudence (Liberty) and in 1964 by Skeeter Davis (RCA Victor). Revived in 1967 with best-selling record by Trini Lopez (Reprise). Source: *Popular Music 1920-1979, Volume 1*, Nat Shapiro and Bruce Pollock, editors. Gale Research Company, Detroit, Michigan, 1985.

Bibliography

Beattie, Melody, *Beyond Codependency and Getting Better All the Time,* San Francisco: Harper/Hazelden, 1989.

Berzon, Betty, *The Intimacy Dance: A Guide to Long-Term Success in Gay and Lesbian Relationships,* New York: Dutton, 1996.

Berzon, Betty, *Permanent Partners: Building Gay and Lesbian Relationships That Last,* New York: Plume, 1988.

Buscaglia, Leo, *Love,* New York: Ballantine, 1972.

Fanning, Patrick, and Mckay, Matthew, *Prisoners of Belief: Exposing and Changing Beliefs That Control Your Life*, Oakland, California: New Harbinger Publications, Inc., 1991.

Fanning, Patrick, and Mckay, Matthew, *Self-Esteem*, Oakland, California: St. Martin's, 1995.

Goleman, Daniel, *Emotional Intelligence: Why It Can Matter More Than IQ,* New York: Bantam, 1995.

Isensee, Rik, *Growing Up Gay in a Dysfunctional Family: A Guide for Gay Men Reclaiming Their Lives,* New York: Simon & Schuster, 1991.

Island, David, and Letellier, Patrick, *Men Who Beat the Men Who Love Them: Battered Gay Men and Domestic Violence,* Binghamton, New York: The Haworth Press, 1991.

Mellody, Pia, *Facing Love Addiction: Giving Yourself the Power to Change the Way You Love,* New York: HarperCollins Publishers, 1992.

Tessina, Tina, *Gay Relationships: How to Find Them; How to Improve Them; How to Make Them Last,* Los Angeles: Jeremy P. Tarcher, Inc., 1989.

Vaughn, Diane, *Uncoupling: How Relationships Come Apart,* New York: Vintage Books, 1987.

Index

Order Your Own Copy of
This Important Book for Your Personal Library!

WHEN IT'S TIME TO LEAVE YOUR LOVER
A Guide for Gay Men

_____ in hardbound at $39.95 (ISBN: 0-7890-0497-6)

_____ in softbound at $24.95 (ISBN: 1-56023-938-7)

COST OF BOOKS_____	☐ **BILL ME LATER:** ($5 service charge will be added)
	(Bill-me option is good on US/Canada/Mexico orders only; not good to jobbers, wholesalers, or subscription agencies.)
OUTSIDE USA/CANADA/ MEXICO: ADD 20%_____	
	☐ Check here if billing address is different from shipping address and attach purchase order and billing address information.
POSTAGE & HANDLING_____ *(US: $3.00 for first book & $1.25 for each additional book)* *Outside US: $4.75 for first book & $1.75 for each additional book)*	
	Signature _____
SUBTOTAL_____	☐ **PAYMENT ENCLOSED: $**_____
IN CANADA: ADD 7% GST_____	☐ **PLEASE CHARGE TO MY CREDIT CARD.**
STATE TAX_____ *(NY, OH & MN residents, please add appropriate local sales tax)*	☐ Visa ☐ MasterCard ☐ AmEx ☐ Discover ☐ Diner's Club
	Account # _____
FINAL TOTAL_____ *(If paying in Canadian funds, convert using the current exchange rate. UNESCO coupons welcome.)*	Exp. Date _____
	Signature _____

Prices in US dollars and subject to change without notice.

NAME _____

INSTITUTION _____

ADDRESS _____

CITY _____

STATE/ZIP _____

COUNTRY _____ COUNTY (NY residents only) _____

TEL _____ FAX _____

E-MAIL_____

May we use your e-mail address for confirmations and other types of information? ☐ Yes ☐ No

Order From Your Local Bookstore or Directly From
The Haworth Press, Inc.
10 Alice Street, Binghamton, New York 13904-1580 • USA
TELEPHONE: 1-800-HAWORTH (1-800-429-6784) / Outside US/Canada: (607) 722-5857
FAX: 1-800-895-0582 / Outside US/Canada: (607) 772-6362
E-mail: getinfo@haworthpressinc.com
PLEASE PHOTOCOPY THIS FORM FOR YOUR PERSONAL USE.

BOF96